T0367659

Real Options in Energy and Commodity Markets

World Scientific–Now Publishers Series in Business

ISSN: 2251-3442

Published:

The complete list of titles in the series can be found at
http://www.worldscientific.com/series/ws-npsb

World Scientific – Now Publishers Series in Business: **Vol. 12**

Real Options in Energy and Commodity Markets

Nicola Secomandi

Tepper School of Business, Carnegie Mellon University

Published by

World Scientific Publishing Co. Pte. Ltd.

5 Toh Tuck Link, Singapore 596224

USA office: 27 Warren Street, Suite 401-402, Hackensack, NJ 07601

UK office: 57 Shelton Street, Covent Garden, London WC2H 9HE

and

now publishers Inc.
PO Box 1024
Hanover, MA 02339
USA

Library of Congress Cataloging-in-Publication Data
Names: Secomandi, Nicola, editor.
Title: Real options in energy and commodity markets / [edited by] Nicola Secomandi
    (Carnegie Mellon University, USA).
Description: New Jersey : World Scientific, [2016] | Series: World Scientific-Now Publishers .
    series in business ; 12 | Includes bibliographical references and index.
Identifiers: LCCN 2016035723 | ISBN 9789813149403
Subjects: LCSH: Commodity exchanges. | Real options (Finance) | Energy industries--Finance.
Classification: LCC HG6046 .R4155 2016 | DDC 332.64/4--dc23
LC record available at https://lccn.loc.gov/2016035723

British Library Cataloguing-in-Publication Data
A catalogue record for this book is available from the British Library.

Desk Editor: Shreya Gopi

Typeset by Stallion Press
Email: enquiries@stallionpress.com

Printed in Singapore

Preface

Energy and commodity markets play fundamental roles in the worldwide economy. The field of real options is concerned with the management and financial valuation of operational flexibility in business endeavors. From the outset of this field, energy and commodity markets have provided a relevant context for real option analysis, both in theory and practice. These markets continue to play an important role for real options.

This volume is a collection of six chapters on recent research on real options in energy and commodity markets. This book is divided into two parts: The first part on theory and the second part on methods and applications.

The first part of this volume includes two chapters: Chapter 1 by Evans and Guthrie and Chapter 2 by Martínez-de-Albéniz and Vendrell Simón. These chapters develop and analyze theoretical models of commodity storage and shipping, respectively. Chapter 1 provides a novel economic perspective on the concept of convenience yield, a modeling construct that has received enormous attention in the field of real options, in the context of the real option to store a commodity. Chapter 2 investigates how the impact of a trader's own activity on market prices affects the classical management of the real option to ship a commodity, such as jet fuel, between two spot markets for this commodity, e.g., the New York Harbor and Los Angeles.

The second part of this volume includes four chapters: Chapter 3 by Benth, Eriksson, and Westgaard, Chapter 4 by Caldentey, Epstein, and Sauré, Chapter 5 by Nadarajah, Secomandi, Sowers, and Wassick, and Chapter 6 by Adelman and Wang. These chapters propose and apply real option models in various application domains. Chapter 3 uses data from the European Union Emission Trading System to investigate the empirical performance of two models of the evolution of futures prices of emission certificates, which are relevant for the real option management of fossil-fueled power plants when accounting for the cost of emissions. Chapter 4 develops a methodology to optimize the management of the real option to extract copper from a mine and applies it to the management of a project at Codelco, Chile, the largest copper producer in the world. Chapter 5 illustrates the core ideas behind real option analysis in the context of the merchant management of hydrocarbon cracking operations. Chapter 6 puts forth a dynamic model, which embeds a model of the evolution of commodity prices commonly used in real option analysis, for optimizing the portfolio of contracts used by oil refineries to sell their gasoline production.

This book includes a highly select collection of chapters. This volume originated with a call to a broad set of researchers in the field of real options for contributions in June 2014 with submission due date by May 2015. This call was followed by the submission of 22 chapter proposals during the summer of 2014. Between August 2014 and May 2015 14 chapters were submitted for possible publication. Of these chapters, 10 moved on to the refereeing stage. The authors of three of these chapters elected to not submit revised versions of their work. Of the seven remaining chapters, five were accepted for publication in this volume. I thank all the individuals who expressed interest in participating in this project as prospective authors, the authors of all the submitted chapters, and the reviewers for their work in assessing the quality of these chapters and the constructive feedback they provided to these authors. This book includes, by permission of the series editor, one additional chapter that was previously refereed and accepted for publication in a separate volume, which ultimately did not reach the publication stage.

I would like to thank Zac Rolnik, the publisher of this volume, for his support of this project and making it a highly enjoyable experience.

I hope you will enjoy reading the chapters in this volume. Ideally, this book will be a source of inspiration for further research or applications in energy and commodity markets.

N. Secomandi
Pittsburgh, PA
April 2016

Contents

About the Editor

Nicola Secomandi is Professor of Operations Management at the Tepper School of Business, Carnegie Mellon University, and a Faculty Affiliate of the Carnegie Mellon Scott Institute for Energy Innovation. His current research involves energy and commodity merchant operations, real options, and approximate dynamic programming. His work has been published in leading operations management/research and management science journals. He is or has been an associate editor for various journals. Secomandi currently teaches MBA courses on real options and risk management and PhD courses on dynamic programming and energy merchant operations. His graduate studies at the University of Houston earned him a PhD in Operations Research and Statistics from the Bauer College of Business and an MS in Computer Science from the College of Natural Sciences and Mathematics. He did postdoctoral work at Cornell University in Civil and Environmental Engineering. He was a senior scientist at PROS Revenue Management and a quantitative analyst at El Paso Merchant Energy, both in Houston, TX.

About the Contributors

Daniel Adelman is the Charles I. Clough Jr. Professor of Operations Management at The University of Chicago Booth School of Business. He conducts research in dynamic stochastic optimization and approximate dynamic programming. Recent projects include work on the electricity smart grid, gasoline supply chains, and software-release planning. He also leads the Healthcare Analytics Laboratory at Chicago Booth, working on real-world projects with providers to improve healthcare delivery through the analysis of large datasets. He serves as Area Editor for *Operations Research*. Adelman received a PhD in Industrial Engineering and Operations Research in 1997 from the Georgia Institute of Technology.

Fred Espen Benth is a full professor of mathematics at the University of Oslo, Norway. His research interests focus around stochastic analysis and its applications to energy finance. He has written more than one hundred research papers and co-authored two monographs on energy and weather markets published by World Scientific. Benth is a fellow at the Wolfgang Pauli Institute in Vienna, where he manages thematic periods in mathematical finance and energy. Recently, Benth was a co-leader of a Center of Advanced Studies at the Academy of Sciences in Norway.

René Caldentey is a Professor of Operations Management at the University of Chicago Booth School of Business. His primary research interests include stochastic modeling with applications to revenue and retail management and natural resource operations. He serves on the editorial board of *Management Science, Manufacturing and Services Operations Management, Operations Research, Production and Operations Management*, and the *Journal of Systems and Engineering*. Before joining Booth, Caldentey was a professor in the department of Information, Operations and Management

Science at New York University Stern School of Business. Prior to that he worked for the Chilean Central Bank and taught at the University of Chile and The Sloan School of Management at the Massachusetts Institute of Technology (MIT). Professor Caldentey received his Master of Arts in Civil and Industrial engineering from the University of Chile and his Doctor of Philosophy in Operations Management from MIT.

Rafael Epstein is an Associate Professor in the Department of Industrial Engineering at the University of Chile. After graduating from the University of Chile in Industrial Engineering, he obtained a PhD in Operations Research at the Massachusetts Institute of Technology. Since then he has conducted relevant applied research in the fields of logistics and production planning, focusing mainly on applications in the forestry, mining, and maritime transport industries. Professor Epstein has achieved prominence for his design of combinatorial auction models that have been used by Chile's school meal tender system. His work has earned him a number of distinctions, including the INFORMS Franz Edelman Award (1998, finalist in 2011), the IFORS OR for Development Prize (2002), the Innovator of the Year Award in Chile (2008), and the Best Engineering Paper of 2011 conferred by the Chilean Institute of Engineers. Dr. Epstein has published numerous academic papers and books that are well cited in the scientific community.

Marcus Eriksson earned his PhD in Mathematics, focusing on stochastic analysis, at the University of Oslo in 2014. Previously he studied engineering physics at Uppsala University. His research interest is on mathematical modeling, in particular of power markets. From 2015 he has been a senior analyst in power markets for continental Europe at ThomsonReuters. This position includes analysis and modeling of power prices and their underlying fundamentals, such as wind and solar energy and consumption.

Lewis Evans is Professor (Emeritus) of the School of Economics and Finance, Victoria University. He has a PhD in economics from the University of Wisconsin Madison. He has published more than fifty journal articles, and has other publications. Awards include Distinguished Fellow of NZ Association of Economists, Fellow of the Law and Economics Association, and appointment as an Officer of the New Zealand Order of Merit (ONZM). His interests lie in industrial and financial economics, and law and economics. He is a lay member of the New Zealand High Court for matters of commerce.

Graeme Guthrie is a professor in the School of Economics and Finance at Victoria University of Wellington, New Zealand. He is the author of *Real Options in Theory and Practice* (Oxford University Press, 2009). His research, which focuses on corporate finance, corporate governance, and the microeconomic foundations of investment behavior, has appeared in the *Journal of Finance, Journal of Financial and Quantitative Analysis, RAND Journal of Economics*, and the *Journal of Economic Literature*. As a consultant he has provided advice on a wide variety of issues in relation to agriculture, electricity, gas, real estate, and telecommunications, much of it using real options analysis.

Víctor Martínez de Albéniz is a full professor in IESE's Department of Production, Technology and Operations Management. He joined IESE in 2004 after earning a PhD from the Operations Research Center of the Massachusetts Institute of Technology and an engineering degree at École Polytechnique in France. His research focuses on supply chain management, where procurement, production and distribution decisions can help companies compete more successfully in the global arena. In particular, he has studied in depth procurement and supply issues, where a balanced sourcing portfolio can provide low cost flexibility and innovation opportunities. He has published his work in journals such as *Management Science, Operations Research, Manufacturing and Services Operations Management*, and *Production and Operations Management*. His projects have been supported by the European Research Council. In 2015 he received the Sabadell Herrero award for Economic Research.

Selvaprabu (Selva) Nadarajah is an Assistant Professor of Operations Management at the University of Illinois at Chicago (UIC) College of Business. Before joining UIC, he obtained his PhD in Operations Research from the Tepper School of Business at Carnegie Mellon University. Selva's research focuses on energy operations and revenue management. In particular, it involves modeling dynamic and stochastic decision making problems that arise in these areas, developing math programming based approximate dynamic programming algorithms, and benchmarking the performance of these methods on realistic models of uncertainty.

Denis Sauré is an assistant professor in the Industrial Engineering Department at the University of Chile (UCH). Prior to joining UCH, he was an assistant professor at the University of Pittsburgh. He holds an MS and a PhD from Columbia University. His research interests lie in the general area of stochastic modeling and its applications to service operations and revenue management. In particular, his research focuses on data-driven approaches to decision-making under uncertainty, and their application in the retail industry, online advertisement, and service systems.

Nicola Secomandi is Professor of Operations Management at the Tepper School of Business, Carnegie Mellon University, and a Faculty Affiliate of the Carnegie Mellon Scott Institute for Energy Innovation. His current research involves energy and commodity merchant operations, real options, and approximate dynamic programming. His work has been published in leading operations management/research and management science journals. He is or has been an associate editor for various journals. Secomandi currently teaches MBA courses on real options and risk management and PhD courses on dynamic programming and energy merchant operations. His graduate studies at the University of Houston earned him a PhD in Operations Research and Statistics from the Bauer College of Business and an MS in Computer Science from the College of Natural Sciences and Mathematics. He did postdoctoral work at Cornell University in Civil and Environmental Engineering. He was a senior scientist at PROS Revenue Management and a quantitative analyst at El Paso Merchant Energy, both in Houston, TX.

Gary Sowers is a Senior Global Technology Manager for The Dow Chemical Company, headquartered in Midland, Michigan. He has spent his twenty-five year career at Dow working on applications of mathematical modeling and optimization for the Hydrocarbons business, one of the largest ethylene producers in the world. He developed and now supports the models used by Dow to select hydrocarbon feedstocks for eleven ethylene manufacturing plants in the US and Europe. He holds a PhD in Chemical Engineering from the University of Delaware.

Josep-Maria Vendrell-Simón is the Director of Financial Environment in the Research Department of Banc Sabadell. Previously he worked at the European Central Bank (ECB) in both the General Directorate of Macroprudential Policy and Financial Stability and the General Directorate of Statistics. Prior to ECB, Josep was a consultant for Advanced Logistics Group and as research assistant at IESE Business School. Josep holds MS degrees in Mathematics and Operations Research from the Polytechnic University of Catalonia, Spain. His research interests include macroprudential policy and systemic risk analysis.

Shanshan Wang currently works for BNP Paribas APAC Corporate and Institutional Banking Consulting. Prior to joining BNP Paribas, she worked with the Boston Consulting Group in the Greater China Region. She holds a Master Degree in Economics from the University of British Columbia and a PhD Degree in Management Science and Operations Management from The University of Chicago Booth School of Business.

John M. Wassick is a Research Fellow and Senior Supply Chain Consultant in the Supply Chain Center of Excellence at The Dow Chemical Company. He has extensive experience in all aspects of control and optimization of chemical processes and he has worked in a wide variety of process technologies. John has also led the application of model-based techniques for supply chain optimization across numerous businesses in Dow. These applications span production scheduling, business planning, network design, and logistics. He holds two patents on nonlinear model predictive control. John has strong ties to academic researchers and he has numerous publications in scholarly journals. In addition to the many technology awards received in Dow, John has been recognized twice by *Computers & Chemical Engineering* as the author of a most cited article and has received the 2014 Computing Practice Award from the Computing and Systems Technology Division of the American Institute of Chemical Engineering. His current research activities include supply chain automation and optimization, enterprise-wide optimization, and batch process optimization. John holds a PhD in Electrical Engineering from Michigan State University.

Sjur Westgaard earned an MS and a Phd in Industrial Economics from the Norwegian University of Science and Technology and an MS in Finance from the Norwegian School of Business and Economics. He has been an investment portfolio manager for an insurance company, a project manager for a consulting company, and a credit analyst for an international bank. He is now a Professor at the Norwegian University of Life Sciences and the Norwegian University of Science and Technology. His teaching involves managerial economics, financial accounting, corporate finance, derivatives and real options, empirical finance, and financial risk management. His main research interests involve risk modeling of commodity markets. He is one of the founders and editors of the *Journal of Commodity Markets*. He is also an associate editor for the *Journal of Energy Markets* and the *Journal of Banking and Finance*.

PART 1
Theory

Chapter 1

Commodity Prices and the Option Value of Storage

Lewis Evans* and Graeme Guthrie[†]

*School of Economics and Finance, Victoria University of Wellington,
PO Box 600, Wellington, New Zealand*

*lew.evans@vuw.ac.nz
[†]graeme.guthrie@vuw.ac.nz

Commodities are physical, not financial assets. We investigate the effects on equilibrium spot-price behavior of frictions in the storage process, which introduce an element of irreversibility to storage decisions and lead to periods when storage operators do not trade in the spot market. We value the real option to delay selling a stored commodity, which comes bundled with the stored commodity itself and generates a convenience yield. The latter arises if the spot price is incorrectly used to measure the market value of the stored commodity, ignoring the embedded real option. It can be interpreted as the expected excess return on the real option to delay selling the stored commodity. Rather than equaling a flow of benefits received during the period over which the return from storage is being calculated, it actually represents changes in the present value of benefits that will be received only some time after the measurement period, when the commodity is released from storage. Storage frictions also generate heteroskedastic spot prices, with volatility being much higher when storage operators decide not to trade in the spot market.

1.1.   Introduction

Commodities are physical, not financial assets, and transporting them between spot markets and storage facilities is costly. In this chapter, we investigate the implications for spot prices and storage policies of frictions in the storage process. In the presence of such frictions, there are actually two distinct goods: the commodity being traded in the spot market and the commodity being held in storage. The market value of the stored commodity is determined in the market for ownership of storage operators. This ensures that the expected growth rate in the market value of the stored commodity, adjusted for ongoing costs of holding the commodity in storage, equals the appropriate risk-adjusted discount rate.[a] The spot price inherits this property as long as storage operators are trading in the spot market. However, whenever they do not participate in the spot market, the items traded there are created and consumed instantaneously, so that there are no intertemporal restrictions on the spot price. In this situation, the expected growth rate in the spot price, adjusted for ongoing storage costs, deviates from the risk-adjusted discount rate, giving the appearance of a convenience yield. Spot price volatility also varies according to whether or not storage operators are trading in the spot market. If they are trading, they will help dampen shocks. However, when storage operators withdraw, the spot price will bear the full impact of shocks. This results in periods of relatively low price volatility while storage operators are trading in the spot market, interrupted by relatively brief periods of much higher volatility when they do not participate.

The convenience yield and spot-price heteroskedasticity stem from a small cost that is incurred each time a unit of the commodity is moved into storage. This friction introduces an element of irreversibility into storage decisions; it is costly to move the commodity into and then immediately out of storage (and also to empty and then immediately refill a storage facility). As a result, the real option to delay selling the stored commodity can be valuable, and this option drives a wedge between the spot price

---

[a]We will assume that all individuals are risk neutral, so that the expected growth rate in the market value of the stored commodity, adjusted for the ongoing cost of storage, equals the risk-free interest rate. However, relaxing this assumption is straightforward, requiring only that we replace the actual process for the harvest in our model with its "risk-neutral" counterpart.

and the market value of the stored commodity.[b] A storage operator that wishes to increase its inventory by one unit must buy that unit in the spot market, as well as incur the cost of moving it into storage. In return, the operator receives one unit of the commodity ready for immediate sale, as well as the real option to wait and sell it at some future date. It is optimal for the operator to buy the commodity in the spot market only when the value of this delay option is at least as great as the cost of moving the commodity into storage. In contrast, a storage operator that wishes to reduce its inventory by one unit must sell that unit in the spot market. Because such a sale destroys the real option to wait and sell at a later date, it is optimal for the operator to sell the commodity in the spot market only when this delay option is worthless. Thus, storage operators will be buyers in the spot market when the delay option's value reaches some strictly positive threshold, and they will be sellers when its value is zero. When the value of the delay option lies anywhere between zero and the positive threshold, storage operators do not trade in the spot market.[c]

In our model, the owner of the stored commodity receives no benefits, pecuniary or otherwise, other than the capital gain. The expected rate of return from storage equals the risk-adjusted discount rate, provided the rate of return is calculated using the market value of the stored commodity. However, if the calculation uses the spot price to (incorrectly) measure the value of the stored commodity, then the expected rate of return from storage differs from the risk-adjusted discount rate whenever storage operators are not trading in the spot market. The difference between the expected rate of return and the risk-adjusted discount rate would normally be attributed to a convenience yield.[d] Thus, our model generates an endogenous convenience yield that is the result of mis-measuring the return from storage and is nonzero only when storage operators are not active in the spot market.[e]

---

[b]The real option associated with holding a commodity in storage is analyzed in [1–4]. The role of ownership, timing options, and stock-outs is analyzed in [5].

[c]Optimal trading strategies for price-taking individuals facing transaction costs are derived in [6–8], which show that no-trade situations result. However, these papers do not derive equilibrium prices.

[d]The convenience yield also arises as a convenient model-fitting device when pricing derivatives with payoffs that are sensitive to a commodity's spot price [9].

[e]Positive inventory in the presence of low expected returns to storage can also be explained by mismeasurement [10]. Commodities that are aggregated for reporting purposes are often economically distinct. If the cost of transforming one commodity into another is higher when carried out in a later period, then one commodity may be stored in positive quantities even though (apparent) excess returns are available from storing

At all times, the market value of the stored commodity equals the sum of the spot price and the market value of the real option to delay selling the stored commodity in the spot market. The expected rate of return on storage is therefore a weighted average of the expected growth rates in the spot price and the option value, adjusted for ongoing storage costs. Equilibrium in the market for ownership of the stored commodity ensures that the (adjusted) weighted average always equals the risk-adjusted discount rate, so if the (adjusted) expected growth rate in the spot price is lower than this, the (adjusted) expected growth rate in the option value must be higher. Because the convenience yield equals the amount by which the (adjusted) expected growth rate in the spot price falls short of the risk-adjusted discount rate, it must also equal the amount by which the (adjusted) expected growth rate in the option value exceeds this level. That is, the convenience yield can be interpreted as the expected excess return on the real option to delay selling the stored commodity.

This interpretation of the convenience yield can be extended beyond our particular model set-up. Different motivations for the convenience yield ultimately reduce to different reasons why timing flexibility might be valuable. In our model, the ultimate source of the timing option's value is the friction in storage, but it could also arise from frictions in production, for example. Rather than equaling a flow of benefits received during the period over which the return from storage is being calculated — which is the standard interpretation — we argue that it actually represents changes in the present value of benefits that will be received only some time after the measurement period, when the commodity is released from storage. This contrasts with the usual interpretation, which is that the convenience yield is a flow of nonpecuniary benefits that firms receive as long as they store the commodity [11–13]. A variety of sources have been suggested for these benefits, including producers' ability to reduce the costs of producing at a given level and of varying output [14] and the ability to avoid costs associated with the frequent deliveries of inputs needed to cope with fluctuating demand and spot prices [15]. One flaw with these motivations of the convenience yield, which we address in this chapter, is that they involve benefits that are received only when the commodity is consumed, transformed as part of a production process, or otherwise destroyed: they are not received while the

---

the other commodity. Such a situation will appear in the data as positive industry-wide storage with a negative expected return to storage.

commodity continues to be stored. Our convenience yield relates to benefits generated while the commodity is being stored.

Our starting point is the competitive storage model generally used to analyze commodity price behavior, in which speculators buy a commodity from producers and store it for subsequent sale to consumers.[f] The key driver of the behavior in this model is the inability of inventory to be negative; storage is frictionless in all other respects. In particular, there are no costs associated with moving the commodity into or out of storage (although there are usually ongoing costs of holding the commodity in storage for a period of time). By introducing a friction into the storage process and investigating the predicted behavior of the equilibrium spot price, we add to a growing literature that uses continuous-time equilibrium models to analyze the behavior of commodity prices. These models have been used to show that there is a U-shaped relationship between spot price volatility for an exhaustible resource and the slope of the term structure of forward prices [25]. A similar result holds for futures price volatility in a model that features irreversible investment and a capacity constraint, a result that it is claimed cannot be captured by standard storage-based models of commodity prices [26]. The competitive storage model has been adapted to investigate important aspects of electricity markets dominated by hydroelectric generation [2].

Section 1.2 introduces the model and describes its general properties. Section 1.3 analyzes price behavior, starting by comparing the spot price and the market value of the stored commodity, and then focusing on the qualitative properties of spot prices. One particular case of the model is solved numerically, allowing us to document some of the quantitative price behavior. Section 1.4 offers some concluding remarks. Our numerical solution approach is summarized in Appendix A.

1.2. Solving for the Equilibrium Commodity Spot Price

Section 1.2.1 describes the components of our model and Sec. 1.2.2 derives a storage policy that a welfare-maximizing social planner would choose.

---

[f]The existence and uniqueness of rational expectations equilibria are considered in [16–21]. The empirical performance of competitive equilibrium storage models is evaluated in [5, 22–24].

Section 1.2.3 proves that the resulting spot price can be achieved in an equilibrium setting where individual storage operators take the spot price as given and adopt storage policies that maximize the value of their business.

1.2.1.   *Model Set-up*

Our model, which contains three types of agents, is summarized in Fig. 1.1. Storage operators purchase the commodity in the spot market and store it for later sale. Producers sell in the spot market, but these sales occur immediately after production (that is, only storage operators can store the commodity). All agents are risk neutral and storage capacity is infinite. Let s_t denote the total quantity of the commodity held in storage at date t and suppose that inventory decays at the constant rate $\varepsilon > 0$. Each unit of the commodity purchased by storage operators increases inventory by only $1 - \kappa$ units, for some positive constant $\kappa < 1$, but the commodity can be removed from storage for sale in the spot market without any additional cost.[g] Thus, total storage evolves according to

$$ds_t = -(\pi(z_t) + \varepsilon s_t)dt, \tag{1.1}$$

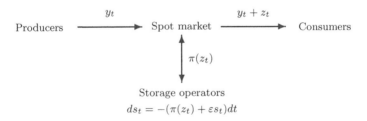

Fig. 1.1   Model structure: The commodity is produced at rate y_t. If the stored commodity is sold in the spot market at rate $z_t \lessgtr 0$, then inventory, s_t, falls at rate $\pi(z_t) \lessgtr 0$.

---

[g]This particular friction is the specific source of the main results in our model. However, anything that introduces an element of irreversibility into the decision to change storage levels will lead to valuable timing options embedded in the stored commodity, and therefore to qualitatively similar results.

where z_t is the rate at which storage operators sell the commodity in the spot market[h] and

$$\pi(z) = \begin{cases} (1 - \kappa)z, & \text{if } z < 0, \\ z & \text{if } z \geq 0. \end{cases}$$

The market-clearing spot price at date t is $p_t = \psi(y_t + z_t)$, where the consumers' inverse demand function ψ satisfies $\psi' < 0$ and $\lim_{q \to \infty} \psi(q) = 0$, and y_t is the rate at which the commodity is produced by producers. We suppose that y_t evolves according to the diffusion process

$$dy_t = \nu(y_t)dt + \phi(y_t)d\xi_t, \tag{1.2}$$

for some functions ν and ϕ, and some Wiener process ξ_t. The risk-free interest rate, r, is constant.

1.2.2. *Solving the Social Planner's Problem*

The main focus of this chapter is the commodity price that results from the competitive interaction between storage operators. We will see that a relatively simple way to determine an equilibrium storage policy is to first consider the problem facing a hypothetical social planner who maximizes the present value of the incremental flow of total surplus attributable to storage, which equals[i]

$$TS(z_t; y_t) = \int_{y_t}^{y_t + z_t} \psi(q) \, dq.$$

If $z_t > 0$ (so that consumption of the commodity at date t is raised due to storage activities) then the sum of consumers' and storage operators' incremental surpluses is the increased area under the demand curve, which is the part lying between consumption levels y_t and $y_t + z_t$. In contrast, if $z_t < 0$ (so that consumption of the commodity at date t is reduced due to storage activities) then the sum of consumers' and storage operators' surpluses falls by an amount equal to the area under the demand curve between consumption levels $y_t + z_t$ and y_t.

---

[h]If $z_t < 0$, then $-z_t$ is the rate at which storage operators purchase the commodity in the spot market.

[i]Deriving a competitive equilibrium by solving an associated "surplus" maximization problem has a long history in studies of commodity markets [18, 19].

The planner takes s and y as given and chooses the level of sales from storage $z_t = z(s_t, y_t)$ at all future dates t in order to maximize the present value of total surplus,

$$W(s, y) = E\left[\left. \int_0^\infty e^{-rt} TS(z(s_t, y_t); y_t)\, dt \,\right|\, (s_0, y_0) = (s, y)\right].$$

The corresponding Hamilton–Jacobi–Bellman equation is

$$0 = \max_z\ -(\pi(z) + \varepsilon s)\frac{\partial W}{\partial s} + \nu\frac{\partial W}{\partial y} + \frac{1}{2}\phi^2\frac{\partial^2 W}{\partial y^2} - rW + TS(z; y). \quad (1.3)$$

The choice of z in (1.3) is constrained by the requirements that consumption and storage cannot be negative; that is, $y + z \geq 0$ for all (s, y) and $z \leq 0$ whenever $s = 0$. If $z^*(s, y)$ maximizes the argument on the right-hand side of (1.3) then W satisfies

$$0 = -(\pi(z^*(s, y)) + \varepsilon s)\frac{\partial W}{\partial s} + \nu\frac{\partial W}{\partial y}$$

$$+ \frac{1}{2}\phi^2\frac{\partial^2 W}{\partial y^2} - rW + \int_y^{y + z^*(s, y)} \psi(q)\, dq. \quad (1.4)$$

The policy function z^* and the value function W must be solved simultaneously. However, we are able to express the optimal inventory management policy, $z^*(s, y)$, in terms of the marginal social value of the stored commodity, $\partial W/\partial s$, by solving the maximization problem in (1.3).

Proposition 1.1. *The socially optimal storage policy depends on the marginal social value of the stored commodity, $\partial W/\partial s$, as follows. When $s > 0$:*

- *if $\partial W/\partial s \leq \psi(y)$ then the planner reduces inventory, choosing $z^* \geq 0$ defined implicitly by $\psi(y + z^*) = \partial W/\partial s$;*
- *if $\psi(y) < \partial W/\partial s \leq \psi(y)/(1 - \kappa)$ then the planner does not adjust inventory, so that $z^* = 0$;*
- *if $\psi(y)/(1 - \kappa) < \partial W/\partial s \leq \psi(0)/(1 - \kappa)$ then the planner raises inventory, choosing $z^* \in [-y, 0]$ defined implicitly by $\psi(y + z^*) = (1 - \kappa)\partial W/\partial s$;*
- *if $\partial W/\partial s > \psi(0)/(1 - \kappa)$ then the planner stores the entire harvest, so that $z^* = -y$.*

When $s = 0$:

- *if $\partial W/\partial s \leq \psi(y)/(1 - \kappa)$ then the planner sells the entire harvest to consumers, so that $z^* = 0$;*

- *if $\psi(y)/(1-\kappa) < \partial W/\partial s \le \psi(0)/(1-\kappa)$ then the planner stores some of the harvest, choosing $z^* \in [-y,0]$ defined implicitly by $\psi(y+z^*) = (1-\kappa)\partial W/\partial s$;*
- *if $\partial W/\partial s > \psi(0)/(1-\kappa)$ then the planner stores the entire harvest, so that $z^* = -y$.*

Proof. The marginal benefit of sales from storage equals $\psi(y+z) - (1-\kappa)\partial W/\partial s$ when $z < 0$ and $\psi(y+z) - \partial W/\partial s$ when $z \ge 0$.

The simpler of the two cases in the proposition is where $s = 0$, since then we need to consider only the behavior of the marginal benefit of sales from storage over the interval $z \in [-y,0]$. If $\psi(0) < (1-\kappa)\partial W/\partial s$ then the marginal benefit of sales from storage is negative for all $z \in [-y,0)$, so that the planner should choose $z^* = -y$. If $\psi(y) > (1-\kappa)\partial W/\partial s$ then the marginal benefit of sales from storage is positive for all $z \in [-y,0]$, so that the planner should choose $z^* = 0$. In all other cases, the planner should choose $z^* \in [-y,0]$ defined implicitly by $\psi(y+z^*) = (1-\kappa)\partial W/\partial s$.

Now we turn to the case where $s > 0$. This is more complicated, as we need to consider the behavior of the marginal benefit of sales from storage over both the intervals $z \in [-y,0]$ and $z \in [0,\infty)$. If $\psi(0) < (1-\kappa)\partial W/\partial s$ then the marginal benefit of sales from storage is negative for all $z \in [-y,\infty)$, so that the planner should choose $z^* = -y$. If $\psi(y) \le (1-\kappa)\partial W/\partial s \le \psi(0)$ then the marginal benefit of sales from storage is zero for some $z^* \in [-y,0]$, so that the planner should choose this z^*, which is defined implicitly by $\psi(y+z^*) = (1-\kappa)\partial W/\partial s$. If $(1-\kappa)\partial W/\partial s < \psi(y) < \partial W/\partial s$ then the marginal benefit of sales from storage is positive for any allowable $z < 0$ and negative for all $z > 0$, implying that $z^* = 0$ is socially optimal. Finally, if $\psi(y) \ge \partial W/\partial s$ then the marginal benefit of sales from storage is zero for some $z^* \ge 0$, so that the planner should choose this z^*, which is defined implicitly by $\psi(y+z^*) = \partial W/\partial s$. □

Proposition 1.1 shows that for any particular level of the marginal value of storage, there will be three distinct ranges for the harvest. The three cases are shown in Fig. 1.2. If the harvest is sufficiently low (for example, y^l in Fig. 1.2) then the planner will sell the commodity out of storage at a rate such that consumers' willingness to pay for one additional unit of consumption, $\psi(y^l + z^l)$, equals the increase in overall welfare from storing one additional unit, $\partial W/\partial s$. In contrast, when the harvest is sufficiently high (for example, y^h in Fig. 1.2), the planner will purchase the commodity and store it at a rate such that consumers' willingness to pay for one additional unit of consumption, $\psi(y^h + z^h)$, equals the increase in overall

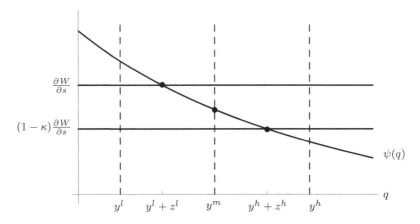

Fig. 1.2 Social planner's storage decisions: The figure illustrates the socially optimal storage policy for three different harvest levels, y^l, y^m, and y^h. Inventory is positive in all cases. As $\psi(y^l) > \partial W/\partial s$, the planner chooses $z^l > 0$ and reduces inventory. As $(1-\kappa)\partial W/\partial s \le \psi(y^m) \le \partial W/\partial s$, the planner chooses $z^m = 0$ and does not adjust inventory. As $\psi(y^h) < (1-\kappa)\partial W/\partial s$, the planner chooses $z^h < 0$ and increases inventory.

welfare from storing $1 - \kappa$ additional units, $(1 - \kappa)\partial W/\partial s$. Between these two ranges (for example, y^m in Fig. 1.2), the harvest is not high enough to justify diverting any from the spot market and it is not low enough to justify boosting it with sales from storage.[j]

1.2.3. *Competitive Equilibrium*

We now show that if $z^*(s, y)$ denotes a socially optimal storage policy then there exists a competitive equilibrium with spot price equal to

$$p_t = P(s_t, y_t) \equiv \psi(y_t + z^*(s_t, y_t)) \tag{1.5}$$

at date t. Our first step is to consider a firm that currently holds x units of the commodity in storage and takes the spot price process in (1.5) as given. The firm chooses its own storage policy in order to maximize its market value. Specifically, the firm chooses its rate of sales from storage at each

---

[j]In the frictionless case (that is, when $\kappa = 0$), it is socially optimal for storage operators to not trade in the spot market only when either (i) inventory is positive and $\partial W/\partial s = \psi(y)$, or (ii) inventory is zero and $\partial W/\partial s \le \psi(y)$.

date t, $w_t = w(x_t; s_t, y_t)$, in order to maximize

$$G(x; s, y) = E \left[\int_0^\infty e^{-rt} w(x_t; s_t, y_t) P(s_t, y_t) \, dt \ \middle| \ (x_0, s_0, y_0) = (x, s, y) \right],$$

where its total inventory evolves according to

$$dx_t = -(\pi(w(x_t; s_t, y_t)) + \varepsilon x_t) dt.$$

The choice of w is constrained by the requirement that $w \leq 0$ whenever $x = 0$; that is, the firm's storage cannot be negative.[k] Solutions to this equation, one of which is described in the following proposition, correspond to optimal storage policies for a price-taking storage operator.

Proposition 1.2. *An optimal storage policy for a price-taking storage operator with x units of the commodity in storage is to sell from storage at the rate*

$$w(x; s, y) = x \cdot \frac{z^*(s, y)}{s}. \tag{1.6}$$

(Negative values of w correspond to spot market purchases.) The market value of such a storage operator equals $x \cdot \partial W / \partial s$.

Proof. We begin by proving that if the market value of a storage operator equals $x \cdot \partial W / \partial s$ then $w = xz^*/s$ is an optimal storage policy. We then show that if a storage operator adopts this policy, its market value equals $x \cdot \partial W / \partial s$.

Suppose that the market value of a storage operator equals $G(x; s, y) = x \cdot \partial W / \partial s$ whenever it holds x units of the commodity in storage. If the firm sells $w \, dt$ units of the commodity over the next interval of time lasting dt years, then it has current market value

$$wp \, dt + e^{-r \, dt} E[G(x + dx; s + ds, y + dy)],$$

---

[k]In keeping with standard competitive equilibrium models, we assume that the firm believes it can always buy and sell as much of the commodity as it wishes. In particular, the firm's choice of w is unaffected by the non-negativity constraints on consumption and aggregate storage.

which reduces to

$$G(x; s, y) + \left(wp - (\pi(w) + \varepsilon x)\frac{\partial G}{\partial x} \right.$$
$$\left. -(\pi(z^*) + \varepsilon s)\frac{\partial G}{\partial s} + \nu\frac{\partial G}{\partial y} + \frac{1}{2}\phi^2\frac{\partial^2 G}{\partial y^2} - rG \right) dt.$$

It therefore chooses w in order to maximize $wp - \pi(w)\partial G/\partial x = wp - \pi(w)\partial W/\partial s$. From Proposition 1.1, if $z^*(s, y) < 0$ then $p = (1 - \kappa)\partial W/\partial s$ and the firm chooses w in order to maximize

$$(w(1 - \kappa) - \pi(w))\frac{\partial W}{\partial s} = \begin{cases} 0 & \text{if } w < 0, \\ -\kappa w\frac{\partial W}{\partial s} & \text{if } w \geq 0. \end{cases}$$

It follows that any $w^* < 0$ is optimal when $z^*(s, y) < 0$. Similarly, if $z^*(s, y) > 0$ then $p = \partial W/\partial s$ and the firm chooses w in order to maximize

$$(w - \pi(w))\frac{\partial W}{\partial s} = \begin{cases} \kappa w\frac{\partial W}{\partial s} & \text{if } w < 0, \\ 0 & \text{if } w \geq 0. \end{cases}$$

It follows that any $w^* > 0$ is optimal when $z^*(s, y) > 0$. Finally, if $z^*(s, y) = 0$ then $(1 - \kappa)\partial W/\partial s \leq p \leq \partial W/\partial s$ and the firm chooses w in order to maximize

$$wp - \pi(w)\frac{\partial W}{\partial s} = \begin{cases} (p - (1 - \kappa)\frac{\partial W}{\partial s})w & \text{if } w < 0, \\ (p - \frac{\partial W}{\partial s})w & \text{if } w \geq 0. \end{cases}$$

Since this function is increasing in w for $w < 0$ and decreasing in w for $w \geq 0$, it follows that $w^* = 0$ is optimal when $z^*(s, y) = 0$. Optimality of the proposed storage policy $w = xz^*/s$ follows immediately.

Now we value a firm that manages its storage facility according to the policy described by $w^* = xz^*/s$. Since it sells $w^* dt$ units of the commodity over the next interval of time lasting dt years, its market value, G, satisfies

$$G(x; s, y) = w^*p\, dt + e^{-r\, dt}E[G(x + dx; s + ds, y + dy)],$$

which reduces to

$$0 = \frac{x}{s}z^*p - \left(\frac{x}{s}\pi(z^*) + \varepsilon x\right)\frac{\partial G}{\partial x} - (\pi(z^*) + \varepsilon s)\frac{\partial G}{\partial s}$$
$$+ \nu\frac{\partial G}{\partial y} + \frac{1}{2}\phi^2\frac{\partial^2 G}{\partial y^2} - rG. \tag{1.7}$$

The form of the storage policy, together with the constant returns to scale of the storage technology, implies that the market value of the firm will equal $G(x; s, y) = xV(s, y)$ for some function V to be determined. Substituting this expression for G into (1.7) shows that V must satisfy

$$0 = -(\pi(z^*) + \varepsilon s)\frac{\partial V}{\partial s} + \nu\frac{\partial V}{\partial y} + \frac{1}{2}\phi^2\frac{\partial^2 V}{\partial y^2} - (r + \varepsilon)V + \frac{z^*}{s}\left(p - \frac{\pi(z^*)}{z^*}V\right).$$

The form of π allows us to rewrite this as

$$0 = -(\pi(z^*) + \varepsilon s)\frac{\partial V}{\partial s} + \nu\frac{\partial V}{\partial y} + \frac{1}{2}\phi^2\frac{\partial^2 V}{\partial y^2} - (r + \varepsilon)V$$
$$+ \frac{z^*\pi'(z^*)}{s}\left(\frac{\partial W}{\partial s} - V\right) + \frac{z^*}{s}\left(p - \pi'(z^*)\frac{\partial W}{\partial s}\right).$$

The last term on the right-hand side is identically equal to zero,[1] so that V is determined by

$$0 = -(\pi(z^*) + \varepsilon s)\frac{\partial V}{\partial s} + \nu\frac{\partial V}{\partial y} + \frac{1}{2}\phi^2\frac{\partial^2 V}{\partial y^2} - (r + \varepsilon)V + \frac{z^*}{s}\pi'(z^*)\left(\frac{\partial W}{\partial s} - V\right).$$

It is straightforward to show that $V = \partial W/\partial s$ is a solution to this equation. □

If each storage operator i, who has x_t^i units of the commodity in storage, follows the policy described in Proposition 1.2, then total inventory is $\sum_i x_t^i = s_t$ and total sales from storage equals

$$\sum_i w_t^i = \sum_i x_t^i \cdot \frac{z^*(s_t, y_t)}{s_t} = z^*(s_t, y_t).$$

The spot price at date t would equal $\psi(y_t + z^*(s_t, y_t))$, which is the expression in (1.5). That is, if each firm takes the price in (1.5) as given and maximizes its own market value using the policy in Proposition 1.2, then the market-clearing spot price equals the one in (1.5). That is, the price in (1.5) can arise in a competitive equilibrium. Proposition 1.3 summarizes this result.

Proposition 1.3. *There exists a competitive equilibrium in which the aggregate storage policy is given in Proposition 1.1, the market-clearing spot price is given by (1.5), and the market value of each unit of the stored commodity is $V(s, y) \equiv \partial W/\partial s$.*

---

[1]This is obviously the case when $z^* = 0$. Moreover, Proposition 1.1 shows that $p = \pi'(z^*)\partial W/\partial s$ whenever $z^* \neq 0$, so that the last term vanishes whenever $z^* \neq 0$ as well.

The form of the policy in Proposition 1.1 determines the behavior of aggregate storage in this equilibrium. In particular, the presence of frictions means that the periods when storage operators appear on the demand side of the spot market are separated from those when they appear on the supply side by discrete intervals with no trading activity. In contrast, when there are no frictions, storage operators switch from one side of the market to the other instantaneously and repeatedly.

The equilibrium behavior of individual storage operators can be understood in terms of the real options associated with storage, as we explain in the next section. A storage operator that wishes to increase its inventory by one unit must buy that unit in the spot market, as well as incur the cost of moving it into storage (in our model, an amount equal to the product of $\kappa/(1 - \kappa)$ and the spot price). In return, the operator receives one unit of the commodity ready for immediate sale, as well as the real option to wait and sell it at some future date. It is optimal for the operator to buy the commodity in the spot market only when the value of this delay option is at least as great as the cost of moving the commodity into storage. In contrast, a storage operator that wishes to reduce its inventory by one unit must sell that unit in the spot market. Because such a sale destroys the real option to wait and sell at a later date, it is optimal for the operator to sell the commodity in the spot market only when this delay option is worthless. Thus, storage operators will be buyers in the spot market when the delay option's value is greater than or equal to some strictly positive threshold, and they will be sellers when its value is zero. When the value of the delay option lies anywhere between zero and this threshold, storage operators do not trade in the spot market.

1.3.   Price Behavior

Section 1.3.1 compares the spot price and the market value of the stored commodity. This comparison is used to analyze the convenience yield in Sec. 1.3.2 and spot price volatility in Sec. 1.3.3. One particular case of the model is solved numerically in Sec. 1.3.4, allowing us to document some of the quantitative price behavior.

1.3.1.   *The Real Option to Delay Selling the Stored Commodity*

The financial market for ownership of the storage operators plays an important role in understanding spot price behavior. Equilibrium in this market requires that the expected rate of return earned by storage operators equals the risk-free interest rate, which determines the market value of storage firms, as well as their behavior and ultimately the spot price. Thus there are actually two goods in our model — the commodity being traded in the spot market and the commodity being held in storage. Their respective prices are the spot price and the market value of a firm holding one unit of the stored commodity, where (from Proposition 1.3) the latter is equal to the marginal value that the planner attributes to inventory. These prices are not equal, but storage operators' ability to transform one good into the other means that they are closely related.

The spot price will never fall below $(1 - \kappa)V(s, y)$. If it did, the ability to instantaneously move the commodity into storage implies that storage operators would demand an infinite amount of the commodity in the spot market, making an immediate gain of $(1 - \kappa)V(s, y) - P(s, y)$ on each unit purchased. Except during stock-outs, it will never climb above $V(s, y)$, because if it did storage operators would instantaneously sell their total inventory in the spot market, making an immediate gain of $P(s, y) - V(s, y)$ on each unit sold. The spot price is thus constrained to a band bounded below by $(1 - \kappa)V(s, y)$ and above by $V(s, y)$.[m] When storage operators are selling the commodity in the spot market, the spot price lies at the top of this band; when they are buying the commodity in the spot market, it lies at the bottom. However, if the spot price lies above the lower bound and below the upper one then storage operators do not trade in the spot market at all: the spot price is too high for purchasing the commodity in the spot market to be profitable, and too low for selling the stored commodity to be profitable. These results are summarized in the following proposition.

Proposition 1.4. *As long as inventory is positive, the market-clearing spot price satisfies*

$$(1 - \kappa)V(s, y) \leq P(s, y) \leq V(s, y),$$

with $P(s, y)$ equaling the lower bound if $z^*(s, y) < 0$ and the upper bound if $z^*(s, y) > 0$, and otherwise equaling $P(s, y) = \psi(y)$.

Proof. Proposition 1.1 shows that

$$V(s, y) = \frac{\partial W}{\partial s} = \frac{\psi(y + z^*(s, y))}{1 - \kappa} = \frac{P(s, y)}{1 - \kappa}$$

---

[m]The upper and lower bounds are equal to each other if there are no transaction-cost frictions, in which case the spot price always equals $V(s, y)$.

when $z^*(s, y) < 0$, and that

$$V(s, y) = \frac{\partial W}{\partial s} = \psi(y + z^*(s, y)) = P(s, y)$$

when $z^*(s, y) > 0$. $\square$

It is useful to think of each unit of the stored commodity being a bundle comprising a unit of the commodity committed to immediate sale in the spot market and the real option to delay this sale until a future date of the owner's choosing. The value of the first component is the spot price $P(s, y)$ and the value of the second component, which we denote by $U(s, y)$, satisfies

$$V(s, y) = P(s, y) + U(s, y). \tag{1.8}$$

Proposition 1.4 shows that $U(s, y)$ equals zero when storage operators are selling in the spot market, equals $(\kappa/(1 - \kappa))P(s, y)$ when they are buying in the spot market, and is otherwise somewhere between these two bounds.

1.3.2. *Convenience Yield and the Expected Return to Storage*

The expected return from storage is typically calculated as the sum of the expected growth rate in the spot price and the so-called convenience yield, which is a flow of nonpecuniary benefits that firms receive as long as they store the commodity [27]. The convenience yield is believed to compensate investors for any expected rate of return shortfall. In this section, we analyze the convenience yield that arises endogenously in our model and we interpret it in terms of the decomposition of the stored commodity into the commodity committed for immediate sale and the real option to delay that sale.

Although the rate of return from storage is usually calculated using the spot price to value the stored commodity, Sec. 1.3.1 shows that the correct approach is to use V. Moreover, because the owner of the stored commodity receives no cash flows or benefits other than the capital gain, the total expected rate of return from storage equals the expected growth rate in V, adjusted for the decay associated with storage. As V is the price of a traded asset — ownership of one unit of the stored commodity — equilibrium in the market for ownership of this asset will ensure that the expected rate of return from buying the stored commodity and holding it for later sale equals the risk-free interest rate. As inventory decays at rate ε, the expected growth rate in the price of the stored commodity must exceed the risk-free interest rate by this amount.

Proposition 1.5. *The expected growth rate in the price of the stored commodity equals*

$$\frac{1}{V}\frac{E[dV]}{dt} = r + \varepsilon. \tag{1.9}$$

Proof. Differentiating (1.3) with respect to s shows that $V = \partial W/\partial s$ satisfies

$$0 = -(\pi(z^*(s,y)) + \varepsilon s)\frac{\partial V}{\partial s} + \nu\frac{\partial V}{\partial y} + \frac{1}{2}\phi^2\frac{\partial^2 V}{\partial y^2} - (r+\varepsilon)V + \theta,$$

where

$$\theta = \left(\psi(y + z^*(s,y)) - \pi'(z^*(s,y))\frac{\partial W}{\partial s}\right)\frac{\partial z^*}{\partial s}.$$

Note that (i) $\partial z^*/\partial s = 0$ in the region where $z^* = 0$ and (ii) the term in large brackets equals zero in the region where $z^* \neq 0$. Thus $\theta = 0$ for all (s,y), implying that

$$\frac{E[dV]}{dt} - (r+\varepsilon)V = -(\pi(z^*) + \varepsilon s)\frac{\partial V}{\partial s} + \nu\frac{\partial V}{\partial y}$$

$$+ \frac{1}{2}\phi^2\frac{\partial^2 V}{\partial y^2} - (r+\varepsilon)V = 0.$$

This implies that (1.9) holds. $\qquad\square$

Proposition 1.5 shows that, if the stored commodity is valued correctly, a convenience yield is not needed to equate the expected rate of return from storage to the risk-free interest rate.

As long as storage operators are active in the spot market, the spot price is proportional to V and so will share the same expected growth rate. However, in the region where $z^* = 0$, the lack of storage-operator involvement means that the spot price is equal to the level at which demand for consumption of the commodity equals the level of the harvest. In this case, there is no intertemporal smoothing on either the demand or supply sides of the market, and so nothing prevents the expected growth rate in the spot price from deviating from $r + \varepsilon$. Trends in the harvest therefore flow through directly into trends in the spot price. The next proposition gives the precise form of the expected growth rate in the spot price.

Proposition 1.6 (Spot-price drift). *The expected growth rate in the spot price equals*

$$\frac{1}{P}\frac{E[dP]}{dt} = \begin{cases} r + \varepsilon & \text{if } z^*(s,y) \neq 0, \\ (\nu\psi'(y) + \frac{1}{2}\phi^2\psi''(y))/\psi(y) & \text{if } z^*(s,y) = 0. \end{cases} \quad (1.10)$$

Proof. When $z^*(s,y) = 0$, the spot price is $P(s,y) = \psi(y)$ and Itô's Lemma implies that

$$\frac{E[dP]}{dt} = \nu\psi'(y) + \frac{1}{2}\phi^2\psi''(y).$$

When $z^*(s,y) > 0$, Proposition 1.1 shows that the spot price is $P(s,y) = \psi(y + z^*) = \partial W/\partial s$. Itô's Lemma implies that

$$\frac{E[dP]}{dt} = \left(-(\pi(z^*) + \varepsilon s)\frac{\partial^2 W}{\partial s^2} + \nu\frac{\partial^2 W}{\partial s\partial y} + \frac{1}{2}\phi^2\frac{\partial^3 W}{\partial s\partial y^2}\right).$$

The Hamilton–Jacobi–Bellman equation (1.3) implies that

$$0 = -(\pi(z^*) + \varepsilon s)\frac{\partial W}{\partial s} + \nu\frac{\partial W}{\partial y} + \frac{1}{2}\phi^2\frac{\partial^2 W}{\partial y^2} - rW + TS(z^*; y).$$

Differentiating with respect to s shows that

$$0 = -(\pi(z^*) + \varepsilon s)\frac{\partial^2 W}{\partial s^2} + \nu\frac{\partial^2 W}{\partial s\partial y} + \frac{1}{2}\phi^2\frac{\partial^3 W}{\partial s\partial y^2} - (r + \varepsilon)\frac{\partial W}{\partial s},$$

where we have used the Envelope Theorem to remove the terms involving $\partial z^*/\partial s$. It follows that

$$\frac{E[dP]}{dt} = -(\pi(z^*) + \varepsilon s)\frac{\partial^2 W}{\partial s^2} + \nu\frac{\partial^2 W}{\partial s\partial y} + \frac{1}{2}\phi^2\frac{\partial^3 W}{\partial s\partial y^2}$$

$$= (r + \varepsilon)\frac{\partial W}{\partial s} = (r + \varepsilon)P.$$

The case when $z^*(s,y) < 0$ can be treated in the same way. □

We will see that, in the frictionless case, the region where $z^*(s,y) = 0$ has measure zero during periods when inventory is positive. The expected growth rate in the spot price is therefore almost always equal to $r + \varepsilon$, except during stock-outs.

In the region where storage operators are active in the spot market, the expected growth rate in the spot price is independent of the current level of the spot price: there is no short-run mean reversion in this case. However, when the spot market separates from the market for ownership of the stored commodity, the expected growth rate varies with the current level of the equilibrium spot price, $\psi(y)$, by (1.5). Given this complex behavior, tests for mean reversion using high-frequency spot-price data that are based on simple autoregressive processes, for example, are inappropriate [28].

Proposition 1.6 shows that there will be situations in which the expected growth rate in the spot price differs from $r + \varepsilon$. The usual approach to dealing with this *apparent* violation of equilibrium behavior is to posit a convenience yield [29, 30]. It follows immediately from Proposition 1.6 that in our model this convenience yield (CY) equals

$$
\mathrm{CY} \equiv (r + \varepsilon)P - \frac{E[dP]}{dt} = \begin{cases} 0 & \text{if } z^*(s, y) \neq 0, \\ (r + \varepsilon)\psi(y) - \nu\psi'(y) & \text{if } z^*(s, y) = 0. \\ \quad - \dfrac{1}{2}\phi^2\psi''(y) \end{cases}
$$

It is nonzero only when storage operators are not trading in the spot market. In the frictionless case, the convenience yield is almost always equal to zero as long as inventory is positive; that is, it is a stock-out phenomenon.

There are no nonpecuniary benefits from storage in our model. The only gain from holding the stored commodity is the capital gain, and when the stored commodity is valued correctly the expected capital gain, adjusted for storage-related decay, is the risk-free interest rate. Thus, the convenience yield in our model is the result of the stored commodity being misvalued when the "return" from storage is being calculated.

Nevertheless, it is possible to interpret the convenience yield as more than simply the consequence of a valuation error. Recall that the value of the stored commodity is equal to the sum of the spot price and the value of the real option to delay selling the commodity: $V = P + U$. Using this decomposition to eliminate V from (1.9) shows that

$$
\frac{E[dP]}{dt} + \frac{E[dU]}{dt} = (r + \varepsilon)(P + U),
$$

which can be rearranged to give

$$
\mathrm{CY} \equiv (r + \varepsilon)P - \frac{E[dP]}{dt} = \frac{E[dU]}{dt} - (r + \varepsilon)U.
$$

That is, the convenience yield is actually the expected excess return on the real option to delay selling the stored commodity. If the spot price is expected to increase at a rate less than $r + \varepsilon$, then the option will be expected to grow in value at a greater rate, because the value of the bundle corresponding to the stored commodity will grow at rate $r + \varepsilon$ on average.

1.3.3. *Spot-price Volatility*

While the previous subsection focuses on the drift in the spot price, this one concentrates on spot-price volatility. It follows from (1.5) and Itô's Lemma that the spot price has volatility

$$\phi(y)\frac{\partial P}{\partial y} = \phi(y)\psi'(y + z^*)\left(1 + \frac{\partial z^*}{\partial y}\right).$$

If storage operators are currently active in the spot market ($z^* \neq 0$), then the effect of a positive harvest shock on the spot price will be partly offset by storage operators either buying more (if $z^* < 0$) or selling less (if $z^* > 0$). Thus, spot-price volatility will be relatively low when $z^* \neq 0$. In contrast, if storage operators are not trading in the spot market ($z^* = 0$), then a positive harvest shock will flow directly through to the spot market. Thus, spot-price volatility will be relatively high when $z^* = 0$. Moreover, although z^* is continuous at the boundaries between the regions where $z^* = 0$ and $z^* \neq 0$, $\partial z^*/\partial y$ will not be, so that there will be a (discontinuous) jump in volatility when the system moves between these regions.

It follows that the spot price will experience distinct periods of especially high volatility, which begin when storage operators withdraw from the spot market and end when they return. Whenever storage operators are trading in the spot market, spot price shocks will be relatively small and — as the result of the smoothing effects of storage — more persistent than harvest shocks. In contrast, whenever storage operators are absent, spot price shocks will be relatively large and less persistent than harvest shocks. In the special case where the friction is zero, the region where $z^*(s, y) = 0$ has measure zero, so that the high-volatility/low-persistence periods will be absent (except during stock-outs).

1.3.4. *Numerical Analysis*

In this section, we present the details of a particular implementation of our model. We assume that the harvest evolves according to

$$dy_t = \eta(\mu - y_t)dt + \sigma y_t^{1/2}d\xi_t$$

and that the inverse demand curve is described by $\psi(x) = (\mu/x)^\alpha$, where η, μ, σ, and α are positive constants. The harvest flow generated by this process is mean-reverting with unconditional mean and variance of μ and $\sigma^2\mu/(2\eta)$, respectively. Deviations from the long-run level are expected to decline at rate η, the harvest can never become negative and, provided

$2\eta\mu \geq \sigma^2$, the harvest will always be positive.[n] We set $\mu = 1$, $\eta = \log 2$, and $\sigma = (\log(2^{1/2}))^{1/2}$, so that the long-run average harvest level is unity, the half-life of harvest shocks is one year, and the unconditional standard deviation of the harvest is half the unconditional mean. The units in which the price is measured are chosen so that the price is unity when consumption equals the long-run average harvest. We set $\alpha = 2$ (so that the price-elasticity of demand equals $-1/2$), $\varepsilon = 0.03$, and $r = 0.04$. We consider two different values for the costs of moving the commodity into storage: $\kappa = 0$ and $\kappa = 0.05$.

We present the model's main outputs by plotting them as functions of the harvest level for various levels of storage. As time evolves, the harvest level changes; as long as $z^* \neq 0$, then the level of storage changes as well. However, changes in storage behave like dt, whereas harvest changes behave like $dt^{1/2}$.[o] When dt becomes infinitesimally small, dt goes to zero faster than $dt^{1/2}$ goes to zero. It is therefore reasonable to treat the storage level as constant for small changes in the harvest.

We begin by solving for the equilibrium storage policy using the approach described in Appendix A. Figure 1.3 illustrates the resulting policy for two different levels of the friction, $\kappa = 0$ in the left-hand graph and $\kappa = 0.05$ in the right-hand one. The three curves plot $z^*(s, y)$ as a function of the harvest, y, for different levels of total storage: the dotted curves correspond to $s = 0$, the dashed curves to $s = 0.25$, and the solid curves

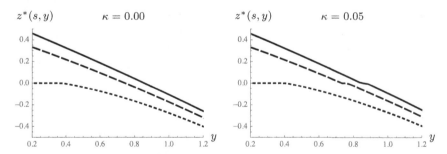

Fig. 1.3 Equilibrium storage policy: Each graph plots $z^*(s, y)$ as a function of the harvest, y, for three different levels of total storage: the dotted curves correspond to $s = 0$, the dashed curves to $s = 0.25$, and the solid curves to $s = 0.50$.

---

[n]This process is also used to model interest rates, where properties of mean reversion and non-negativity are also important [31].

[o]This follows from (1.1) for storage and from (1.2) for the harvest. See Chapter 3 of [29] for an introduction to relevant properties of Itô processes.

to $s = 0.50$. When the harvest is poor, storage operators sell the commodity from storage (that is, $z^* > 0$) as long as storage is positive; when the harvest is good, storage operators buy the commodity and store it (that is, $z^* < 0$); when inventory is high, inventory is either sold more aggressively (that is, positive values of z^* are larger) or bought more cautiously (that is, negative values of z^* are smaller). The right-hand graph shows that when a friction is introduced, a range of harvest values appears for which storage operators temporarily withdraw from the spot market — they neither buy nor sell the commodity until the harvest moves out of this region.

Fig. 1.4 uses the same format as Fig. 1.3, but plots the market clearing spot price. The graphs show that the spot price is decreasing in both the level of the harvest and total storage. When the storage technology contains a friction, the spot price is especially sensitive to the harvest in the region, where $z^* = 0$, corresponding to the kinks in each of the curves in Fig. 1.4, which are aligned with the "flat spots" in Fig. 1.3.

Finally, Fig. 1.5 illustrates the behavior of the expected growth rate in the spot price (the top two graphs) and the volatility (the bottom two graphs), where the latter is expressed as a proportion of the spot price. The graphs have the same format as Fig. 1.3. Consistent with the discussion in Sects.1.3.2 and 1.3.3, in the frictionless case, as long as inventory is positive the expected growth rate in the spot price equals $r + \varepsilon$ (so that the convenience yield is zero) and volatility is approximately constant. During a stock-out, if the harvest is sufficiently low then the inability of storage operators to offset poor harvests results in high spot-price volatility (storage operators cannot buffer harvest shocks) and expected growth rates that deviate from $r + \varepsilon$. Including the friction in the model has little

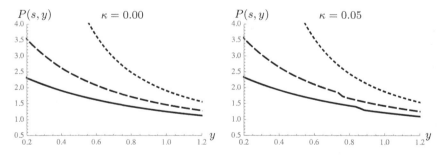

Fig. 1.4   Spot-price behavior: Each graph plots the spot price, $P(s, y)$, as a function of the harvest, y, for three different levels of total storage: the dotted curves correspond to $s = 0$, the dashed curves to $s = 0.25$, and the solid curves to $s = 0.50$.

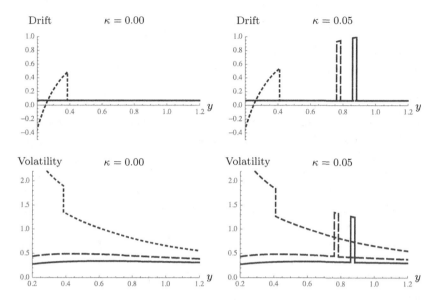

Fig. 1.5   Spot-drift, drift and volatility: Each graph in the top panel plots the expected growth rate in the spot price as a function of the harvest, y, for three different levels of total storage: the dotted curves correspond to $s = 0$, the dashed curves to $s = 0.25$, and the solid curves to $s = 0.50$. Each graph in the bottom panel plots the instantaneous volatility of the spot price for the same three storage levels.

impact on spot-price behavior during stock-outs. However, differences are clearly evident when inventory is positive. Although the expected growth rate still equals $r + \varepsilon$ and spot-price volatility is still low and approximately constant when storage operators are trading in the spot market, neither of these properties hold when storage operators withdraw from the spot market: the top right-hand graph shows that the expected growth rate differs from $r + \varepsilon$ and the bottom right-hand one shows that volatility increases dramatically.

1.4.   Concluding Remarks

This chapter extends the standard competitive storage model of commodity prices by incorporating a transaction cost reflecting the costs of moving a commodity into storage. We derive the conditions for a competitive equilibrium, showing that the real option to delay selling the stored commodity can be valuable and that this leads to a range of spot prices in which storage operators do not trade in the spot market. They will be buyers in the spot market when the delay option's value is at least as great as the cost of moving the commodity into storage, and they will be sellers when its value is zero. When the value of the delay option lies anywhere between zero and the cost of moving the commodity into storage, storage operators do not trade in the spot market. It follows that there are actually two goods in our model — the commodity being traded in the spot market and the commodity being held in storage — with the market value of the stored commodity being determined in the market for ownership of storage operators. The spot price inherits the properties of the market value of the stored commodity when storage operators are active in the spot market: small and relatively persistent price shocks, and an expected growth rate (adjusted for ongoing storage costs) that equals the risk-free interest rate. However, when storage operators are not trading in the spot market, the spot price is decoupled from the market value of the stored commodity, resulting in a period of large and relatively transient shocks to the spot price.

Although our model is framed in terms of three distinct types of agents — consumers, producers, and storage operators — our results apply to a variety of situations that better match some real-world arrangements, where the distinctions between these agents may be blurred. For example, producers might operate their own storage facilities, as is common in markets for agricultural commodities. Producer-storers will send their produce directly to the spot market when the spot price is in the no-trade region, and hold onto whatever inventory they have. Where there is no market for ownership of stand-alone storage operators, as envisaged in our model, the market value of the stored commodity will be determined in the market for ownership of producer-storers.

The results in this chapter have implications for the way we think about and model commodity spot-price behavior. The traditional story is that the convenience yield represents a flow of nonpecuniary benefits received during the period over which the return from storage is being calculated. In contrast, we argue that it represents changes in the present value of benefits that will be received only some time after the measurement period, when the commodity is released from storage. In our model, the convenience yield is the expected excess return on the real option to delay selling the stored commodity. Moreover, if the expected rate of return on storage was measured correctly — using the market value of the stored commodity rather than the spot price — the convenience yield would be zero whenever inventory is positive.

Second, our model makes several predictions about spot-price behavior that are not captured by the stochastic processes typically used when valuing commodity derivatives and other contingent claims. The simplest models assume that the commodity price follows geometric Brownian motion with a constant convenience yield, while other models use a mean-reverting stochastic process to model the behavior of the convenience yield [32, 33]. Our results suggest that neither approach is consistent with a theory of equilibrium spot-price behavior incorporating frictions in the storage and trading process. For example, our results indicate that the spot price will experience periods of unusually low volatility (when the convenience yield is zero), interrupted by periods of unusually high volatility (during which the convenience yield is nonzero). This behavior is not consistent with the approaches described above, although it could be captured in a regime-switching framework [34, 35]. Investigation of such possibilities is left as a topic for future research.

Acknowledgments

We gratefully acknowledge the helpful suggestions of the editor, who also refereed this chapter, which significantly improved the exposition of this chapter.

Appendix A. Numerical Solution Method

We use policy iteration to solve for the social planner's optimal storage policy on a discrete grid in (s, y)-space. The starting point is an initial guess for the social planner's storage policy, denoted $z^{(0)}(s, y)$, which we calculate using Proposition 1.1 for the case where $\partial W/\partial s = 1$ (that is, we set $\partial W/\partial s$ equal to the price when consumption equals the long-run average harvest). Given the storage policy $z^{(n)}(s, y)$, we solve the finite difference approximation of the partial differential equation (1.4) after making the substitution $z^* = z^{(n)}$, using central differences to approximate $\partial W/\partial y$ and $\partial W/\partial s$. We impose numerical boundary conditions along the boundaries of the grid. Once we have found the finite difference approximation to the social planner's objective function, which we denote $W^{(n)}(s, y)$, we use

Proposition 1.1 to calculate the new storage policy $z^{(n+1)}(s,y)$. We repeat this sequence of steps until convergence occurs.

References

[1] L. Evans and G. Guthrie, How options provided by storage affect electricity prices, *Southern Economic Journal*. **75**(3), 681–702 (2009).

[2] L. Evans, G. Guthrie, and A. Lu, The role of storage in a competitive electricity market and the effects of climate change, *Energy Economics*. **36**, 405–418 (2013).

[3] G. Lai, M. X. Wang, S. Kekre, A. Scheller-Wolf, and N. Secomandi, Valuation of storage at a liquefied natural gas terminal, *Operations Research*. **59**(3), 602–616 (2011).

[4] M. Thompson, M. Davison, and H. Rasmussen, Natural gas storage valuation and optimization: A real options application, *Naval Research Logistics*. **56** (3), 226–238 (2009).

[5] B. R. Routledge, D. J. Seppi, and C. S. Spatt, Equilibrium forward curves for commodities, *Journal of Finance*. **55**(3), 1297–1338 (2000).

[6] J.-P. Chavas, P. M. Despins, and T. R. Fortenbery, Inventory dynamics under transaction costs, *American Journal of Agricultural Economics*. **82** (2), 260–273 (2000).

[7] G. M. Constantinides, Capital market equilibrium with transaction costs, *Journal of Political Economy*. **94**(4), 842–862 (1986).

[8] B. Dumas and E. Luciano, An exact solution to a dynamic portfolio choice problem under transaction costs, *Journal of Finance*. **46**(2), 577–595 (1991).

[9] N. Secomandi and D. J. Seppi, Real options and merchant operations of energy and other commodities, *Foundations and Trends in Technology, Information and Operations Management*. **6**(3–4), 161–331 (2014).

[10] B. D. Wright and J. C. Williams, A theory of negative prices for storage, *Journal of Futures Markets*. **9**(1), 1–13 (1989).

[11] N. Kaldor, Speculation and economic stability, *Review of Economic Studies*. **7**(1), 1–27 (1939).

[12] H. Working, Theory of the inverse carrying charge in futures markets, *Journal of Farm Economics*. **30**(1), 1–28 (1948).

[13] H. Working, The theory of price of storage, *American Economic Review*. **39** (6), 1254–1262 (1949).

[14] L. G. Telser, Futures trading and the storage of cotton and wheat, *Journal of Political Economy*. **66**(3), 233–255 (1958).

[15] M. J. Brennan, The supply of storage, *American Economic Review*. **48**(1), 50–72 (1958).

[16] M. Kohn, Competitive speculation, *Econometrica*. **46**(5), 1061–1076 (1978).

[17] J. F. Muth, Rational expectations and the theory of price movements, *Econometrica.* **29**(3), 315–335 (1961).

[18] P. A. Samuelson, Stochastic speculative price, *Proceedings of the National Academy of Sciences.* **68**(2), 335–337 (1971).

[19] J. A. Scheinkman and J. Schechtman, A simple competitive model with production and storage, *Review of Economic Studies.* **50**(3), 427–441 (1983).

[20] B. D. Wright and J. C. Williams, The economic role of commodity storage, *Economic Journal.* **92**(367), 596–614 (1982).

[21] B. D. Wright and J. C. Williams, The welfare effects of the introduction of storage, *Quarterly Journal of Economics.* **99**(1), 169–192 (1984).

[22] M. J. Chambers and R. E. Bailey, A theory of commodity price fluctuations, *Journal of Political Economy.* **104**(5), 924–957 (1996).

[23] A. Deaton and G. Laroque, On the behaviour of commodity prices, *Review of Economic Studies.* **59**(1), 1–23 (1992).

[24] A. Deaton and G. Laroque, Competitive storage and commodity price dynamics, *Journal of Political Economy.* **104**(5), 826–923 (1996).

[25] M. Carlson, Z. Khokher, and S. Titman, Equilibrium exhaustible resource price dynamics, *Journal of Finance.* **62**(4), 1663–1703 (2007).

[26] L. Kogan, D. Livdan, and A. Yaron, Oil futures prices in a production economy with investment constraints, *Journal of Finance.* **54**(3), 1345–1375 (2009).

[27] M. J. Brennan and E. S. Schwartz, Evaluating natural resource investments, *Journal of Business.* **58**(2), 135–157 (1985).

[28] D. A. Dickey and W. A. Fuller, Distribution of the estimators for autoregressive time series with a unit root, *Journal of the American Statistical Association.* **74**(366), 427–431 (1979).

[29] A. K. Dixit and R. S. Pindyck, *Investment Under Uncertainty.* Princeton University Press, Princeton, NJ, USA (1994).

[30] L. Trigeorgis, *Real Options: Managerial Flexibility and Strategy in Resource Allocation.* The MIT Press, Cambridge, MA, USA (1996).

[31] J. C. Cox, J. E. Ingersoll, Jr., and S. A. Ross, A theory of the term structure of interest rates, *Econometrica.* **53**(2), 385–407 (1985).

[32] J. Casassus and P. Collin-Dufresne, Stochastic convenience yield implied from commodity futures and interest rates, *Journal of Finance.* **50**(5), 2283–2331 (2005).

[33] E. S. Schwartz, The stochastic behavior of commodity prices: Implications for valuation and hedging, *Journal of Finance.* **52**(3), 923–973 (1997).

[34] Z. Chen and P. A. Forsyth, Implications of a regime-switching model on natural gas storage valuation and optimal operation, *Quantitative Finance.* **10**(2), 159–176 (2010).

[35] J. D. Hamilton, A new approach to the economic analysis of non-stationary time series and the business cycle, *Econometrica.* **57**(2), 357–384 (1989).

Chapter 2

A Capacitated Commodity Trading Model with Market Power

Victor Martínez-de-Albéniz[*,‡] and Josep Maria Vendrell Simón[†,§]

*IESE Business School, University of Navarra, Av. Pearson 21,
08034 Barcelona, Spain
†European Central Bank, Sonnemannstrasse 20,
60314 Frankfurt am Main Germany

‡valbeniz@iese.edu
§josep-maria.vendrell-simon@ecb.int

In commodity markets, physical traders can take advantage of geographical price spreads by buying a commodity at the location where the price is low and reselling it where it is high. These trading decisions may have an impact on future prices, which we refer to as market power. They are also subject to operational capacity constraints. Our objective in this chapter is to understand how to best utilize this capacitated locational spread option in the presence of market power. We model the trader's market power by altering the drifts of the underlying price stochastic processes. We find that the optimal policy is similar to the classical case without market power: there are two thresholds that determine three regions where it is optimal to: (1) move as much as possible from one market to the other; (2) do the the same in the opposite direction; or (3) do nothing. The values of the thresholds depend on operational costs, as usual, but also on market power and price uncertainty. We characterize these thresholds both in isolation and in a competitive equilibrium.

2.1. Introduction

Commodities are the building blocks of a large part of our economy. Examples include energy, minerals, metals and agricultural products such as oil, natural gas, iron ore, aluminum, silver, gold, sugar, coffee, rice and wheat, as well as intermediate or manufactured products, such as chemicals or generic drugs. They are nowadays relatively easily traded, can be physically delivered anywhere in the world and sometimes can be stored for a reasonable length of time. The volume of commodity trading in the world is colossal: for instance, in 2014 more than 99 million 60 kg coffee bags were exported, out of 141 million produced bags [1], and more than 56 million barrels of oil were traded daily [2]. Commodities are traded in organized markets, such as the Chicago Board of Trade (CBOT), the New York Mercantile Exchange (NYMEX) or the London Metal Exchange (LME), as well as over-the-counter markets.

The price of a commodity can depend on the location where it is traded, because it reflects logistics costs and the local balance of supply and demand. For example, a coffee producer with several factories in Europe pays different prices for delivery of coffee berries to its different factories. Interestingly, for most commodities the price *spread*, that is, the difference between prices at two geographical locations, is usually quite variable over time. In the short term, this spread can significantly deviate from its

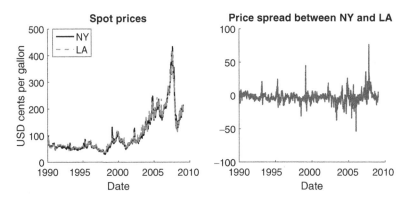

Fig. 2.1   Left panel: jet-fuel daily spot prices (in USD cents per Gallon) at the New York Harbor (NY) and Los Angeles (LA). Right panel: corresponding spread between them Source.

Source: The source of the data is the Energy Information Administration of the U.S. Government (http://www.eia.doe.gov).

long-term average. As an example, Fig. 2.1 illustrates the daily spot price evolution of jet fuel (kerosene) at two locations, the New York Harbor and Los Angeles, from January 1991 to December 2009. The commodity traded in these two markets is exactly the same, since customers (airlines) require a standard chemical composition everywhere. As can be seen in the left-hand panel of this figure, the evolution of the price at these two locations is almost always the same, suggesting that the average spreads are small. However, upon closer examination we observe in the right-hand panel of this figure that the spread can occasionally be quite large. Specifically, the observed price spread is on average $-\$0.025$ (USD) but has a minimum of $-\$0.54$ and a maximum of $\$0.765$. These statistics suggest that although the average price spread between the New York Harbor and Los Angeles is small, at times it can be very large.

Positive, even if transitory, geographical price spreads create profit opportunities for players that can buy a commodity in one market, ship it to a different market, and sell it at this other market. In practice, commodity trading firms such as Bunge, Cargill or Louis Dreyfus, and commodity desks of investment banks are quite active in this area and often own physical resources, such as shipping and storage capacity, to be able to perform these trades.

Deciding how much commodity to trade between two geographically separated markets at a particular time requires consideration of the current price spread, shipping capacity, and how the trader's action might affect the price dynamics at both markets. In particular, if a trade is large enough, it will deflate/inflate the market where the sale/purchase occurs. This price impact is what we call *market power*.

The objective of this chapter is to integrate market power considerations into the operational decision-making of a trader that operates between two geographically separated markets. In this context, finding the optimal trading policy must consider how the stochastic evolution of prices is influenced by the trader's actions. That is, we consider the management of a locational spread option by taking into account a trader's market power. We establish that the commodity price spread dynamics are driven by both exogenous supply and demand shocks and the endogenous rational trader's actions. Our work combines elements from two major streams of research in commodity price modeling (reviewed in Sec. 2.2). On the one hand, one can find reduced-form models of the firm where prices evolve exogenously of trading decisions. These models are extremely practical and easy to use because they only require estimating a few parameters. On the other hand, there exist equilibrium models where the commodity price evolution is endogenously set by the actions of different players in the industry, typically assuming perfect competition (that is, no market power). These models are appealing because they capture the basic economic elements from which market prices emerge. We propose a "hybrid" modeling approach that retains the tractability of the reduced-form models and some of the appeal of the equilibrium models, while also taking into account market power.

For analytical tractability, we focus on a simple setting with a fixed trading capacity. This capacity can be thought of as the maximum possible amount of commodity that the trader can ship per period between the two locations given its logistics resources. In addition, we assume that the inventory in transit between the two markets is constant. This assumption is reasonable when the shipping is done through a pipeline (e.g., gas, oil) or for commodities whose storage capacity is very limited (e.g., electricity). We establish the structure of the trading policy that maximizes the trader's total expected discounted profit over an infinite horizon: given a realization of the current price spread, there exist two thresholds such that the trader buys in the low-price market and sells in the high-price market up to capacity when the spread is below the lower threshold or above the upper threshold, and otherwise does not trade. We characterize these optimal thresholds and study their sensitivity with respect to some model parameters. The structure of this optimal policy is similar to that in the case of no market power, where the thresholds only depend on trading costs, but the thresholds of our optimal policy are also driven by the market power intensity and the volatility of the price processes.

Furthermore, with many traders present in the market, each trader's policy depends on what its competitors do. We analyze with game-theoretical tools the corresponding equilibrium, which we characterize in a symmetric setting. Finally, we discuss how our model can be extended to more general price evolution processes than the one we consider, and the case with more than two markets.

In summary, this chapter makes two main contributions. First, it proposes a novel hybrid modeling approach that incorporates the effect of large trades on the price spread dynamics, characterizing the resulting equilibrium spread evolution process. Second, it provides guidelines to traders, in particular quantifying the potential benefit of optimizing their trading strategies when they have market power, compared to using simple policies that ignore this feature. Our work can potentially be relevant for the management of other energy and commodity real options, including different types of spread options (see Secomandi and Seppi [3]).

The rest of this chapter is organized as follows. In Sec. 2.2 we review the related literature. In Sec. 2.3 we describe our model. In Sec. 2.4 we characterize the structure of the optimal policy. In Sec. 2.5 we present extensions. In Sec. 2.6 we conclude and discuss future research directions. Appendix A includes the proofs of our results.

2.2. Literature Review

There is a significant amount of research on commodity price modeling and commodity trading, with at least two different literature streams: the first in economics and finance; the second in operations management.

Researchers in economics and finance have developed various models of the evolution of prices in commodity markets. As pointed out in the introduction, there are typically two ways of modeling this evolution.

The first approach describes spot prices with reduced-form (non-equilibrium) models where the price evolution is determined in an exogenous manner. Gibson and Schwartz [4] model the convenience yield (a measure of the benefits from owning a commodity asset versus holding a long futures contract on the asset) and the spot price as separate, possibly correlated, stochastic processes (see also [5] for a different interpretation of convenience). Schwartz [6] develops three variations of a stochastic model driven by one, two or three factors taking into account mean reversion, convenience yields, and stochastic interest rates. Schwartz and Smith [7] propose a two-factor stochastic spot-price model determined by the combination of short-term and long-term factors. Collectively, the authors apply their models to copper, gold, and crude oil price data. These models are commonly used in the energy and commodity real options literature [8–12].

The second approach develops industry equilibrium models, which endogenously determine the evolution of commodity prices by capturing the underlying evolution of supply and demand. These models usually assume perfect competition, which results in social welfare being maximized. One of the first papers in this area is that of Deaton and Laroque [13]. These authors develop a rational expectations model for commodity prices that explains the high observed autocorrelation and variability of these prices. They base their model on the existence of competitive speculators that hold inventory of the commodity: they accumulate inventory when the price is low, and deplete it when the price is high. As a result, speculators act as regulators of the commodity prices. These authors extend this work [14], finding that speculation alone is not sufficient to explain the high observed positive autocorrelation of commodity prices: part of it must be caused by the underlying processes of supply and demand. The works of Chambers and Bailey [15] and Routledge *et al.* [16] also use a competitive rational expectations model to explain the properties of commodity prices.

Some equilibrium models have also been developed to explain geographical price differences, but, in contrast to our work, typically do not consider market power. Williams and Wright [17, Chapter 9] propose an equilibrium model of commodity shipping between two locations, with or without storage at each of these two locations. Routledge *et al.* [18] study the correlation between prices of different commodities within broad families (e.g., natural gas and electricity in energy). They model the substitutability of these commodities and find existence of equilibrium price processes, in a setting where rational agents convert one commodity into another. In particular, they focus on the price difference between natural gas and electricity, known in the industry as the *spark spread*, which is used extensively by commodity traders. De Vany and Walls [19] study the natural gas price evolution at different points of the United States. pipeline network system. They show that geographical price spreads are bounded by the transmission costs within the network, except when the capacity of some links is fully utilized. Their analysis suggests that the U.S. natural gas market is generally competitive, with arbitrage opportunities limited to short-term imbalances when flow is constrained.

Our work is an attempt at bridging these two main streams of work. Specifically, we incorporate equilibrium aspects in a reduced-form price evolution model, by adding an endogenous component to this model to account for the effect of large trades on the future price evolution.

Our research is also related to the operations management literature that deals with commodities under price or demand uncertainty, because we consider operational constraints on the trader's activity. Golabi [20] proves that a sequence of critical price levels determines the optimal ordering strategy when the purchase price is uncertain and demand is deterministic. Wang [21] proves that a myopic inventory policy is optimal in a multi-period model with stochastic demand and purchase prices that decrease over time. Berling and Martínez-de-Albéniz [22] describe the optimal ordering policy when the purchase price follows a geometric Brownian motion or is mean-reverting. Berling and Xie [23] develop approximations for this problem. Goel and Gutierrez [24] focus on the management of the inventory of a commodity, in the presence of both price and demand uncertainty. They establish the structure of the optimal inventory policy and apply their policy using the price model of Schwartz and Smith [7]. Secomandi [25] considers commodity trading modeling the details of the operations involved in managing storage assets, that is, storage facilities or contracts on their capacity. He derives the structure of the optimal trading policy and assesses the benefit of optimally managing the storage asset flow constraints in a natural gas application. The same author [26] shows the equivalence of different models for valuing contracts on the transport capacity of natural gas pipelines and provides empirical support for the use of real option models to value such contracts in practice. Lai *et al.* [27] derive a related structure in the context of liquefied natural gas shipping and storage. Caldentey *et al.* [28] develop a heuristic for managing copper mining operations under price uncertainty and apply it to a real project in Chile.

Our work also combines price evolution models from economics and finance, together with detailed operational models. In particular, we include equilibrium aspects in the real option model of Secomandi [25].

2.3. Model

In Sec. 2.3.1 we describe our model setup with a trader that operates in two geographically separated commodity markets. In Sec. 2.3.2 we specify the price processes of the commodity in these markets. In Sec. 2.3.3 we characterize the price spread distribution as a function of the trader policies and formulate the trader's optimization problem when there is market power.

2.3.1. *Setup*

Consider two markets for a given commodity at two geographically distinct locations A and B. Trading of the commodity may occur between A and B. In particular, traders may choose to buy the commodity at one location and ship it, at a cost, to the other location. Shipping of physical commodities is not simultaneous, that is, it incurs a positive lead-time. For the sake of simplicity and tractability, we assume that this lead-time is zero, implicitly assuming that at any given time what is bought at one location is immediately sold at the other. Thus, our model describes a pipeline with fixed content, so that shipping of the commodity between the two locations simply entails opening a faucet at either one of the two ends of the pipeline. Our model could also handle a shipping process that does not

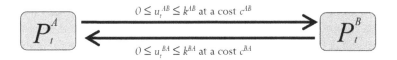

Fig. 2.2   Summary of model features.

involve a pipeline, as long as the inventory level along the route remains constant. For instance, consider a set of trucks or ships that on each day can move towards A or towards B in a coordinated manner. The quantity originating at A and arriving at B will be identical and will be constrained by the maximum speed in the system.

The pipeline capacity is the maximum achievable flow per unit of time. We denote by k^{AB} the trader's controlled shipping capacity from A to B, per period, and k^{BA} the one from B to A, which might be different.

We model time as a continuous variable and denote it by $t \geq 0$. We denote the price at time t of the commodity at markets A and B as P_t^A and P_t^B, respectively. We consider time-independent and constant marginal shipping costs: c^{AB} is the cost of moving one unit of commodity from A to B, and c^{BA} is the analogue when shipping the commodity from B to A. Using constant marginal costs is a strong assumption but it has been made before in the literature [26].

Let u_t^{AB} and u_t^{BA} be the quantity of commodity shipped from A to B and from B to A respectively, at time t. These quantities are constrained as follows:

$$0 \leq u_t^{AB} \leq k^{AB} \text{ and } 0 \leq u_t^{BA} \leq k^{BA}.$$

The incurred shipping cost is equal to $c^{AB} u_t^{AB} + c^{BA} u_t^{BA}$. Figure 2.2 summarizes the main model features.

2.3.2.   *Price Processes*

We let $u_t := u_t^{AB} - u_t^{BA}$ denote the trader's *net trading quantity*, and $v_t := v_t^{AB} - v_t^{BA}$ the other players' aggregate net trading quantity at time t, where v_t^{AB} and v_t^{BA} are their aggregate trading quantities at time t from location A to location B and vice versa, respectively.

We model the price processes at A and B as correlated arithmetic processes:

$$\begin{pmatrix} dP_t^A \\ dP_t^B \end{pmatrix} = \begin{bmatrix} \alpha(P_t^A, P_t^B) + \beta_A(u_t + v_t) \\ \alpha(P_t^A, P_t^B) - \beta_B(u_t + v_t) \end{bmatrix} dt + \begin{pmatrix} \sigma_{A1} & \sigma_{A2} \\ \sigma_{B1} & \sigma_{B2} \end{pmatrix} \begin{pmatrix} dW_t^1 \\ dW_t^2 \end{pmatrix},$$

$$\tag{2.1}$$

where W_t^1 and W_t^2 are independent Wiener processes, α can be any exogenous function, and β_A, β_B, σ_{A1}, σ_{A2}, σ_{B1}, and σ_{B2} are positive constants.

The net flow $u_t + v_t$ between A and B at time t has a direct impact on the drift of the price processes: when positive, it increases the drift of the price at A and decreases the drift of the price at B. This feature is qualitatively intuitive. Furthermore, we model this dependency as *linear* for tractability.

The function α can be freely specified. In particular, it can incorporate mean-reverting prices, as long as the mean-reverting effect is the same in both markets. For example, one could let $\alpha(P_t^A, P_t^B) = \kappa[\mu - (\lambda^A P_t^A + \lambda^B P_t^B)]$, where κ, μ, λ^A, and λ^B are non-negative parameters.

In contrast to common reduced-form price models [6], we consider arithmetic processes instead of geometric processes. Our assumption guarantees the analytical tractability of our model. However, geometric processes can be dealt with numerically as shown in Sec. 2.5.1.

The trader's margin at time t depends on the corresponding price spread, which we define as $G_t := P_t^B - P_t^A$. From (2.1), we have $dG_t = -(\beta_A + \beta_B)(u_t + v_t)dt + (\sigma_{B2} - \sigma_{A2})dW_t^2 - (\sigma_{A1} - \sigma_{B1})dW_t^1$. Thus, G_t is a stochastic process that can be expressed as

$$dG_t = -\beta(u_t + v_t)dt + \sigma dW_t, \qquad (2.2)$$

where β is defined as $\beta_A + \beta_B$, σ^2 as $(\sigma_{B2} - \sigma_{A2})^2 + (\sigma_{A1} - \sigma_{B1})^2$, and W_t is a Wiener process.

2.3.3. *Relating the Spread Distribution and the Trader's Policy*

In the remainder of this chapter, we assume that the traded quantities u_t (net flow from the trader) and v_t (net flow from the rest of the market) only depend on G_t, and that these quantities are piecewise constant functions of G_t with a finite number of jumps. This assumption guarantees analytical tractability. As a result, both revenue and cost depend only on G_t. We can thus write u_t and v_t as $u_t = u(G_t)$ and $v_t = v(G_t)$. Expression (2.2) implies that the price spread G satisfies the stochastic differential equation $dG_t = A(G_t)dW_t + B(G_t)dt$, with $A(G) = \sigma$ and $B(G) = -\beta[u(G) + v(G)]$. The solution to this equation can be characterized as the following proposition states.

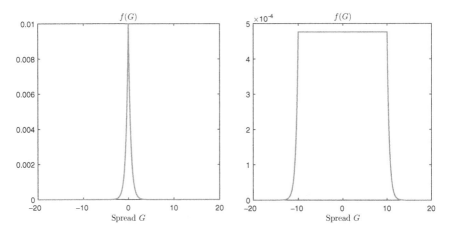

Fig. 2.3   Stationary p.d.f. of G, with $v \equiv 0$, $\beta = 1$, and $\sigma = 1$. On the left panel, $u = -2$ for $G < 0$ and $u = +2$ for $G \geq 0$; on the right panel, $u = -2$ for $G < -10$, $u = 0$ for $-10 \leq G < 10$, and $u = +2$ for $G \geq 10$.

Proposition 2.1. *If for a certain $\epsilon > 0$,* $\lim\limits_{G \to -\infty} B \geq \epsilon$ *and* $\lim\limits_{G \to +\infty} B \leq -\epsilon$, *the price spread G has a stationary probability density function (p.d.f.), denoted $f(G)$, which satisfies*

$$\frac{1}{2}A^2(G)\frac{d^2f}{dG^2} - B(G)\frac{df}{dG} = 0. \tag{2.3}$$

Equation (2.3) is known as the Chapman–Kolmogorov equation and is a backward parabolic partial differential equation [29]. In our case, it can be written as

$$\frac{1}{2}\sigma^2\frac{d^2f}{dG^2} + \beta[u(G) + v(G)]\frac{df}{dG} = 0. \tag{2.4}$$

Thus, the control $u(G)$ has a direct influence on the p.d.f. of the spread, $f(G)$, which we sometimes denote as $f(G|u)$ to make this dependency apparent. This link is central to the optimization of the trader's shipping decisions, because the trader can capture profit now at the expense of reducing future spreads and, hence, future profits. As an illustration, Fig. 2.3 shows the stationary p.d.f. $f(G|u)$ for two controls $u(G)$ with $v \equiv 0$.

2.3.4.   *Optimization of the Trading Policy*

Given a realization of the price spread at time t, G_t, and given the capacities k^{AB} and k^{BA}, we are interested in finding the optimal shipping decision

u_t that maximizes the trader's profits. Because the evolution of the system is governed by the price spread G_t, the optimal policy is a rule that dictates u_t, that is, how much product to buy and sell depending on G_t. In other words, the trader must decide on a function $u(G_t)$ that maximizes its profit (this friction is stationary in our infinite horizon model, introduced next).

Under a given policy, the profit at time t is calculated from the revenue $G_t u(G_t)$ and the trading cost $c(u) := c^{AB}u^+ + c^{BA}u^-$ evaluated at $u = u(G_t)$, where for any scalar a we define $a^+ := \max\{a, 0\}$ and $a^- := \max\{-a, 0\}$. We focus here on maximizing the trader's expected total discounted profit over an infinite horizon, although similar results can be derived for the expected average profit per unit of time. We assume that the trader is risk-neutral. We discount future cash flows at a rate $r > 0$. At time 0, given G_0, the trader seeks to find a function $u(G_t)$ that maximizes

$$J(u, G_0) := \mathbb{E}\left[\left.\int_0^\infty \left(G_t u(G_t) - c^{AB}u^+(G_t) - c^{BA}u^-(G_t)\right)e^{-rt}dt \right| G_0\right].$$
(2.5)

The discounted profit $J(u, G_0)$ depends on the current price spread G_0 and the function $u(G_t)$, but the optimal policy $u(G_t)$ does not depend on G_0, as shown in Sec. 2.4.

2.4. Analysis

In this section, we solve the maximization of the objective function in (2.5). We consider the case with no market power in Sec. 2.4.1, then consider the general case in Sec. 2.4.2, discuss comparative statics in Sec. 2.4.3 and characterize the market equilibrium Sec. 2.4.4.

2.4.1. *Optimal Policy without Market Power*

If the current trading activity does not influence the future prices, that is, $\beta = 0$, then $f(G|u)$ is independent of u. In this case, the trader's optimal policy simply maximizes the profit from trading at t, that is, it solves the optimization

$$\max_{0 \le u_t^{AB} \le k^{AB}, \; 0 \le u_t^{BA} \le k^{BA}} (P_t^B - P_t^A)(u_t^{AB} - u_t^{BA}) - c^{AB}u_t^{AB} - c^{BA}u_t^{BA}.$$

It is easy to see that the optimal policy for this case is such that at most one of the two flow variables u_t^{AB} and u_t^{BA} is nonzero and at optimality the net flow u_t is

$$
u_t^* = \begin{cases} k^{AB}, & G_t \geq c^{AB}, \\ 0, & c^{AB} \geq G_t \geq -c^{BA}, \\ -k^{BA}, & -c^{BA} > G_t, \end{cases} \tag{2.6}
$$

where the superscripted $*$ denotes optimality. In words, a trader that does not influence future prices will trade at maximum capacity provided that the price spread exceeds the trading cost, as in the model of Secomandi [26]. If the trader's activity does influence future prices, the structure of the trader's optimal shipping policy generalizes (2.6), as we establish in Sec. 2.4.2.

2.4.2. *Optimal Policy with Market Power*

We use optimal control theory to maximize (2.5). We denote $J^*(G_0)$ as the value function evaluated at the initial price spread G_0. The trader's maximization problem can be written as

$$
J^*(G_0) = \sup_u J(u, G_0), \tag{2.7}
$$

where the supremum is taken over all functions such that $u(G) \in [-k^{BA}, k^{AB}]$. The optimality conditions for (2.7) are given by the Hamilton–Jacobi–Bellman (HJB) equation (see [30] for more details). They allow us to characterize the optimal policy in Proposition 2.2.

Proposition 2.2. *The value function satisfies*

$$
\frac{\sigma^2}{2} \frac{d^2 J^*}{dG^2} - \beta v \frac{dJ^*}{dG} - r J^*
$$
$$
+ \max_{-k^{BA} \leq x \leq k^{AB}} \left\{ Gx - c^{BA} x^- - c^{AB} x^+ - \beta x \frac{dJ^*}{dG} \right\} = 0. \tag{2.8}
$$

In addition, a maximizer in (2.8) corresponds to the control determined by an optimal policy $u^*(G)$ and $J^* = J(u^*, \cdot)$.

The value returned by the optimal control function $u^*(G)$ can thus be obtained by solving

$$
\max_{-k^{BA} \leq x \leq k^{AB}} \left(G - \beta \frac{dJ^*}{dG} \right) x - c^{BA} x^- - c^{AB} x^+. \tag{2.9}
$$

Since the objective is piecewise-linear in x, we obtain that $u^*(G)$ can take on only three values: $-k^{\mathrm{BA}}, 0,$ or k^{AB}. Hence, a bang–bang policy is optimal when trading occurs. In fact, under mild assumptions, the structure of the optimal policy is to apply one of these three values in three adjacent price spread intervals, as stated in Theorem 2.1.

Theorem 2.1. *Assume that $v(G)$ is non-decreasing, $v(G) \geq 0$ for $G \geq 0$, $v(G) \leq 0$ for $G \leq 0$, $\lim_{G\to+\infty} v(G) > 0$ and $\lim_{G\to-\infty} v(G) < 0$. Then there exist m^{BA} and m^{AB} with $m^{\mathrm{BA}} \leq m^{\mathrm{AB}}$ so that the optimal policy for (2.7) is*

$$
u^*(G) = \begin{cases} -k^{\mathrm{BA}}, & G \leq m^{\mathrm{BA}}, \\ 0, & m^{\mathrm{BA}} < G \leq m^{\mathrm{AB}}, \\ k^{\mathrm{AB}}, & G > m^{\mathrm{AB}}. \end{cases}
$$

According to Theorem 2.1, the optimal policy is characterized by three distinct and constant decisions, in three price spread regions: if $G \in (-\infty, m^{\mathrm{BA}}]$ then it is optimal to move as much product as possible from market B to market A (k^{BA}); if $G \in (m^{\mathrm{AB}}, \infty)$ then it is optimal to move as much commodity as possible in the opposite direction, from A to B (k^{AB}); and if $G \in (m^{\mathrm{BA}}, m^{\mathrm{AB}}]$ then it is optimal to wait for larger spreads to occur. This structure resembles the one for case with no market power, (see expression (2.6)) but with different thresholds. Indeed, with no market power the optimal thresholds are $-c^{\mathrm{BA}}$ and c^{AB}. Hence, market power changes the optimal trading policy by modifying the values of the price spreads that trigger when a trader should begin to ship product from one market to the other. Theorem 2.1 requires certain regularity conditions on v. These conditions are quite natural: since v represents the drift of the spread process when the trader is absent, that is, $u = 0$, essentially they state that when the spread is positive or negative it tends to get closer to zero over time.

Proposition 2.3 characterizes the optimal thresholds.

Proposition 2.3. *The thresholds that define the optimal policy satisfy*

$$
m^{\mathrm{BA}} + c^{\mathrm{BA}} = \beta \frac{dJ^*}{dG}(m^{\mathrm{BA}}),
$$

$$
m^{\mathrm{AB}} - c^{\mathrm{AB}} = \beta \frac{dJ^*}{dG}(m^{\mathrm{AB}}). \tag{2.10}
$$

In addition, it holds that $-c^{\mathrm{BA}} - \beta k^{\mathrm{BA}}/r \le m^{\mathrm{BA}} \le -c^{\mathrm{BA}}$ *and* $c^{\mathrm{AB}} \le m^{\mathrm{AB}} \le c^{\mathrm{AB}} + \beta k^{\mathrm{AB}}/r$.

Although no closed-form expression is available for the thresholds, Proposition 2.3 provides an implicit condition to compute them numerically by simple search. It also states that it is never optimal to ship below cost, that is, that if $u^*(G) > 0$ then $G > c^{\mathrm{AB}}$ and if $u^*(G) < 0$ then $G < -c^{\mathrm{BA}}$, which is intuitive. Indeed, trading below cost would, on the one hand, yield immediate negative profits and, on the other hand, reduce the probability of large spreads in the future, which would both be detrimental to the trader. If the trader has no market power ($\beta = 0$), then $m^{\mathrm{BA}} = -c^{\mathrm{BA}}$ and $m^{\mathrm{AB}} = c^{\mathrm{AB}}$, and we hence recover the result shown in (2.6).

Corollary 2.1, which is a direct consequence of Proposition 2.3, identifies the asymptotic behavior of the optimal thresholds when the trader is small compared to the market.

Corollary 2.1. *If* $k^{\mathrm{AB}}, k^{\mathrm{BA}} \to 0$, *then* $m^{\mathrm{BA}} \to -c^{\mathrm{BA}}$ *and* $m^{\mathrm{AB}} \to c^{\mathrm{AB}}$.

This result states that in the limit (when $k^{\mathrm{AB}} = k^{\mathrm{BA}} = 0$), our optimal policy is the same as that of a rational trader with no market power. Proposition 2.4 provides additional properties of the optimal thresholds m^{BA} and m^{AB} in a symmetric system.

Proposition 2.4. *If* $c^{\mathrm{AB}} = c^{\mathrm{BA}}$, $k^{\mathrm{AB}} = k^{\mathrm{BA}}$ *and* $v(-G) = -v(G)$ *for all* G, *then* $m^{\mathrm{BA}} = -m^{\mathrm{AB}}$ *and* $J^*(-G) = J^*(G)$ *for all* G.

This result states that in a symmetric system, where in particular the trader has the same shipping marginal cost and capacity from A to B and from B to A, the optimal policy is also symmetric. Hence, the search for the optimal policy in symmetric systems simplifies to effectively finding only one threshold instead of two.

2.4.3. *Comparative Statics*

We now investigate numerically the sensitivity of the optimal policy and value function with respect to the model parameters, namely the trader's shipping capacities k^{AB} and k^{BA}, the shipping marginal cost c^{AB} and c^{BA}, the price volatility σ, and the price elasticity to trading β.

The results are obtained by computing, for each threshold policy u, the corresponding value function $J(u, G)$. The optimal policy is identified from (2.10) and corresponds to the policy that, for a given G_0, maximizes

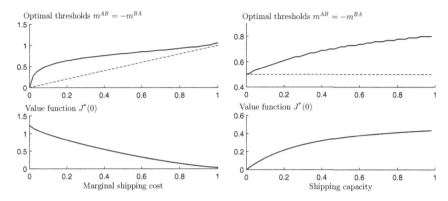

Fig. 2.4 Optimal thresholds (top panels) and value function, evaluated at $G = 0$ (bottom panels). In the left panel, $c^{AB} = c^{BA}$ is varied; in the right panel, $k^{AB} = k^{BA}$ is varied. We use $c^{AB} = c^{BA} = 0.5$, $k^{AB} = k^{BA} = 1$, $v(G) = 1$ when $G \geq 1$, $v(G) = -1$ when $G \leq -1$ and $v(G) = 0$ otherwise, $\beta = 1$, $\sigma = 0.5$, and $r = 10\%$. In the top panels, the dotted line corresponds to the shipping cost.

$J(u, G_0)$ over u. For simplicity, we focus on the symmetric case where $c^{AB} = c^{BA} = c$, $k^{AB} = k^{BA} = k$, and $v(-G) = -v(G)$ for all G. According to Proposition 2.4, we have that $J^*(-G) = J^*(G)$ and only one threshold needs to be calculated.

We first depict the impact of marginal cost and capacities in Fig. 2.4. This figure shows the optimal values for the thresholds $m^{AB} = -m^{BA}$ and the value function $J^*(G)$, evaluated at the value $G = 0$. This case corresponds to a starting situation where the trader must wait for to make a trade. On the left panel, the shipping capacity is fixed and the shipping marginal cost varies; on the the right panel, the shipping marginal cost is fixed and the shipping capacity varies.

Not surprisingly, we observe that the value functions are decreasing and convex in shipping cost $c^{AB} = c^{BA}$, and increasing and concave in shipping capacity $k^{AB} = k^{BA}$. More interestingly, the optimal threshold increases steeply initially but less so thereafter. Thus, the difference $m^{AB} - c^{AB}$ increases quickly and then progressively decreases to zero. Thus, when the marginal shipping cost is large, the optimal threshold is close to this cost and the trader's optimal policy resembles that for the case of no market power. The optimal threshold increases in the shipping capacity k^{AB}. This behavior suggests that a trader with larger shipping capacity will wait for large spreads before trading, thereby exerting more market power than a

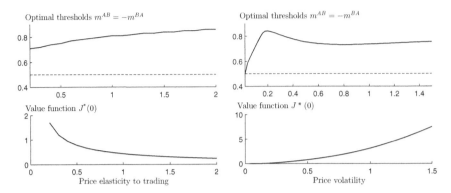

Fig. 2.5   Optimal thresholds (top panels) and value function, evaluated at $G = 0$ (bottom panels). In the left panel, β is varied; in the right panel, σ is varied. We use $c^{AB} = c^{BA} = 0.5$, $k^{AB} = k^{BA} = 1$, $v(G) = 1$ when $G \geq 1$, $v(G) = -1$ when $G \leq -1$ and $v(G) = 0$ otherwise, $\beta = 1$, $\sigma = 0.5$, and $r = 10\%$. In the top panels, the dotted line corresponds to the shipping cost.

trader with smaller shipping capacity. In particular, when k^{AB} is close to zero a trader behaves as in the case of no market power, cf. Proposition 2.1.

Figure 2.5 illustrates the impact of the price evolution parameters: elasticity to trading (β, the impact of a one traded unit on the future spread variation, and volatility σ). The value function decreases in β and increases in σ, because lower elasticity to trading and higher volatility magnify spreads, thereby making trading more valuable. This numerical finding is not surprising given that real option values usually increase in the volatility of the underlying price processes [31].

The behavior of the optimal threshold in Fig. 2.5 is less intuitive. The larger the β, the more the trader's impact on the price spreads, which reduces the probability of seeing large spreads in the future. As a result, a trader chooses to increase the absolute value of the thresholds that makes shipping the commodity optimal. The dependency of the optimal thresholds on σ is non-monotonic. For small volatility, the price process is very concentrated around zero, and hence it is optimal to ship the commodity as soon as the spread exceeds the marginal shipping cost. As σ increases, the probability of seeing larger spreads (above the trader's marginal shipping cost) also increases and hence the trader can benefit from these large spreads by increasing the absolute value of the optimal thresholds. But as σ becomes larger, given that the competing traders are assumed to act as soon as $G > 1$

and $G < -1$, large spreads (above their own traders' threshold, which is equal to 1 in this case) do not occur frequently. As a result, the trader finds it in its best interest to reduce the absolute value of its thresholds, so as to benefit more often from nonzero spreads.

2.4.4. *Market Equilibrium*

So far we have considered the optimization problem of a trader given that all the other traders follow a fixed trading policy, the function denoted as $v(G)$. However, it is natural to model them as rational players that optimize their own actions. Hence, the optimal policy $u^*(G)$ derived in Sec. 2.4.2 is in fact the best-response of one trader to the competitors' trading strategies. We now study the strategic interactions among n players in the market, with trader $i = 1, \ldots, n$ trading $u_t^i = u^i(G_t)$ units of the commodity when the spread is G_t. The rule $u^i(\cdot)$ is the best-response of trader i to the competitors' actions, which are captured via the function

$$v_t^i \equiv v^i(G_t) := \sum_{j \neq i} u^j(G_t).$$

We analyze the equilibria of the game in pure strategies. We focus here on the symmetric case, where all traders have the same marginal shipping costs c^{BA} and c^{AB}, the same shipping capacities k^{BA} and k^{AB}, and they all maximize total expected profit discounted at the same rate r. In addition, for simplicity we assume that $c^{BA} = c^{AB}$ and $k^{BA} = k^{AB}$, although the results can be extended to the more general case.

When all traders are identical, there is a unique symmetric equilibrium. Indeed, in such an equilibrium all players use the same trading strategy $u^i(\cdot) = u(\cdot)$, and hence $v^i(G) = (n-1)u(G)$. Since $v(\cdot)$ satisfies the assumptions of Theorem 2.1, there exist two common optimal thresholds m^{BA} and m^{AB} that determine how all players trade. Hence, the equilibrium value function J^* of each trader satisfies

$$\frac{\sigma^2}{2} \frac{d^2 J^*}{dG^2} = \begin{cases} \beta n k^{AB} \dfrac{dJ^*}{dG} + rJ^* - k^{AB}(G - c^{AB}), & m^{AB} \leq G, \\ rJ^*, & m^{BA} \leq G \leq m^{AB}, \\ -\beta n k^{BA} \dfrac{dJ^*}{dG} + rJ^* - k^{BA}(-G - c^{BA}), & G \leq m^{BA}. \end{cases}$$

In addition, it holds that

$$m^{BA} + c^{BA} = \beta \frac{dJ^*}{dG}(m^{BA}),$$

$$m^{AB} - c^{AB} = \beta \frac{dJ^*}{dG}(m^{AB}).$$

These equations can be solved to derive the equation stated in Theorem 2.2 that implicitly provides the equilibrium thresholds.

Theorem 2.2. *If $c^{AB} = c^{BA} = c$ and $k^{AB} = k^{BA} = k$, there is a unique symmetric equilibrium such that $m^{BA} = -m^{AB} = m^{eq}$ where*

$$m^{eq} = c + \frac{\beta\theta \left(e^{\theta m^{eq}} - e^{-\theta m^{eq}}\right)\left(-\frac{\nu\beta n k^2}{r^2} + \frac{k}{r}\right)}{\left(\theta + \nu - \frac{\beta\theta\nu k}{r}\right)e^{\theta m^{eq}} - \left(\theta - \nu - \frac{\beta\theta\nu k}{r}\right)e^{-\theta m^{eq}}}$$

with $\nu = \left[\sqrt{(n\beta k)^2 + 2r\sigma^2} - n\beta k\right]/\sigma^2$ and $\theta = \sqrt{2r}/\sigma$.

Theorem 2.2 provides an equation that can be solved numerically to obtain the values of the price spreads at which all traders in equilibrium use their shipping capacity. This result can be used to investigate the sensitivity of the equilibrium threshold m^{eq} with respect to the model parameters. In particular, in accordance with Corollary 2.1, one can check that m^{eq} is decreasing in n, so that as competition becomes more intense each trader sets its own optimal threshold closer and closer to its marginal shipping cost, and in the limit $n \to \infty$ all traders behave as if they had no market power.

2.5.   Extensions

In this section, we present two extensions of our model. In Sec. 2.5.1 we consider alternative price processes and cost structures. In Sec. 2.5.2 we focus on the case of a network of geographical locations connected by the traders' shipping capacities.

2.5.1.   *Alternative Price Processes*
and Cost Structures

In Sec. 2.3.2 we recast the two stochastic processes for the prices P_t^A and P_t^B into a single stochastic process for the price spread $G_t = P_t^B - P_t^A$. This simplification is possible under the following two assumptions:

- The term dG_t can be expressed only as a function of G_t, which occurs, for instance, when the actions of the competitors v_t only depend on G_t, rather than on (P_t^A, P_t^B);
- The cost function of the trader is the product of a constant times the quantity of commodity being shipped, which implies that the marginal shipping cost is independent of (P_t^A, P_t^B).

These assumptions may not be valid when one considers general cost functions found in the literature, for example those including shipping losses [26]. Unfortunately, when either one of these two assumptions is not satisfied, then the approach developed in this chapter becomes significantly more complicated. We can nevertheless provide guidelines on how to deal with such more general settings. In such cases, the generic formulation for the price processes extends (2.1) to

$$dP_t^A = \left[\alpha^A(P_t^A, P_t^B) + \beta^A(P_t^A, P_t^B)\left(u_t + v_t(P_t^A, P_t^B) \right) \right] dt$$
$$+ \sigma^A(P_t^A, P_t^B)dW_t^A,$$
$$dP_t^B = \left[\alpha^B(P_t^A, P_t^B) - \beta^B(P_t^A, P_t^B)\left(u_t + v_t(P_t^A, P_t^B) \right) \right] dt$$
$$+ \sigma^B(P_t^A, P_t^B)dW_t^B. \tag{2.11}$$

The objective function thus becomes

$$J(u, P_0^A, P_0^B) := \mathbb{E}\left[\int_0^\infty \left\{ (P_t^B - P_t^A)u_t - c\left(P_t^A, P_t^B, u_t \right) \right\} \right.$$
$$\left. \times e^{-rt}dt \middle| P_0^A, P_0^B \right],$$

where P_t^A and P_t^B evolve following (2.11) and $u_t = u(P_t^A, P_t^B)$. In this case, the analysis becomes two-dimensional and the solution cannot be easily computed.

One particular case of this extended formulation is geometric Brownian motion, in which, for $i \in \{A, B\}$, $\alpha^i = 0$, $\beta^i = \bar{\beta}^i P_t^i$, and $\sigma^i = \bar{\sigma}^i P_t^i$, with $\bar{\beta}^i$ and $\bar{\sigma}^i$ given constants. Figure 2.6 shows the optimal policy for this case under constant marginal shipping costs. We observe that the bang–bang nature of the policy is preserved, but the optimal threshold is a function of (P_t^A, P_t^B) instead of $G_t = P_t^B - P_t^A$.

Another particular case of interest is that of mean-reverting prices. Indeed, the price in a given location may revert to a "local" average. For instance, consider the case $\alpha^i = \kappa^i \left[(\bar{\alpha}^i - \ln \left(P_t^i \right) \right] P_t^i$, $\beta^i = \bar{\beta}^i P_t^i$, and

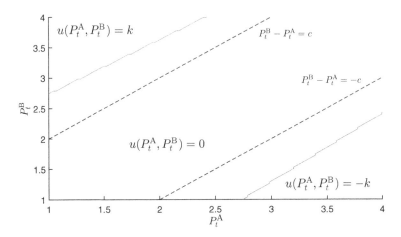

Fig. 2.6   Optimal policy for the geometric Brownian motion, with $\bar{\beta}^i = 1$, $\bar{\sigma}^i = 0.2$. Marginal shipping costs are set to $c(P_t^A, P_t^B, u) = c|u|$ with $c = 1$, and shipping capacity to $k^{AB} = k^{BA} = 1$. The competitor is assumed to ship $v_t(P_t^A, P_t^B) = 1$ if $P_t^B - P_t^A \geq 2$, $v_t(P_t^A, P_t^B) = -1$ if $P_t^B - P_t^A \leq -2$, and zero otherwise. The interest rate is set to $r = 10\%$.

$\sigma^i = \bar{\sigma}^i P_t^i$ for $i \in \{A, B\}$. Figure 2.7 shows that the bang–bang nature of the policy is preserved, but again the optimal threshold depends on (P_t^A, P_t^B) rather than $G_t = P_t^B - P_t^A$.

2.5.2.   *Trading in a Network*

The model developed in this chapter considers trading between two locations. Trading opportunities may be possible between many potential markets, e.g., Routledge *et al.* [18] consider the case of a network. We can extend our model to a connected graph with n locations. For this purpose, define the trader's shipping quantity between markets i and j as u^{ij}, the competitors' shipping quantity as v^{ij}, the trader's shipping capacity as k^{ij} and its marginal shipping cost as c^{ij}. We must also redefine the price process evolution as

$$
dP_t^i = \left[\alpha(\mathbf{P}_t) + \sum_{j \neq i} \beta^{ij}(u_t^{ij} + v_t^{ij}) - \sum_{j \neq i} \beta^{ji}(u_t^{ji} + v_t^{ji}) \right] dt
$$
$$
+ \sigma^i dW_t^i, \forall i \in \{1, \ldots, n\}, \tag{2.12}
$$

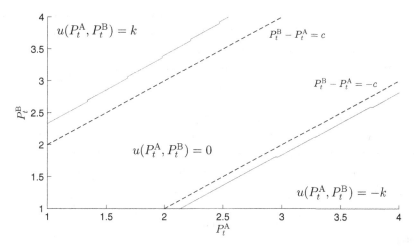

Fig. 2.7   Optimal policy for a scenario with mean-reverting prices, with $\kappa^i = 0.5$, $\bar{\alpha}^A = 0.8$, $\bar{\alpha}^B = 1$, $\bar{\beta}^i = 1$, and $\bar{\sigma}^i = 0.2$. Marginal shipping costs are set to $c(P_t^A, P_t^B, u) = c|u|$ with $c = 1$, and shipping capacity to $k^{AB} = k^{BA} = 1$. The competitor does not trade, that is, $v = 0$. The interest rate is set to $r = 10\%$.

where $\mathbf{P}_t = (P_t^1, \ldots, P_t^n)$ and the W_t^i's are (possibly correlated) Wiener processes.

With this new formulation, similar to Sec. 2.5.1, it is no longer possible to transform the optimization problem into a single-dimensional state space (the price spread). Analytical tractability is consequently lost and numerical methods must be used. Under constant marginal shipping costs, the findings from numerical experiments, the details of which are not discussed here for brevity, suggest that the bang–bang nature of the optimal trading policy is preserved. The main difference between these results and the ones obtained with our original model is that in the former case the regions in which u^{ij} is either equal to 0 or k^{ij} are now defined by n-dimensional sets that are no longer simple to characterize.

2.6.   Conclusions

In this chapter, we model and analyze the optimal strategy of a trader that can ship a commodity between two geographically separated markets, up to a certain shipping capacity. We assume that prices evolve following correlated arithmetic Brownian processes and are influenced by the trader's actions, that is, they are subject to market power. Under this assumption, we show that it is possible to model the trader's optimal policy as depending on the price spread $G_t = P_t^B - P_t^A$. We characterize the structure of this optimal trading policy. It is described by two thresholds $m^{BA} \leq m^{AB}$ such that it is optimal to ship as much quantity as possible (up to capacity) from B to A when $G_t \leq m^{BA}$, do nothing when $m^{BA} < G_t \leq m^{AB}$, and again ship as much as possible from A to B when $G_t > m^{AB}$. This structure is similar to the optimal policy for the case with no market power. We show that the thresholds are close to the marginal shipping costs c^{BA} and c^{AB} when the shipping capacity is small, whereas the thresholds can significantly deviate from these costs when the trading capacity is large. We also examine the equilibrium that arises when several traders determine their trading policies in response to their competitors' optimal strategies, and characterize the equilibrium thresholds in a symmetric setting.

Besides further analysis of the two extensions presented in Sec. 2.5, there are several directions for future research that are worth commenting. The empirical validity of the model presented here could be tested along the lines of De Vany and Walls [19]. Such a study could aim at establishing the relationship between shipping capacity and the speed at which spreads return to zero. Another possible extension is to model inventory considerations associated with trade. We consider here a shipping system where the quantity bought at A is equal to the one sold at B. This modeling assumption is fair for a pipeline, for instance. However, if the shipping system is a serial network of warehouses, then one should consider the possibility of storing inventory somewhere in that network. The analysis of this case rather than ours becomes significantly more complex. In our model, the markets A and B correspond to geographical locations where an identical commodity is traded. The trading capacity represents the available shipping capacity per period. There is an alternative interpretation of our results: A and B could represent *two different commodities* traded at the same location and the trading capacity represents the conversion capacity per period of one commodity into the other, e.g., natural gas into electricity. This line of work would complement the work of Routledge *et al.* [18].

Acknowledgments

We thank a reviewer and the book editor for their helpful comments in improving the exposition of this chapter.

Appendix A. Proofs

A.1. *Proof of Proposition 2.1*

In steady state, it is not necessary to consider the transients solutions of the Chapman–Kolmogorov equation that involve $\partial f/\partial t$. We consider the backward problem: the probability that the spread is G at time $t + dt$ is the same as that in time t and depends only on the spread at time t, because this is a Markovian process. We thus have

$$f(G) = \mathbb{E}\Big[f(G - B(G)dt - A(G)\sqrt{dt}\epsilon, t)\Big],$$

where $\epsilon = 1$ with probability $1/2$ and -1 otherwise. When the p.d.f. is stationary, a second-order Taylor approximation yields

$$f(G) = f(G) - \frac{df}{dG}B(G)dt + \frac{1}{2}\frac{d^2f}{dG^2}A^2(G)dt.$$

This expression leads to (2.3). We refer the reader to [32] for details on this methodology.

A.2. *Proof of Proposition 2.2*

Proposition 2.2 is an adaptation of Propositions 3.2.1 and 3.3.1 in [30].

A.3. *Proof of Theorem 2.1*

This proof is similar to the proofs of the propositions in [33], but with different costs and dynamics.

We start the proof by describing the optimal objective value of the objective $J^*(G)$ for $G \to \infty$, denoted here as J to simplify the notation. Consider $G = G^\infty$, a large enough value of G such that $v(G) = v^\infty > 0$, a constant (which is true if v is piecewise constant with a finite number of pieces). Given a starting value of the price spread $G_0 \gg G^\infty$, the spread tends to revert to smaller values. Thus, the trader is better off shipping the maximum quantity from A to B to avoid losing a potential profit. As a result, the value of J can be computed as the following expected net present value of the trading margins:

$$J(G_0) = \mathbb{E}\int_0^\infty e^{-rt}\Big[G_t u(G_t) - c\Big(u(G_t)\Big)\Big]\,dt$$

$$\approx \int_0^\infty e^{-rt}k^{\mathrm{AB}}\left(\mathbb{E}G_t - c^{\mathrm{AB}}\right)dt$$

$$\approx J^{\mathrm{AB}}(G_0),$$

where $J^{AB}(G_0) := k^{AB}G_0/r - \beta k^{AB}(k^{AB} + v^\infty)/(r^2)$ because $\mathbb{E}G_t = G_0 - \beta(k^{AB} + v^\infty)t$. Thus, J is asymptotically linear as G_0 approaches $+\infty$. The same holds true at $-\infty$.

Consider now the solution to (2.8). This is a second-order homogeneous differential equation. Its solution is continuously differentiable everywhere. In addition, J is infinitely differentiable at points G where u and v remain fixed. The solution to the HJB equation has two degrees of freedom, which will be determined by the boundary conditions, that is, the fact that J is asymptotically linear as G_0 approaches $+\infty$ or $-\infty$. We also know that $J(G) \geq 0$ for all G.

We define the functions

$$\phi^{AB}(G) := J(G) - \left(\frac{k^{AB}(G - c^{AB})}{r} - \frac{\beta k^{AB}\left(k^{AB} + v(G)\right)}{r^2} \right),$$

which is piecewise linear with jumps up at points where v jumps up;

$$\phi^{BA}(G) := J(G) - \left(-\frac{k^{BA}(G + c^{BA})}{r} - \frac{\beta k^{BA}\left(k^{BA} - v(G)\right)}{r^2} \right),$$

which is piecewise linear with jumps down; and $\phi^0(G) := J(G)$. From (2.8) we know that if $u(G) = 0$ then

$$\frac{\sigma^2}{2} \frac{d^2\phi^0}{dG^2} = \beta v \frac{d\phi^0}{dG} + r\phi^0;$$

if $u(G) = k^{AB}$ then

$$\frac{\sigma^2}{2} \frac{d^2\phi^{AB}}{dG^2} = \beta(k^{AB} + v)\frac{d\phi^{AB}}{dG} + r\phi^{AB};$$

and if $u(G) = -k^{BA}$ then

$$\frac{\sigma^2}{2} \frac{d^2\phi^{BA}}{dG^2} = \beta(-k^{BA} + v)\frac{d\phi^{BA}}{dG} + r\phi^{BA}.$$

The asymptotic conditions at $G \to +\infty$ and $G \to -\infty$ can be expressed as $\lim_{G \to +\infty} \phi^{AB}(G) = 0$ and $\lim_{G \to -\infty} \phi^{BA}(G) = 0$, respectively.

We focus on $G \geq 0$ first. We prove that there exists m^{AB} such that once $u(m^{AB}) = k^{AB}$, any $G \geq m^{AB}$ dictates $u(G) = k^{AB}$. We first show that when $u(G) = 0$ then $d^2 J/dG^2 > 0$. Then we establish that if we reach a point where $u(G) = k^{AB}$ then u remains equal to k^{AB} for larger values of G.

Take G_0 such that doing nothing is optimal, that is, $u^*(G_0) = 0$ and $J(G) = \phi^0(G)$. Suppose that $(d^2 J/dG^2)(G_0) \leq 0$. This assumption implies that $(dJ/dG)(G_0) \leq 0$ since $v(G) \geq 0$ for $G \geq 0$. We then have

$$\frac{\sigma^2}{2} \frac{d^3 J}{dG^3} = \beta v \frac{d^2 J}{dG^2} + r \frac{dJ}{dG} \leq 0.$$

Thus, when J becomes concave at G_0, it is decreasing and concave for $G \geq G_0$ while $u(G) = 0$, because the jumps up $v(G)$ can only make $d^2 J/dG^2$ more negative. Eventually, since $G - \beta dJ/dG$ increases, there exists G_1 such that $u(G_1) = k^{AB}$. At this point it holds that

$$J(G) = \phi^{AB}(G) + \left(\frac{k^{AB} G}{r} - \frac{\beta k^{AB} \left(k^{AB} + v(G) \right)}{r^2} \right)$$

and

$$\frac{\sigma^2}{2} \frac{d^2 \phi^{AB}}{dG^2} = \beta(k^{AB} + v) \frac{d\phi^{AB}}{dG} + r\phi^{AB}.$$

By continuity of dJ/dG and $d^2 J/dG^2$ at G_1 (because $\max_{u} \{Gu - c(u) - \beta u dJ/dG\}$ is continuous), ϕ^{AB} is decreasing and concave at G_1. By the inequality

$$\frac{\sigma^2}{2} \frac{d^3 \phi^{AB}}{dG^3} = \beta(k^{AB} + v) \frac{d^2 \phi^{AB}}{dG^2} + r \frac{d\phi^{AB}}{dG} \leq 0,$$

ϕ^{AB} is decreasing and concave and $u(G) = k^{AB}$ for $G > G_1$. Eventually, for sufficiently large G we have $J(G) < 0$ which is a contradiction. Hence, when $u(G_0) = 0$ then $(d^2 J/dG^2)(G_0) > 0$.

Let G_1 be the lowest $G \geq G_0$ such that $u(G_1) = k^{AB}$. At this point it holds that

$$G_1 - \beta \frac{dJ}{dG}(G_1) = c^{AB} \quad \text{and} \quad 1 - \beta \frac{d^2 J}{dG^2}(G_1) > 0.$$

Moreover, for $G > G_1$, provided that $u(G) = k^{AB}$, we have

$$\frac{\sigma^2}{2} \frac{d^2 \phi^{AB}}{dG^2} = \beta \left(k^{AB} + v \right) \frac{d\phi^{AB}}{dG} + r\phi^{AB}.$$

At $G = G_1$, by continuity, $(d^2\phi^{AB}/dG^2)(G_1) \geq 0$. Suppose that

$$\frac{\sigma^2}{2}\frac{d^3\phi^{AB}}{dG^3}(G_1) = \beta\left(k^{AB} + v\right)\frac{d^2\phi^{AB}}{dG^2}(G_1) + r\frac{d\phi^{AB}}{dG}(G_1) \geq 0.$$

Then, $\phi^{AB}(G)$ would become more and more convex as G increases. Hence, as G tends to $+\infty$ the function $\phi^{AB}(G)$ cannot converge to zero, a contradiction. Thus, $(d^3\phi^{AB}/dG^3)(G_1) < 0$ and, consequently, $(d\phi^{AB}/dG)(G_1) < 0$ since $(d^2\phi^{AB}/dG^2)(G_1) \geq 0$. These inequalities also imply that $\phi^{AB}(G_1) > 0$.

We thus know that at $G = G_1$ and its vicinity the function ϕ^{AB} is positive, decreasing, convex but less and less convex. The same argument applies as G increases, even when $v(G)$ jumps up. After a jump in $v(G)$, ϕ^{AB} jumps up, $d\phi^{AB}/dG$ is continuous and as a result $d^2\phi^{AB}/dG^2$ jumps down. This second derivative cannot become negative since in that case it would hold that $J(G) < 0$ for sufficiently large values of G. Hence, $G - \beta dJ/dG$ is increasing at a rate $1 - \beta d^2J/dG^2$, which is larger than zero at $G = G_1$ and thus remains larger than zero for $G > G_1$. This argument shows that for $G \geq G_1$, the equality $u(G) = k^{AB}$, and thus the existence of $m^{AB} > 0$ is established.

For $G < 0$, the same set of arguments applies: Starting from zero, we can find the first $G_2 < 0$ such that $u(G_2) = -k^{BA}$, below which the policy u returns the same value. Hence, there is $m^{BA} < 0$ below which $u(G) = -k^{BA}$. As $G - \beta dJ/dG$ is continuous in G, the function $u(G)$ tends to k^{AB} and $-k^{BA}$ as G tends to $+\infty$ and $-\infty$, respectively. Thus, the function $u(G)$ is equal to zero in between the thresholds m^{AB} and $-m^{BA}$.

A.4.   *Proof of Proposition 2.3*

As stated in Theorem 2.1, the optimal thresholds are precisely determined by (2.10). Using the same notation used in the proof of this result, we know that for $G \geq m^{AB}$, ϕ^{AB} is convex. This behavior implies that $dJ^*/dG = d\phi^{AB}/dG + k^{AB}/r$ is non-decreasing. Furthermore, we have $dJ^*/dG \to k^{AB}/r$ when $G \to \infty$. It follows that

$$m^{AB} - c^{AB} = \beta\frac{dJ^*}{dG}(m^{AB}) \leq \frac{\beta k^{AB}}{r}.$$

Similarly, it holds that

$$m^{BA} + c^{BA} = \beta\frac{dJ^*}{dG}(m^{BA}) \geq -\frac{\beta k^{BA}}{r}.$$

In addition, we have $m^{AB} \geq c^{AB}$ and $m^{BA} \leq -c^{BA}$. Indeed, the trading margin is increasing when the spread is larger than c^{AB} since higher short-term trading margin can be obtained with higher spreads; similarly, the trading margin is decreasing when the spread is below $-c^{BA}$, that is, the trading margin is higher when the negative spread is larger.

A.5. *Proof of Corollary 2.1*

Letting $k^{AB}, k^{BA} \to 0$ in (2.10) yields the claimed result.

A.6. *Proof of Proposition 2.4*

When the costs and capacities are symmetric, it is immediate to observe that $J^*(-G) = J^*(G)$, since if the function $J(G)$ satisfies the optimality HJB equation, then $J(-G)$ also does so.

A.7. *Proof of Theorem 2.2*

When the costs and capacities are the same in both directions, we have $J(-G) = J(G)$ and, hence, $m = m^{AB} = -m^{BA}$. Thus, it holds that $(dJ/dG)(0) = 0$. For $G \geq m$, we have

$$J(G) = \frac{k}{r}(G - c) - \beta n \left(\frac{k}{r}\right)^2 + A_r e^{-\nu G}$$

for some parameter $A_r \geq 0$, and with $\nu = \left[\sqrt{(n\beta k)^2 + 2r\sigma^2} - n\beta k\right]/(\sigma^2)$. For $0 \leq G \leq m$, it holds that

$$J(G) = A_m \left(e^{\theta G} - e^{-\theta G}\right)$$

for some parameters A_m, and with $\theta = \sqrt{2r}/\sigma$. Note that $\theta \geq \nu$. Since J is continuously differentiable at m, we must have that

$$\frac{k}{r}(m - c) - \beta n \left(\frac{k}{r}\right)^2 + A_r e^{-\nu m} = A_m \left(e^{\theta m} + e^{-\theta m}\right),$$

$$\frac{k}{r} - \nu A_r e^{-\nu m} = \theta A_m \left(e^{\theta m} - e^{-\theta m}\right).$$

The first (second) equality comes from equating the value of J (dJ/dG) in the left vicinity of m with that in the right vicinity of m. Thus, we have

$$A_m = \frac{\nu \left(\frac{k}{r}(m - c) - \beta n \left(\frac{k}{r}\right)^2\right) + \frac{k}{r}}{(\theta + \nu)e^{\theta m} - (\theta - \nu)e^{-\theta m}},$$

from which it follows that

$$m - c = \frac{\beta\theta\left(e^{\theta m} - e^{-\theta m}\right)\left[\nu\left(\frac{k}{r}(m-c) - \beta n\left(\frac{k}{r}\right)^2\right) + \frac{k}{r}\right]}{(\theta + \nu)e^{\theta m} - (\theta - \nu)e^{-\theta m}}.$$

Letting $\Delta := m - c$, this expression can be rearranged as

$$\left[(\theta + \nu)e^{\theta m} - (\theta - \nu)e^{-\theta m}\right]\Delta = \beta\theta\left(e^{\theta m} - e^{-\theta m}\right)\left(\frac{\nu k}{r}\Delta - \frac{\nu\beta n k^2}{r^2} + \frac{k}{r}\right),$$

or, equivalently, as

$$\left[\left(\theta + \nu - \frac{\beta\theta\nu k}{r}\right)e^{\theta m} - \left(\theta - \nu - \frac{\beta\theta\nu k}{r}\right)e^{-\theta m}\right]\Delta$$
$$= \beta\theta\left(e^{\theta m} - e^{-\theta m}\right)\left(-\frac{\nu\beta n k^2}{r^2} + \frac{k}{r}\right),$$

so that

$$m - c = \frac{\beta\theta\left(e^{\theta m} - e^{-\theta m}\right)\left(-\frac{\nu\beta n k^2}{r^2} + \frac{k}{r}\right)}{\left(\theta + \nu - \frac{\beta\theta\nu k}{r}\right)e^{\theta m} - \left(\theta - \nu - \frac{\beta\theta\nu k}{r}\right)e^{-\theta m}},$$

which has a unique solution m.

References

[1] International Coffee Organization. Statistics — historical data. Technical report, International Coffee Organization (2015). URL http://www.ico.org/historical/1990%20onwards/PDF/1c-exportable-production.pdf.

[2] E. Holodny, How oil flows in and out of every major region around the world, *Business Insider*. **June 12**, online (2015). URL http://www.businessinsider.com/bp-map-world-oil-trade-movements-2014-2015-6.

[3] N. Secomandi and D. J. Seppi, Real options and merchant operations of energy and other commodities, *Foundations and Trends in Technology, Information and Operations Management*. **6**, 3–4 (2014).

[4] R. Gibson and E. S. Schwartz, Stochastic convenience yield and the pricing of oil contingent claims, *The Journal of Finance*. **45**(3), 959–976 (1990).

[5] L. Evans and G. Guthrie. Commodity Price Behavior With Storage Frictions. In (ed.), N. Secomandi, *Real Options In Energy And Commodity Markets*, 3–29. Now Publishers, Boston, MA, USA and World Scientific Publishing, Hackensack, NJ, USA (2017).

[6] E. S. Schwartz, The stochastic behavior of commodity prices: Implications for valuation and hedging, *The Journal of Finance*. **52**(3), 923–973 (1997).

[7] E. Schwartz and J. E. Smith, Short-term variations and long-term dynamics in commodity prices, *Management Science*. **46**(7), 893–911 (2000).

[8] J. E. Smith and K. F. McCardle, Options in the real world: Lessons learned in evaluating oil and gas investments, *Operations Research.* **47**(1), 1–15 (1999).

[9] A. Eydeland and K. Wolyniec, *Energy and Power Risk Management: New Developments in Modeling, Pricing, and Hedging.* John Wiley & Sons Inc., Hoboken, NJ, USA (2003).

[10] H. Geman, *Commodities and Commodity Derivatives: Modeling and Pricing for Agriculturals, Metals and Energy.* John Wiley & Sons Ltd, Chichester, England, UK (2005).

[11] C. Pirrong, *Commodity Price Dynamics: A Structural Approach.* Cambridge University Press, Cambridge, England, UK (2011).

[12] N. Secomandi and D. Seppi. Energy real options: Valuation and operations. In (ed.), V. Kaminski, *Managing Energy Price Risk*, Fourth edn, 449–477, Risk Books, London, England, UK (2016).

[13] A. Deaton and G. Laroque, On the behaviour of commodity prices, *The Review of Economic Studies.* **59**(1), 1–23 (1992).

[14] A. Deaton and G. Laroque, Competitive storage and commodity price dynamics, *Journal of Political Economy.* **104**(5), 896–923 (1996).

[15] M. J. Chambers and R. E. Bailey, A theory of commodity price fluctuations, *Journal of Political Economy.* **104**(5), 924–957 (1996).

[16] B. R. Routledge, D. J. Seppi, and C. S. Spatt, Equilibrium forward curves for commodities, *The Journal of Finance.* **55**(3), 1297–1338 (2000).

[17] J. C. Williams and B. D. Wright, *Storage and Commodity Markets.* Cambridge University Press, Cambridge, England, UK (2005).

[18] B. R. Routledge, C. S. Spatt, and D. J. Seppi. The spark spread: An equilibrium model of cross-commodity price relationships in electricity. Working paper, Graduate School of Industrial Administration, Carnegie Mellon University, Pittsburgh, PA, USA (2001).

[19] A. De Vany and W. D. Walls, The law of one price in a network: Arbitrage and price dynamics in natural gas city gate markets, *Journal of Regional Science.* **36**(4), 555–570 (1996).

[20] K. Golabi, Optimal inventory policies when ordering prices are random, *Operations Research.* **33**(3), 575–588 (1985).

[21] Y. Wang, The optimality of myopic stocking policies for systems with decreasing purchasing prices, *European Journal of Operational Research.* **133**(1), 153–159 (2001).

[22] P. Berling and V. Martínez-de Albéniz, Optimal inventory policies when purchase price and demand are stochastic, *Operations Research.* **59**(1), 109–124 (2011).

[23] P. Berling and Z. Xie, Approximation algorithms for optimal purchase/inventory policy when purchase price and demand are stochastic, *OR Spectrum.* **36**(4), 1077–1095 (2014).

[24] A. Goel and G. J. Gutierrez, Multiechelon procurement and distribution policies for traded commodities, *Management Science.* **57**(12), 2228–2244 (2011).

[25] N. Secomandi, Optimal commodity trading with a capacitated storage asset, *Management Science.* **56**(3), 449–467 (2010).

[26] N. Secomandi, On the pricing of natural gas pipeline capacity, *Manufacturing & Service Operations Management.* **12**(3), 393–408 (2010).

[27] G. Lai, M. X. Wang, S. Kekre, A. Scheller-Wolf, and N. Secomandi, Valuation of storage at a liquefied natural gas terminal, *Operations Research.* **59**(3), 602–616 (2011).

[28] R. Caldentey, R. Epstein, and D. Sauré. Optimal exploitation of a nonrenewable resource. In (ed.), N. Secomandi, *Real Options In Energy And Commodity Markets*, 117–171. Now Publishers, Boston, MA, USA and World Scientific Publishing, Hackensack, NJ, USA (2017).

[29] C. W. Gardiner, *Handbook of Stochastic Methods*, Vol. 4., Springer, Berlin, Germany (1985).

[30] D. P. Bertsekas, *Dynamic Programming and Optimal Control*, 2nd edn. Athena Scientific, Belmont, MA, USA (2000).

[31] L. Trigeorgis, *Real Options: Managerial Flexibility and Strategy in Resource Allocation.* MIT Press, Cambridge, MA, USA (1996).

[32] P. Wilmott, J. Dewynne, and S. Howison, *Option Pricing: Mathematical Models and Computation.* Oxford Financial Press, Oxford, England, UK (1993).

[33] I. Karatzas, Optimal discounted linear control of the Wiener process, *Journal of Optimization Theory and Applications.* **31**(3), 431–440 (1980).

PART 2
Methods and Applications

Chapter 3

Stochastic Volatility Modeling of Emission Allowances Futures Prices in the European Union Emission Trading System Market

Fred Espen Benth[*,‡], Marcus Eriksson[*,§], and Sjur Westgaard[†,¶]

Department of Mathematics, University of Oslo, P.O. Box 1053, Blindern, N-0316 Oslo, Norway.
†*Department of Industrial Economics and Technology Management, Norwegian University of Science and Technology, N-7491 Trondheim, Norway.*

‡*fredb@math.uio.no*,
§*marcuskveriksson@gmail.com*
¶*sjur.westgaard@iot.ntnu.no*

We conduct an empirical investigation of the logreturns of the futures prices of the European Union Emission Trading System emission certificates traded in the Nord Pool market between 2005 and 2013. We observe heaviness, skewness, and high kurtosis of these logreturns. We thus propose modeling the futures logprices using the Barndorff-Nielsen and Shephard (BNS) or the Heston stochastic volatility models. We carry out an empirical comparison between the performances of these models and investigate their stationary autocorrelation structure. In particular, as a consequence of allowing for skewness in the Heston model, we find analytical expressions for the autocorrelation function of the logreturns and their squares. Our analysis indicates the presence of short-range dependence in the observed futures logprice returns. We conclude that the BNS model better describes the empirical features of the observed futures prices than the Heston model. Our findings have relevance for the real option modeling of fossil-fueled power plants when considering emission costs.

3.1. Introduction

The European Union (EU) Emission Trading System (ETS) is a system to reduce the emissions of greenhouse gases in the EU. EU ETS covers around 45% of EU's greenhouse gas emissions. The participants in the EU ETS can buy and sell emission allowances, called European Union Allowances (EUAs), which permit their holders to emit a certain amount of CO_2. There is a limit on the number of EUAs that can be traded each year. This limit is reduced each year in order to meet desirable emission levels in the future.

High-emitting industry players can buy allowances if needed or sell them if they judge that their current stock is more than needed. In this way companies can cut their emissions in a cost-effective way as the right to emit CO_2 becomes a tradable commodity. For example, coal- or gas-fired power plants in Europe have caps on the maximum amount of CO_2 that they can emit. All the production exceeding the limit must be covered by emission allowances. As production is stochastic, the managers of such power plants face a risk that they can hedge by actively trading in EUAs. Emissions are thus a cost when operating fossil-fueled power plants, the profitability of which depends on both the spread between the power and fuel prices and the emission costs, as recognized in the real option literature. Specifically in the real option modeling of these plants, the so-called clean spark (respectively dark) spread is of fundamental importance, being the difference between the power price, the natural gas (respectively coal) price, and the emission cost (see e.g., [1–6] for real option valuation and energy spark spreads). Secomandi and Seppi [7, S. 7.6] briefly discuss the operations of a power plant as a switching option where the plant produces when it is most profitable according to the spark (dark) spread. They view the usage of emission rights as an inventory disposal asset, whereby the inventory level is reduced when production takes place. Given a market for emission rights, the inventory of permits can vary over time due to consumption, purchases, or sales.

We perform an empirical investigation with the goal of specifying a continuous time model for the futures price evolution of EUAs on the EU ETS market. Our analysis relies on futures price data collected from the Nord

Pool market between April 2005 and August 2013. From our statistical analysis of the logreturns we observe skewness, heavy tails, and leptokurtic behavior in their distribution, rejecting the normal distribution. To capture these observed features we consider logprice models with stochastic volatility. We choose stochastic volatility models, rather than Lévy processes [8], since we observe volatility clustering in the time series for the logreturns, a feature that Lévy models do not capture. Two commonly used models in commodity markets with this property are the Barndorff-Nielsen and Shepard (BNS) model [9,10] and the Heston model [11].

The main objective of this chapter is to compare the empirical performance of the BNS and Heston models in relation to observed data from the EU ETS market. That is, we focus on the calibration of these models to this data. Our comparison centers on how well these models capture key distributional properties of this data as well observed autocorrelations.

We show that it is necessary to introduce an additional parameter in the drift of the Heston model to be able to account for skewness in the conditional price process. As a consequence, the stationary autocorrelation function for the logreturns is nonzero and exhibits short-range dependence. We also derive analytical expressions for the stationary autocorrelation function of the logreturns and their squares for this modified version of the Heston model.

The Heston model, which is a mixture of geometric Brownian motion with volatility modeled by the square root of a Cox–Ingersoll–Ross (CIR) model [12], results in a stationary variance-Gamma (VG) distribution for the logreturns. This distribution is also obtained as a particular case in the BNS model. From the sample distribution of our data we use maximum-likelihood estimation (MLE) to obtain values for the parameters of the VG distribution and use them to estimate the parameters of the BNS and Heston models, respectively. As the BNS model is more flexible than the Heston model, e.g., allowing for generalized-hyperbolic (GH) distributions, we also investigate the fit of the normal inverse Gaussian (NIG) distribution to the sample logreturn distribution. Both the aforementioned distributions possess key features of our data, such as skewness, peakedness, and heavy tails, which the normal distribution cannot capture. However, a fundamental difference between the BNS model and the Heston model is the structure of the respective stationary autocorrelation functions. For the BNS model this function is zero, while it may not be zero for the Heston model. Since the sample stationary autocorrelation function is close to zero and due to a slightly better distributional fit with the NIG distribution compared with the VG distribution, we conclude that the BNS model is a better model of EU ETS futures prices than the Heston model.

The EU ETS market was introduced in January 2005. Its pilot phase, phase 1, occurred between 2005 and 2007. The second phase, the Kyoto commitment period, spanned the years from 2008 to 2012. The post Kyoto period, phase 3, is planned until 2020. Most of the existing empirical studies on EU ETS prices only involve data from phase 1. Recent work investigating the dynamics of CO_2 allowance prices includes [13–16]. In [13] the authors propose Markov-switching and AR-GARCH models of the logprice returns. They find that these models capture key observed features of the data, such as skewness, excess kurtosis, and nonconstant volatility. In [15] the performance of different GARCH models is considered. These papers (and some of those that they cite) also give a description of the underlying market institutions and conduct empirical investigations based on the spot prices in the first phase.

The three main markets for EUAs within EU ETS, Powernext, Nord Pool, and the European Climate Exchange (ECX), are studied in [16]. Banking of permits was prohibited during phases 1 and 2, which made emission allowances worthless at the end of phase 1, and thus not tradable during the whole life of the underlying contract. This issue is addressed in [16]. The authors of this paper also consider the cases of futures traded within a single phase (intra-period futures) and futures traded across phases (inter-period futures). They investigate an augmented cost-of-carry relationship between futures and spot prices (see references therein for other research on EU ETS futures prices). Furthermore, these authors examine the ability of various diffusion and jump diffusion continuous-time processes to capture the dynamics of EUA spot prices. In particular, they find that a geometric Brownian motion augmented with jumps significantly improves on the performance of its diffusion counterpart. The authors of the recent paper [17] use a nonlinear dynamics approach to analyze EUA price volatility based on data from April 2005 to February 2009.

Compared to the existing literature, we perform an extensive and up to date empirical analysis of EU ETS Nord Pool futures prices, investigating the descriptive statistics of their logreturns. Moreover, we consider two continuous stochastic volatility models, specifically the BNS and Heston models for the futures price logreturns. This approach differs from the one of [16], where a jump diffusion model is used to account for the overall volatility. Furthermore, we introduce an additional parameter in the Heston model to capture skewness. As a consequence, this modified model features a nonzero stationary autocorrelation function for the logreturns, distinguished by short-range dependence. To the best of our knowledge, this result is new to the literature.

This chapter is organized as follows. In Sec. 3.2 we present the findings of our statistical analysis of our data set. In Sec. 3.3 we present the BNS and Heston models and their stationary autocorrelation functions. In Sec. 3.4 we investigate the fit of the VG and NIG distributions, estimating their parameters via MLE, and compare the empirical performance of the BNS and Heston models. In Sec. 3.5 we conduct a statistical analysis and study the empirical behavior of the VG and NIG distributions for each individual EU ETS phase. We conclude in Sec. 3.6. Appendix A includes proofs.

3.2. Statistical Analysis of EU ETS Futures Prices

We analyze five time series of futures prices for EUAs observed on the Nordic power exchange Nord Pool. These series pertain to the front contract, the next front contract, and so on. The data is collected on a daily basis (five days a week) from April 22, 2005 to August 27, 2013, yielding 2,148 observed futures prices. Due to the similarity in the data, our analysis focuses on the first time series. However, the statistical characteristics of all time series are collected in the tables presented in this chapter. In this section, we present statistical results, which provide the foundations and motivation for investigating the BNS and Heston models.

We start by analyzing the time series for the futures price $X(t)$ of time series 1, shown in Fig. 3.1. We observe a clear downward trend in the futures prices. The futures prices do not show any seasonal pattern, which is in line with the main finding in [14] for CO_2 spot prices. Table 3.1 reports the first four sample moments of the futures price data series. These prices are slightly skewed. The significant excessive kurtosis suggests a non-Gaussian distribution.

To proceed, we investigate the logreturns $L(t)$, which we now introduce. Define the normalized[a] futures logprice as

$$S(t) := \log \frac{X(t)}{X(0)}. \tag{3.1}$$

---

[a]Normalized in the sense that $S(0) = 0$.

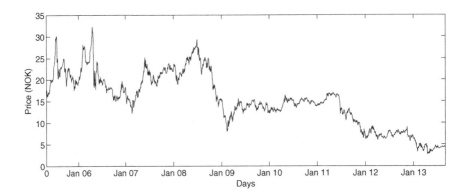

Fig. 3.1   The futures price $X(t)$ for time series 1.

Table 3.1   Sample moments of the futures prices.

Time Series	Mean	Variance	Skew ($\times 10^{-2}$)	Kurtosis
1	15.30	39.30	−2.28	2.31
2	15.55	41.83	−0.65	2.29
3	15.79	44.39	1.57	2.27
4	16.07	47.08	3.77	2.27
5	16.36	50.29	8.16	2.29

The logreturn at time t_i is defined as

$$L(t_i) := S(t_{i+1}) - S(t_i). \tag{3.2}$$

Consistent with our daily data, we consider daily logreturns, so that $t_{i+1} - t_i = 1$. We define the daily logreturns in continuous time as

$$L(t) := S(t + 1) - S(t). \tag{3.3}$$

Figure 3.2 shows a time series of the logreturns. The observed volatility clustering in Fig. 3.2, which seems to have a non-deterministic behavior, indicates that a large (small) absolute change tends to be followed by a large (small) absolute change. In particular, we can observe several absolute changes greater than 10%.[b] This behavior is also consistent

---

[b]Most of the extreme changes in the market prices are due to weather conditions, e.g., dry summers or cold winters and corresponding high or low prices of competing energy commodities, such as oil and gas. However, in 2005 there was a surplus of granted EUAs in the market, which caused a crash in April 2006 (see [13]).

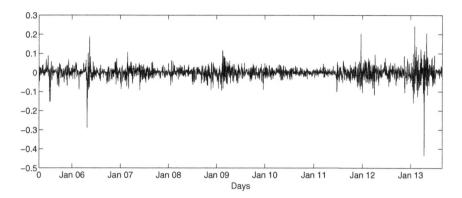

Fig. 3.2 Time series of the logreturns $L(t)$.

with the autocorrelation of the absolute logreturns in Fig. 3.3(b). That the absolute logreturns are slowly decaying to zero is considered as a typical indicator of volatility clustering (see [18]). The slow decay to zero can also be observed in the autocorrelation function for the squared logreturns (see Fig. 3.6), but it is more apparent for the absolute logreturns.

Figure 3.3(a) displays the autocorrelation function of the logreturns, which, as expected, shows a variation around zero. Here, we observe that the correlation tends rapidly towards zero, even for lag 1. The small observed autocorrelation does not necessarily indicate independence, because non-linear dependence may be present. However, this empirical finding suggests a model characterized by small or no-memory effects in the logreturns, i.e., a stationary autocorrelation function close to zero for all lags. This modeling approach excludes any long-range dependence, even though we may have a presence of short-range dependence, i.e., an autocorrelation function decreasing at a geometric rate (see [18]).

The sample moments presented in Table 3.2 show that the logreturns are skewed to the left. Furthermore, the high excessive kurtosis indicates a distribution of the returns that has a strong deviation away from normality. Hence, the increments of $S(t)$, i.e., the logreturns, are clearly not normally distributed. This non-normal behavior is apparent in the density plots in Fig. 3.4, which visualize the deficiency of the normal distribution as a descriptive model of the empirical logreturn distribution.

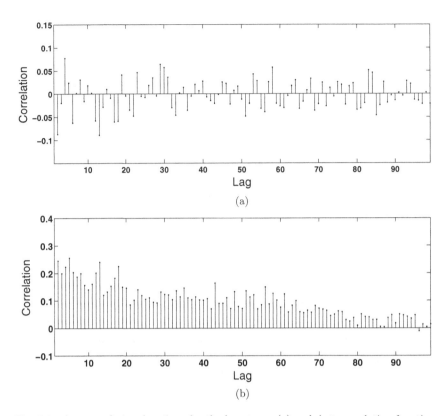

Fig. 3.3   Autocorrelation functions for the logreturns (a) and Autocorrelation function for the absolute logreturns (b).

Table 3.2   Sample moments of the logreturns.

Time Series	Mean ($\times 10^{-4}$)	Variance ($\times 10^{-4}$)	Skew	Kurtosis
1	−6.2	11	−1.19	24.82
2	−6.2	11	−1.16	24.59
3	−6.2	10	−1.15	24.66
4	−6.2	10	−1.14	24.48
5	−6.2	10	−1.17	24.37

3.3.   The BNS and Heston Models

In this section, we investigate distributional and stationary properties of the BNS model and of the Heston model. First we set up a stochastic modeling

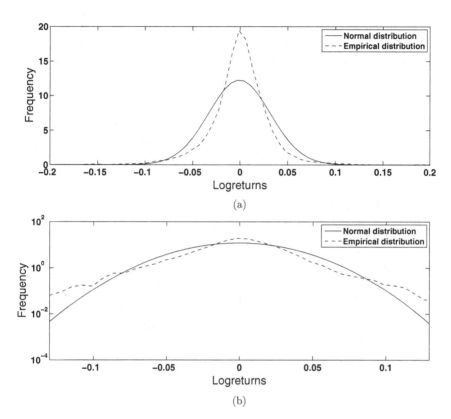

Fig. 3.4   The empirical distribution of the logreturns and a fitted normal distribution with sample mean and variance reported in Table 3.2. (a) Distribution of the logreturns. (b) Distribution of the logreturns (logarithmic scale).

framework. Denote the square of the stochastic volatility process by Y, and define the filtration $\mathcal{F}_t^Y := \{Y(u), u \leq t\}$, i.e., the σ-algebra generated by Y, revealing all the information of the stochastic volatility up to time t. Similarly, we define $\mathcal{F}_t^B$ to be the σ-algebra generated by the Brownian motion B. Let $(\Omega, \mathcal{F}, \mathbb{F}, \mathbf{P})$, where $\mathbb{F} := \{\mathcal{F}_t\}_{t \geq 0}$, be a complete filtered probability space satisfying the usual conditions. We define $\mathcal{F}_t$ as the smallest σ-algebra containing all the information generated by the Brownian motion B and the stochastic volatility Y up to time t, i.e., $\mathcal{F}_t := \mathcal{F}_t^B \vee \mathcal{F}_t^Y$.

Our data analysis in Sec. 3.2 brings to light skewness and clustering in the logreturns and heavier tails in the empirical distribution than the normal distribution. As mentioned in [10], this type of data is at odds with the assumptions in the Black–Scholes model. These statistical features and the empirical logreturn autocorrelation indicate that we need to extend our model to incorporate stochastic volatility. We investigate two models with this property: The model proposed by Barndorff-Nielsen and Shephard, which is known as the BNS model (see [9, 10]), and the Heston model (see [11]). These models can explain stylized facts like heavy tails, skewness, and excessive returns, as observed in the considered time series. We provide the main properties of the BNS and Heston models in Secs. 3.3.1 and 3.3.2, respectively. We refer the reader to [9–11, 19, 20] for a more detailed description of these models.

3.3.1. *The BNS Model*

The BNS model features stochastic volatility. The idea is to model the squared volatility $\sigma^2(t)$ as a superposition of independent stationary positive Ornstein–Uhlenbeck (OU) processes driven by a Background Driving Lévy Process (BDLP) (see [10]). Specifically, we consider the following model for the evolution of the logarithmic futures price $S(t)$:

$$dS(t) = (\mu + \beta\sigma^2(t))dt + \sigma(t)dB(t), \qquad (3.4)$$

with deterministic parameters μ and β. We assume

$$\sigma^2(t) = Y(t), \qquad (3.5)$$

where

$$dY(t) = -\lambda Y(t)dt + dU(\lambda t); \qquad (3.6)$$

here the parameters λ is the speed of mean reversion and the process U is a subordinator, i.e., a Lévy process with positive drift and jumps but no Brownian part, which ensures that $Y(t)$ is a positive process and the volatility $\sigma(t) \equiv \sqrt{Y(t)}$ is well defined. The unusual scaling by the speed of mean reversion λ in the argument of $U(\lambda t)$ ensures that the stationary distribution of U does not depend on λ. Thus, the speed of mean reversion accounts only for the modeling of the autocorrelation function of the squared logreturns. The process $U(t)$ is the BDLP of $Y(t)$.

When using an n-factor model for the stochastic volatility, the process $\sigma^2(t)$ has the form

$$\sigma^2(t) = \sum_{i=1}^{n} w_i Y_i(t), \quad \sum_{i=1}^{n} w_i = 1. \qquad (3.7)$$

Our empirical analysis of the futures price data in Sec. 3.2 suggests that choosing n equal to 1 is sufficient for our purposes (see Sec. 3.4.1.1).

In [10] it is shown that for a self-decomposable distribution D, there exists a stationary OU-process such that $Y \sim D$, satisfying (3.6) with U taken as a Lévy process with positive increments. Moreover, the cumulant generating function, which is defined as the logarithm of the moment generating function, is

$$\psi(u) = -\int_{0+}^{\infty} (1 - e^{-ux})\ell(dx),$$

where ℓ is the Lévy measure of $U(1)$, i.e., a subordinator. The only requirement of a self-decomposable distribution D gives analysts great flexibility in the choice of distributions for Y.

The self-decomposable class of generalized inverse Gaussian (GIG) distributions is considered in [9, 10]. This three parameter class, labeled $GIG(\nu, \delta, \gamma)$, has the following probability density function (pdf):

$$\text{pdf}_{GIG(\nu,\delta,\gamma)}(u) := \frac{(\gamma/\delta)^{\nu}}{2K_{\nu}(\delta\gamma)} u^{\nu-1} \exp\left(-\frac{1}{2}(\delta^2 u^{-1} + \gamma^2 u)\right), \quad u > 0,$$

where K_{ν} is the Bessel function of third kind. By choosing $Y \sim GIG(\nu, \delta, \gamma)$ independent of the Brownian motion B, the resulting logreturns, $L(t) \equiv S(t+1) - S(t)$, are distributed according to a generalized hyperbolic (GH) distribution. The GH distribution is a five parameter family allowing us to control the modeled skewness and kurtosis, which is a desirable feature given our data analysis in Sec. 3.2. Define $\alpha := \sqrt{\beta^2 + \gamma^2}$. The $GH(\nu, \alpha, \beta, \delta, \mu)$ pdf is

$$\text{pdf}_{GH(\nu,\alpha,\beta,\delta,\mu)}(u) := \frac{(\gamma/\delta)^{\nu}}{\sqrt{2\pi}\alpha^{\nu-1/2}K_{\nu}(\delta\gamma)} \left(\delta^2 + (u - \mu)^2\right)^{(\nu-1/2)/2}$$
$$\times K_{\nu-1/2}\left[\alpha\sqrt{\delta^2 + (u - \mu)^2}\right] \exp\left(\beta(u - \mu)\right).$$

$$(3.8)$$

For our purposes, we consider two special cases: $\nu = -\frac{1}{2}$, leading to Y following the Inverse-Gaussian (IG) distribution $IG(\delta, \gamma)$, and $\delta = 0$ and $\nu > 0$, leading to Y following the Gamma distribution $\Gamma(\nu, \gamma)$, with respective densities

$$\text{pdf}_{IG(\delta,\gamma)}(u) := \frac{\delta}{\sqrt{(2\pi)}} \exp(\delta\gamma)u^{-3/2} \exp\left(-\frac{1}{2}(\delta^2 u^{-1} + \gamma^2 u)\right), \quad u > 0,$$

with $\delta > 0$ and $\gamma \geq 0$, and

$$\frac{\text{pdf}_{\Gamma(\nu,\gamma)}}{\sqrt{2\pi}}(u) := \frac{(\gamma^2/2)^\nu}{\Gamma(\nu)}u^{\nu-1}\exp(-u\gamma^2/2), \quad u > 0.$$

Using $Y \sim \text{IG}(\delta,\gamma)$ or $Y \sim \Gamma(\nu,\gamma)$ results in the logreturns having a NIG-distribution or a Γ-distribution, respectively, which are both special cases of the GH distribution. In Sec. 3.4 we estimate the parameters of these distributions on our data and analyze their respective fit.

From our discussions, we see that the BNS model is rather flexible in capturing distributional properties of data. The approach proposed in [10] is to start with a model for the stationary distribution of Y and then construct a BDLP U that gives this desired distribution. Such a BDLP exists whenever Y has a self-decomposable distribution.

We end our discussion of the BNS model by stating a known property (see [10]) of its autocorrelation function, which is useful for parameter estimation.

Proposition 3.1. *The stationary autocorrelation functions of the logreturns defined as in* (3.3) *with logprice given by* (3.4) *and the corresponding squared logreturns for $k = 0, 1, \ldots$ are*

$$\text{AutoCorr}(L(t), L(t+k)) = 0, \tag{3.9}$$
$$\text{AutoCorr}(L^2(t), L^2(t+k)) = e^{-\lambda k}. \tag{3.10}$$

As illustrated in Fig. 3.3(a), the autocorrelation function for the observed logreturns is close to zero for all lags. Because the driving Brownian motion in (3.4) and U are independent, the BNS model exhibits this behavior, as can be seen in (3.9).

3.3.2. *The Heston Model*

The Heston model (see [11, 20]) is a bivariate process (X, Y) in which the dynamics of the futures price $X(t)$ are

$$dX(t) = \left(\mu + \left(\frac{1}{2} - \beta\right)\sigma^2(t)\right)X(t)\,dt + \sigma(t)X(t)\,dB(t), \tag{3.11}$$

where μ and β are constants and the squared of the stochastic volatility $\sigma(t)$ equals $Y(t)$, which evolves according to the CIR process

$$dY(t) = \gamma(\lambda - Y(t))dt + \kappa\sqrt{Y(t)}dW(t), \tag{3.12}$$

where $\lambda > 0$ is the long-time mean of Y, $\gamma > 0$ is the rate of relaxation to this mean, $\kappa > 0$ is the variance noise (the volatility of the volatility), and $W(t)$ is a standard Brownian motion assumed to be independent of $B(t)$ (the independence is not necessary in general, but our investigation will rely on this assumption).The introduction of the constant β in the dynamics (3.11) is necessary for obtaining the desired distributional characteristics (see Remark 3.1 in Sec. 3.4.1.1). We refer to the process for Y in (3.12) as a Heston type volatility model.

By Itô's Formula we obtain the following process for the logprice defined in (3.1):

$$dS(t) = \left(\mu - \beta\sigma^2(t)\right) dt + \sigma(t)dB(t). \tag{3.13}$$

The daily logreturn $L(t) \equiv S(t+1) - S(t)$, defined in (3.3), expressed in terms of Y is then given by

$$L(t) = \int_t^{t+1} (\mu - \beta Y(s))ds + \int_t^{t+1} \sqrt{Y(s)}dB(s), \tag{3.14}$$

or approximately as

$$L(t) \approx (\mu - \beta Y(t)) + \sqrt{Y(t)}\Delta B(t),$$

with $\Delta B(t) := B(t+1) - B(t)$.

We investigate the characteristics of $L(t)$. By conditioning on $Y(t) = y$, $L(t)$ is normally distributed with mean $\mu - \beta y$ and variance y. It is shown in [20] that the stationary pdf $\Pi(y)$ of Y is given by

$$\Pi(y) := \frac{\alpha}{\Gamma(\alpha)} \frac{y^{(\alpha-1)}}{\lambda^\alpha} \exp\left(\frac{-\alpha y}{\lambda}\right), \quad \alpha = \frac{2\gamma\lambda}{\kappa^2}.$$

The characteristic function $\phi_L(u)$ for L can be obtained as

$$\phi_L(u) = \mathbb{E}\left[e^{iuL(t)}\right]$$

$$= \mathbb{E}\left[\mathbb{E}\left[e^{iuL(t)}|Y(t)\right]\right]$$

$$= \mathbb{E}\left[e^{iu(\mu-\beta Y(t))-\frac{1}{2}u^2 Y(t)}\right]$$

$$= \mathbb{E}\left[e^{iu\mu + i(-\beta u + i\frac{1}{2}u^2)Y(t)}\right]$$

$$= e^{iu\mu}\mathbb{E}\left[e^{i\xi Y(t)}\right] = e^{iu\mu}\phi_Y(\xi),$$

where $\xi := -\beta u + i\frac{1}{2}u^2$. The characteristic function $\phi_Y(\xi)$ for Y is obtained via the density $\Pi(y)$. The following calculation shows that the extension to a complex-valued parameter ξ in the Lévy–Khintchine formula is not problematic:

$$\phi_Y(\xi) = \int_0^\infty e^{i\xi y}\frac{\alpha}{\Gamma(\alpha)}\frac{y^{(\alpha-1)}}{\lambda^\alpha}\exp(\frac{-\alpha y}{\lambda})dy$$

$$= \frac{\alpha^\alpha}{\Gamma(\alpha)\lambda^\alpha}\int_0^\infty y^{\alpha-1}e^{-(\frac{\alpha}{\lambda}-i\xi)y}dy$$

$$= \left(1 - i\frac{\lambda}{\alpha}\xi\right)^{-\alpha},$$

where in the last step we use the integral identity

$$\int_0^\infty x^m e^{-qx^n}dx = \frac{\Gamma(p)}{nq^p}, \quad p = \frac{m+1}{n}$$

for $\text{Re}(n) > 0$, $\text{Re}(m) > -1$, and $\text{Re}(q) > 0$. By identification, we have $\text{Re}(n) = 1$, $\text{Re}(m) = \alpha - 1$, and $\text{Re}(q) = \alpha/\lambda + u^2/2$. Hence, the conditions for the integral identity are satisfied. Using the expressions for ξ and α, the characteristic function $\phi_L(u)$ can be expressed as

$$\phi_L(u) = e^{iu\mu}\left(1 + i\frac{\beta\kappa^2}{2\gamma}u + \frac{\kappa^2}{4\gamma}u^2\right)^{-\frac{2\gamma\lambda}{\kappa^2}}. \tag{3.15}$$

The conditional distribution of the CIR model is non-centered chi-squared. Because $\gamma, \lambda > 0$, the CIR model approaches a Gamma distribution in stationarity. Thus, the Heston model has VG distributed logreturns. In Sec. 3.4 we estimate the parameters of the Heston model via MLE. However, rather than directly estimating these parameters, we estimate the parameters of a process that possesses the same key features observed in our statistical data analysis. Furthermore, because we know the stationary characteristic function for the logreturns of the Heston model, we consider a process having a VG distribution with known characteristic function. A natural process with these properties is the VG process.

The VG process is introduced in [21] as a two-parameter model for stock market logreturns. To account for skewness, it is extended in [22] and [23], respectively, to a three and four parameter model for the logreturns of any underlying. This process is obtained by evaluating a Brownian motion with drift at a Γ-distributed random time, leading to a variance mixture model via subordination. Conditioning the underlying process on this random time yields a normally distributed process with two parameters, the drift and (constant) volatility. The pdf of the VG distribution is

$$
\mathrm{pdf}_{\mathrm{VG}(c,\sigma_{\mathrm{VG}},\theta,\nu_{\mathrm{VG}})}(u) := \frac{2\exp\left(\frac{\theta(u-c)}{\sigma_{\mathrm{VG}}^2}\right)}{\sigma_{\mathrm{VG}}\sqrt{2\pi}\nu_{\mathrm{VG}}^{\frac{1}{\nu_{\mathrm{VG}}}}\Gamma(\frac{1}{\nu_{\mathrm{VG}}})} \left(\frac{|u-c|}{\sqrt{\frac{2\sigma_{\mathrm{VG}}^2}{\nu_{\mathrm{VG}}}+\theta^2}}\right)^{\frac{1}{\nu_{\mathrm{VG}}}-\frac{1}{2}}
$$

$$
\times K_{\frac{1}{\nu_{\mathrm{VG}}}-\frac{1}{2}}\left(\frac{|u-c|\sqrt{\frac{2\sigma_{\mathrm{VG}}^2}{\nu_{\mathrm{VG}}}+\theta^2}}{\sigma_{\mathrm{VG}}^2}\right), \tag{3.16}
$$

where K_η is the modified Bessel function of third kind with index η (see [23]), c describes the long-time mean of the process, σ_{VG} is the volatility of the Brownian motion, θ is the drift in the Brownian motion with drift, which introduces skewness, and ν_{VG} is the variance rate of the Gamma-distributed time change.

In Sec. 3.4 we fit the VG distribution on the logreturns of our futures price data and relate the parameters of the VG distribution to those of the Heston model. To do that we need the results stated in Propositions 3.2 and 3.3 on the autocorrelation function of the logreturns and the squared logreturns, respectively (the respective proofs of these propositions are in Appendix A.1 and in Appendix A.2). Specifically, these results allow us to make the characteristic function (3.15) consistent with the pdf (3.16).

Proposition 3.2. *The stationary autocorrelation function of lag $k > 0$ for the logreturns, defined as in (3.14), is of the form*

$$
\mathrm{AutoCorr}(L(t+k),L(t)) = Ce^{-\gamma k}, \tag{3.17}
$$

where the constant C is given by

$$
\frac{\beta^2\kappa^2}{(\beta^2\kappa^2+2\gamma)\gamma^2}(e^\gamma + e^{-\gamma} - 2). \tag{3.18}
$$

This proposition states that although the autocorrelation does not depend on the mean of the stochastic volatility, it does depend on the rate of relaxation γ to this mean and the volatility of the stochastic volatility κ. Furthermore, since $\gamma > 0$ the autocorrelation decays at a geometric rate, indicating short-range dependence (see [18]). The proof of this result shows that the calculation of the non-stationary autocorrelation function is straightforward.

Proposition 3.3. *The stationary autocorrelation function of lag $k > 0$ for the squared logreturns, defined as in (3.14), is of the form*

$$\text{AutoCorr}(L^2(t+k), L^2(t)) = A_0 + A_1 e^{-\gamma k} + A_2 e^{-2\gamma k}, \qquad (3.19)$$

where the constants A_0, A_1, and A_2 depend on the parameters of the distribution of L.

The characteristic function ϕ_L and the autocorrelation in Proposition 3.3 give us a bridge to connect the parameters in the Heston model with the four parameters c, σ_{VG}, θ, and ν_{VG} of the VG distribution.

3.4. Estimation of the Stochastic Volatility Models

As discussed in Sec. 3.2, the normal distribution is unable to capture key features of the EU ETS logprices. In contrast, the class of GH distributions presented in Sec. 3.3 can reproduce these properties. We consider here two special cases of these distributions: The VG distribution in Sec. 3.4.1 and the NIG distribution in Sec. 3.4.2. Specifically, we analyze the BNS and Heston models aiming at establishing their best respective distributional fit. Recall that the Heston model gives VG distributed logreturns, whereas the BNS model is more flexible in terms of the possible distributions. We focus on two cases for the BNS model. First, the case in which the squared stochastic volatility, Y, is IG distributed, resulting in NIG-distributed logreturns. Second, as a "fair" comparison with the Heston model, the case in which this volatility is Γ distributed, yielding VG-distributed logreturns. In the latter case, we also derive expressions for the BNS model parameters. In Sec. 3.4.3 we compare the results of our estimation of the VG and NIG distributions.

Both the Heston and the BNS models require the estimation of five parameters. In order to specify all the parameters of these models, we consider the autocorrelation of the squared logreturns in addition to the sample distributional fit.[c] The density functions used for MLE are given by

---

[c]We have used MLE in R to estimate the parameters discussed in this section, based on the packages "VarianceGamma" and "fBasics." All the figures and the numerical calculations have been generated in Matlab. We have performed the symbolic calculations in Maple.

(3.16) for the VG distribution and by (3.26) for the NIG distribution. In particular, we relate the parameters in the Heston model and in the VG-distributed BNS model to the parameters in (3.16), and the parameters in the NIG-distributed BNS model to (3.26).

3.4.1. *Variance-Gamma Distribution*

Figure 3.5 shows the empirical and estimated VG densities for the logreturns.[d] Table 3.3 displays the estimated parameters of the VG distribution. The VG distribution, with p.d.f given in (3.16), captures the key features

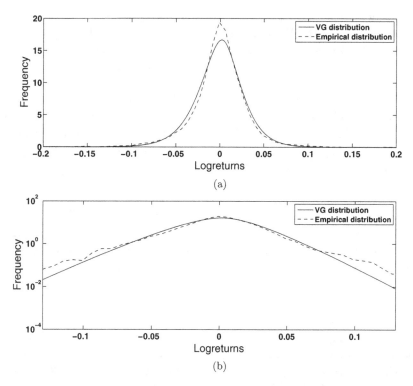

Fig. 3.5   The empirical distribution of the logreturns and the fitted VG distribution with parameter estimates reported in Table 3.3. (a) Distribution of the logreturns. (b) Distribution of the logreturns(logarithmic scale).

---

[d]Figures with logarithmic scale are truncated due to the presence of a few outliers, which make the kernel density estimator in Matlab inaccurate.

Table 3.3   VG parameter estimates for the logreturns.

Time Series	$\hat{c}$	$\hat{\sigma}_{\mathrm{VG}}$	$\hat{\theta}$	$\hat{\nu}_{\mathrm{VG}}$
1	0.00379	0.0282	−0.00441	0.387
2	0.01440	0.0786	−0.01800	0.118
3	0.00732	0.0307	−0.00758	0.118
4	0.01110	0.0296	−0.01160	0.118
5	0.06900	0.0723	−0.07270	0.118

of the data well, even though it exhibits some minor shortcomings in both the tail and the center.

We proceed to obtain the VG distribution of the logreturns assuming stationarity using the BNS model in Sec. 3.4.1.1 and the Heston model in Sec. 3.4.1.2, also estimating the parameters of these models.

3.4.1.1.   *VG Distribution via the BNS Model*

To obtain the VG distribution via the BNS model we take Y to be $\Gamma(\nu, \gamma)$-distributed with $\gamma := \sqrt{\alpha^2 - \beta^2}$. The logreturns are consequently $GH(\nu, \alpha, \beta, 0, \mu)$ distributed, i.e., follow the VG distribution. The corresponding p.d.f is obtained as the limit $\delta \to 0$ of (3.8):

$$\mathrm{pdf}_{\mathrm{BNS-VG}}(u) = \frac{\gamma^{2\nu}|u - \mu|^{\nu-1/2} K_{\nu-1/2}\left(\alpha|u - \mu|\right)}{\sqrt{\pi}\Gamma(\nu)(2\alpha)^{\nu-1/2}} \exp\left(\beta(u - \mu)\right).$$
(3.20)

The construction of such a process Y can be found in [10] using a series representation.

For the BNS model we need to estimate the vector of parameters $(\mu, \beta, \lambda, \nu, \gamma)$, where $\gamma \equiv \sqrt{\alpha^2 - \beta^2}$. To estimate these parameters, we first consider the autocorrelation function for the squared logreturns. By (3.10) in Proposition 3.1, we estimate the λ parameter as the decay coefficient in the autocorrelation for the squared logreturns. The other BNS parameters in (3.20) can be related to the estimated VG parameters in Table 3.3 via the p.d.f (3.16). We find the BNS parameters by identification, i.e., obtaining equality between (3.16) and (3.20) using $\alpha = \sqrt{2\sigma_{\mathrm{VG}}^2/\nu_{\mathrm{VG}} + \theta^2}/\sigma_{\mathrm{VG}}^2$:

$$(\mu, \beta, \lambda, \nu, \gamma) = \left(c, \frac{\theta}{\sigma_{\mathrm{VG}}^2}, \lambda, \frac{1}{\nu_{\mathrm{VG}}}, \sqrt{\frac{2}{\sigma_{\mathrm{VG}}^2 \nu_{\mathrm{VG}}}}\right).$$
(3.21)

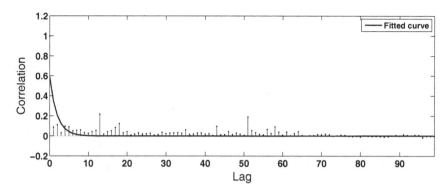

Fig. 3.6 Autocorrelation function for the squared logreturns. The solid curve is the fitted function $\exp(-\hat{\lambda}k)$ with $\hat{\lambda} = 0.526$.

This characterization completely specifies the BNS model (3.4)–(3.6) with $Y \sim \Gamma(\nu, \gamma)$.

The solid curve shown in Fig. 3.6 is the the fitted exponential function $\exp(-\hat{\lambda}k)$ with mean-reversion coefficient estimate $\hat{\lambda} = 0.5260$. Except from some peaks around lags 15 and 50, we observe a nice decay toward zero. The fit is far from perfect, but captures at least the main feature of a fast decaying autocorrelation function. The one-factor BNS model is a "first order" approximation, but using a multi-factor stochastic volatility model would require a much more sophisticated estimation procedure, which we do not pursue here. The estimated mean-reverting coefficients for the other time series are the same up to an accuracy of three decimals. Numerically, using in (3.21) the vector of parameter estimates $(\hat{c}, \hat{\sigma}_{\mathrm{VG}}, \hat{\theta}, \hat{\nu}_{\mathrm{VG}})$ in Table 3.3 and the given estimate $\hat{\lambda}$, we find the following vector of estimates of the parameters of the VG-distributed BNS model:

$$(\hat{\mu}, \hat{\beta}, \hat{\lambda}, \hat{\nu}, \hat{\gamma}) = (0.00379, -5.56, 0.526, 2.59, 80.8).$$

3.4.1.2. *VG Distribution via the Heston Model*

To obtain the parameters of the Heston model we use the characteristic function (3.15). As shown in [22] (see also [23]), the characteristic function $\phi_{L_{\mathrm{VG}}}(u)$ for the logreturns is

$$\phi_{L_{\mathrm{VG}}}(u) = e^{iuc}\left(1 - i\theta\nu_{\mathrm{VG}}u + \frac{\sigma_{\mathrm{VG}}^2\nu_{\mathrm{VG}}}{2}u^2\right)^{-\frac{1}{\nu_{\mathrm{VG}}}}. \qquad (3.22)$$

By comparing the characteristic functions (3.15) and (3.22) we can identify the parameters $(\mu, \beta, \gamma, \lambda, \kappa)$ of model (3.11), with Heston type volatility

(3.12), with the parameters $(c, \sigma_{\mathrm{VG}}, \theta, \nu_{\mathrm{VG}})$ of the VG distribution. We obtain the system of equations

$$c = \mu, \qquad -\frac{\beta \kappa^2}{2\gamma} = \theta \nu_{\mathrm{VG}}, \tag{3.23}$$

$$\frac{\kappa^2}{4\gamma} = \frac{\sigma_{\mathrm{VG}}^2 \nu_{\mathrm{VG}}}{2}, \qquad \frac{2\gamma\lambda}{\kappa^2} = \frac{1}{\nu_{\mathrm{VG}}}. \tag{3.24}$$

There are more unknowns than equations in (3.23) and (3.24), making this system of equations under-determined. Defining $\tilde{\alpha} := \kappa^2/\gamma$, the system (3.23) and (3.24) can then be solved for $\tilde{\alpha}$, β, and λ as follows:

$$(\tilde{\alpha}, \beta, \lambda) = \left(2\sigma_{\mathrm{VG}}^2 \nu_{\mathrm{VG}}, -\frac{\theta}{\sigma_{\mathrm{VG}}^2}, \sigma_{\mathrm{VG}}^2 \right).$$

We can estimate the parameter γ from the autocorrelation function to solve the under-determined system of equations (3.23) and (3.24). The solid curve in Fig. 3.7 is the fitted function $A_0 + A_1 \mathrm{e}^{-\gamma k} + A_2 \mathrm{e}^{-2\gamma k}$. The estimation yields $(\hat{\gamma}, \hat{A}_0, \hat{A}_1, \hat{A}_2) = (1.62, 0.0281, 1.31, 18.4)$. We obtain the following corresponding parameters for the Heston model:

$$(\mu, \beta, \gamma, \lambda, \kappa) = \left(c, -\frac{\theta}{\sigma_{\mathrm{VG}}^2}, \gamma, \sigma_{\mathrm{VG}}^2, \sqrt{2\sigma_{\mathrm{VG}}^2 \nu_{\mathrm{VG}} \gamma} \right). \tag{3.25}$$

This characterization completely specifies the Heston model (3.11) with Heston type volatility (3.12). Numerically, using in (3.25) the vector of parameter estimates $(\hat{c}, \hat{\sigma}_{\mathrm{VG}}, \hat{\theta}, \hat{\nu}_{\mathrm{VG}})$ in Table 3.3 and the estimate $\hat{\gamma}$ we find the following vector of parameter estimates for Heston model:

$$(\hat{\mu}, \hat{\beta}, \hat{\gamma}, \hat{\lambda}, \hat{\kappa}) = (0.00379, 5.56, 1.62, 0.0008, 0.0316).$$

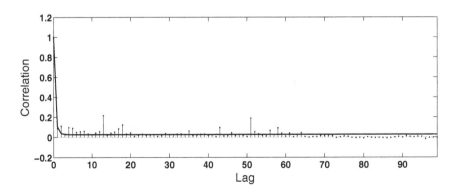

Fig. 3.7   Autocorrelation functions of the squared logreturns fitted with the curve in Proposition 3.3; $(\hat{\gamma}, \hat{A}_0, \hat{A}_1, \hat{A}_2) = (1.62, 0.0281, 1.31, 18.4)$.

The first two parameters in (3.21) and (3.25) are the same (considering the absolute value for β) for the VG-distributed BNS model and Heston model. This equality is clear, because, conditionally on the volatility in (3.4) and (3.13), these models have the same dynamics. The difference in the sign of the β parameter is just a consequence of the different choices of sign in (3.4) and (3.13) for the BNS and Heston models, respectively.

Remark 3.1. It is evident that $\beta = 0$ if and only if $\theta = 0$, where θ is the drift parameter in the VG process that gives rise to skewness. Hence, the introduction of the parameter β is necessary to account for skewness.

3.4.2. *Normal Inverse Gaussian Distribution*

Fig. 3.8 displays the empirical and estimated NIG densities. The pdf for the $\mathrm{NIG}(\alpha, \beta, \mu, \delta)$ distribution is given by (see [9])

$$
\mathrm{pdf}_{\mathrm{NIG}}(u) := \frac{\delta \alpha}{\pi \sqrt{\delta^2 + (u - \mu)^2}} \exp\left(\delta\sqrt{\alpha^2 - \beta^2} + \beta(u - \mu)\right)
$$
$$
\times K_1\left(\alpha\sqrt{\delta^2 + (u - \mu)^2}\right), \tag{3.26}
$$

where K_1 is the modified Bessel function of third order and index 1. The parameter $\alpha > 0$ controls the behavior of the tails. The steepness of the NIG distribution increases with increasing α. Hence, large values of α imply light tails and vice versa. The parameter β, $0 < |\beta| < \alpha$, controls the skewness of the distribution. The terms μ and δ are the location and scale parameters, respectively. The NIG distribution can capture stylized features such as tail and center behavior well. Table 3.4 reports the estimates of these parameters.

By the flexibility of the BNS model, a $\mathrm{NIG}(\alpha, \beta, \mu, \delta)$ distribution is obtained by taking Y to be $\mathrm{IG}(\delta, \sqrt{\alpha^2 - \beta^2})$ distributed, i.e., $\nu = -1/2$ in (3.8). A method to construct and simulate such an IG-process Y is described in [24].

The NIG distribution (3.26) is defined as the distribution of the BNS model when Y is IG distributed with parameters $(\delta, \sqrt{\alpha^2 - \beta^2})$ and the parameters in the NIG distribution exactly correspond to the parameters in that BNS model. Hence, the parameters in the BNS model are obtained by fitting the NIG density (3.26) to the sample density. As in Sec. 3.4.1.1,

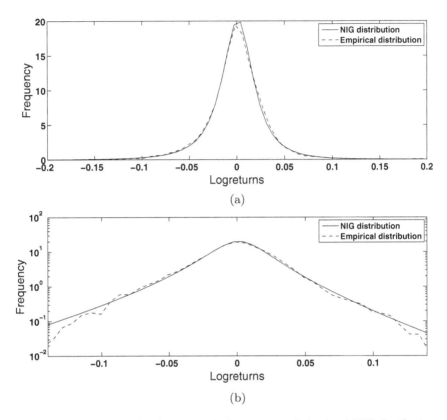

Fig. 3.8   The empirical distribution of the logreturns and the fitted NIG distribution with its estimated parameters given in the row corresponding to time series 1 in Table 3.4. The fitted NIG distribution captures the heavy tails well (a) Distribution of the logreturns. (b) Distribution of the logreturns (logarithmic scale).

the parameter λ is estimated via the autocorrelation function (3.10) for the squared logreturns. This estimation approach completely specifies all the parameters in the BNS model (3.4)–(3.6) with $Y \sim \mathrm{IG}(\delta, \gamma)$. We directly obtain the BNS parameters as follows:

$$(\mu, \beta, \lambda, \delta, \gamma) = \left(\mu_{\mathrm{NIG}}, \beta_{\mathrm{NIG}}, \lambda, \delta_{\mathrm{NIG}}, \sqrt{\alpha_{\mathrm{NIG}}^2 - \beta_{\mathrm{NIG}}^2} \right). \qquad (3.27)$$

The corresponding vector of estimated parameters is

$$(\hat{\mu}, \hat{\beta}, \hat{\lambda}, \hat{\delta}, \hat{\gamma}) = (0.0019, -2.59, 0.526, 0.0210, 21.4).$$

Table 3.4   NIG parameter estimates for the logreturns.

Time Series	$\hat{\alpha}_{\text{NIG}}$	$\hat{\beta}_{\text{NIG}}$	$\hat{\mu}_{\text{NIG}}(\times 10^{-3})$	$\hat{\delta}_{\text{NIG}}(\times 10^{-2})$
1	21.58	-2.59	1.90	2.10
2	21.24	-2.44	1.75	2.05
3	20.94	-2.54	1.83	2.02
4	20.88	-2.56	1.85	2.01
5	21.20	-2.63	1.92	2.04

3.4.3. *Comparison*

It is evident from Fig. 3.9 that the NIG distribution provides a better fit of the tails and center of the sample distribution than the VG distribution. Furthermore, we have tested equality of the sample distribution of the logreturns with the estimated VG and NIG distributions, respectively, using the Kolmogorov–Smirnov test (KS test). Table 3.5 reports the p-values of the KS test.[e] These p-values indicate that it is reasonable to (i) reject the null hypothesis that the logreturns sample distribution arises from a VG distribution and (ii) fail to reject the analogous null hypothesis for the NIG distribution.[f]

3.5.   Empirical Analysis for the Three Individual EU ETS Phases

The three EU ETS phases are distinguished by different regulations. In this section we separately analyze the prices of each such phase, restricting our analysis to the time series of futures 1.We perform a statistical analysis of the observed logreturns of each EU ETS phase in Sec. 3.5.1. We investigate the fit of the VG distribution in Sec. 3.5.2 and of the NIG distribution in Sec. 3.5.3. We compare them in Sec. 3.5.4. For brevity, we do not estimate the parameters for the BNS and Heston models. As in Sec. 3.4, these parameters can be estimated using the autocorrelation functions.

---

[e]We conducted the KS test in R.

[f]A low p-value provides evidence against the null hypothesis.

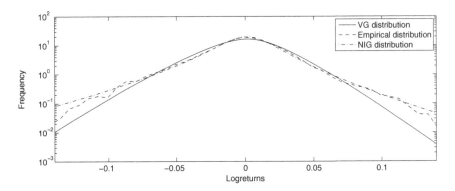

Fig. 3.9   Logarithmic sample distribution of the logreturns and the fitted VG and NIG distributions.

Table 3.5   K-S test: p-values.

Time Series	VG	NIG
1	0.00155	0.318
2	<0.001	0.402
3	n.a.[a]	0.337
4	<0.001	0.231
5	<0.001	0.267

[a]R was unable to calculate the p-value.

3.5.1.   *Statistical Data Analysis*

Phase 1 took place between 2005 and 2007, phase 2 between 2008 and 2012, and phase 3 started in 2013 and is planned until 2020.We thus have 690, 1,289, and 169 observed futures prices for these three phases, respectively. Table 3.6 includes the sample moments of the logreturns for each individual phase and all phases combined. For each phase we observe skewness (most apparent in phases 1 and 3) and high excessive kurtosis. This observation is in line with the features of the time series presented in Fig. 3.2. This deviation from normality is apparent in Fig. 3.10, which displays the empirical distributions of the logreturns for the three EU ETS phases and their respective estimated normal distributions.

The absolute autocorrelation functions presented in Fig. 3.11 indicate volatility clustering, as observed for the full time series displayed in Fig. 3.2.

Table 3.6   Sample moments of the logreturns of time series 1 for the EU ETS phases.

EU ETS Phase(s)	Mean ($\times 10^{-4}$)	Variance ($\times 10^{-4}$)	Skew	Kurtosis
1	4.0	9.1	−1.4700	19.43
2	−10.0	7.3	0.0733	6.97
3	−20.0	43.0	−1.3000	14.62
All	−6.2	11.0	−1.1900	24.82

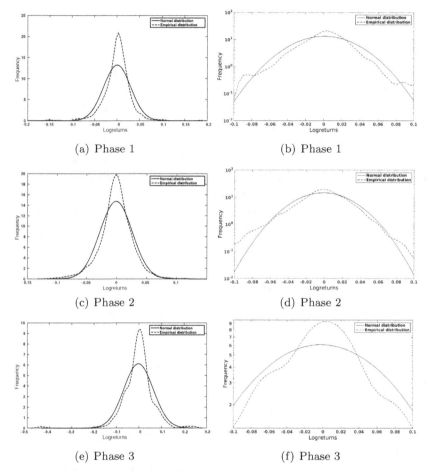

(a) Phase 1   (b) Phase 1

(c) Phase 2   (d) Phase 2

(e) Phase 3   (f) Phase 3

Fig. 3.10   The empirical distributions of the logreturns for the three EU ETS phases and their corresponding fitted normal distributions (logarithmic scale on the right).

For phases 1 and 2 the autocorrelations of the logreturns are close to zero. However, for phase 3 we observe a modest autocorrelation (see Fig. 3.11(f)). Further, the excessive kurtosis is considerably higher in phases 1 and 3. However, each phase has lower excessive kurtosis than the full series, as shown in Table 3.6. Notably, as also indicated in this table, the variance for phase 3 is greater than the variance for the other two phases, as well as the variance for the full time series.

3.5.2. *VG Distribution*

Figure 3.12 plots the empirical density of the logreturns and the estimated VG density. Table 3.7 reports the estimates of the VG distribution parameters. The VG distribution poorly fits the individual empirical densities. It is particularly deficient in capturing the behavior of the center of the empirical density for each phase, as well as its heavy tails in phases 1 and 2 (however it better captures the tail behavior in phase 3). The latter observation is consistent with the lower excessive kurtosis for the individual phases compared to the full time series. Based on these observed distributional properties, the Heston model does not seem adequate as a model of the logreturns for the individual EU ETS phases.

3.5.3. *NIG Distribution*

Fig. 3.13 displays the empirical density of the logreturns and the estimated NIG density. Table 3.8 gives the estimated parameters of the NIG distribution. The NIG distribution does a good job at capturing the observed distributional behavior of the logreturns. The main distributional difference across the three phases is the heaviness of the tails. This behavior is reflected in the estimated value of the α_{NIG} parameter given in Table 3.8. The substantially higher (lower) value of the estimate of α_{NIG} in phase 2 (phase 3) is consistent with the observed time series and the statistics presented in Table 3.6. The BNS model seems adequate as a model for the logreturns of the individual EU ETS phases.

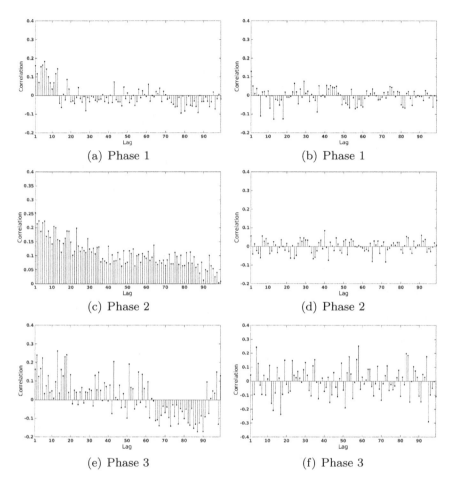

Fig. 3.11   Autocorrelation functions for the absolute logreturns (left) and the logreturns (right) for the three EU ETS phases.

3.5.4.   *Comparison*

Figure 3.14 compares the empirical distribution and the fitted NIG and VG distributions: The NIG distribution seems superior to the VG distribution when considering each phase in isolation. In particular, the NIG distribution is better able to capture the peak behavior than the VG distribution for

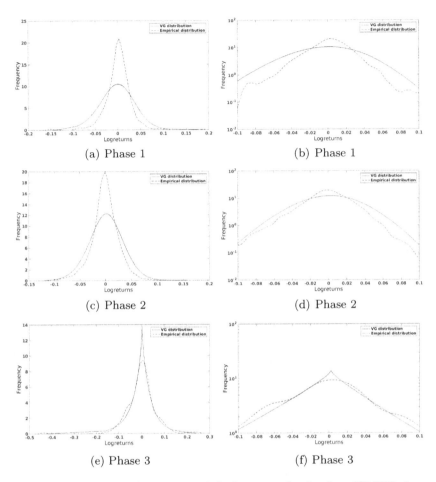

Fig. 3.12   The empirical distributions of the logreturns for the three EU ETS phases and their corresponding fitted VG distributions with parameter estimates in Table 3.7 (logarithmic scale on the right).

Table 3.7   Estimates of the parameters of the VG distribution for the logreturns of time series 1 of the EU ETS phases.

EU ETS Phase(s)	$\hat{c}$	$\hat{\sigma}_{\mathrm{VG}}$	$\hat{\theta}$	$\hat{\nu}_{\mathrm{VG}}$
1	0.01830	0.0392	−0.02120	0.118
2	0.00983	0.0340	−0.00910	0.118
3	0.00232	0.0615	−0.00421	1.190
All	0.00379	0.0282	−0.00441	0.387

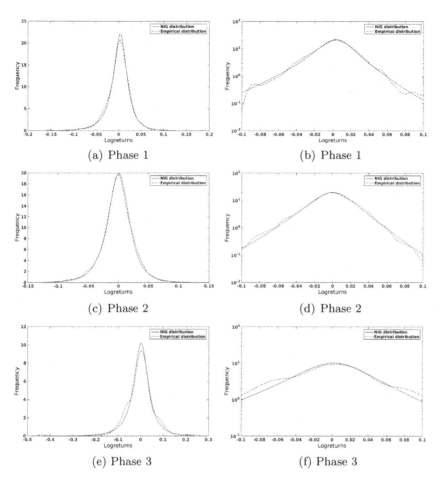

Fig. 3.13   The empirical distributions of the logreturns for the three EU ETS phases and their corresponding fitted NIG distributions with parameter estimates in Table 3.8 (logarithmic scale on the right),

Table 3.8   Estimates of the parameters of the NIG distribution for the logreturns of time series 1 for the EU ETS phases.

EU ETS Phase(s)	$\hat{\alpha}_{\mathrm{NIG}}$	$\hat{\beta}_{\mathrm{NIG}}$	$\hat{\mu}_{\mathrm{NIG}}$ ($\times 10^{-3}$)	$\hat{\delta}_{\mathrm{NIG}}$ ($\times 10^{-2}$)
1	23.75	−4.82	4.34	1.89
2	33.85	−2.56	0.83	2.46
3	10.14	−1.14	2.73	4.06
All	21.58	−2.59	1.90	2.10

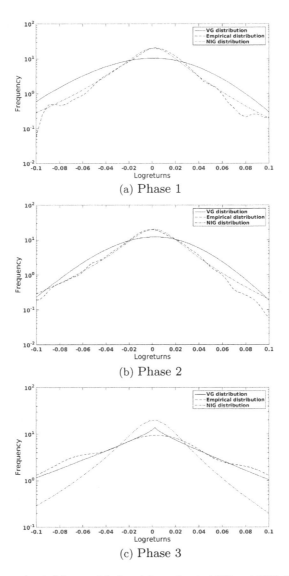

(a) Phase 1

(b) Phase 2

(c) Phase 3

Fig. 3.14   Comparison of the empirical and the estimated VG and NIG distributions of the logreturns for the three EU ETS phases (logarithmic scale).

each phase. This observation is consistent with what observed in Sec. 3.4.3 with respect to Fig. 3.9.

3.6. Conclusions

Both the BNS model and the Heston model can explain key empirical features of EU ETS futures prices observed in the Nord Pool market, such as skewness and heavy tails of the empirical logreturn distribution. Introducing an additional parameter in the Heston model is necessary to obtain a model that incorporates skewness. The resulting Heston model thus has a nonzero autocorrelation function. Compared to this model, the zero autocorrelation function of the BNS model is more consistent with the observed empirical autocorrelation. Furthermore, the NIG distribution obtained from the BNS model by taking the stochastic volatility to be IG distributed fits the data substantially better than the VG distribution associated with the Heston model. Further, the BNS model is more flexible then the Heston model, because we can obtain different distributions for the logreturns by choosing a suitable self-decomposable distribution for the stochastic volatility process. These findings continue to hold when restricting attention to each of the three EU ETS phases, in which case we observe a modest autocorrelation in phase 3 compared to the almost zero autocorrelation in phases 1 and 2 and a substantially higher excessive kurtosis in phases 1 and 3 than in phase 2. Considering both the autocorrelation structure and the distributional properties, we conclude that the NIG distributed BNS model is a more adequate model of the EU ETS allowance futures prices than the Heston model.

Acknowledgments

The authors are grateful to Montel for providing data. Financial support from Elcarbonrisk and Mawrem funded by the Norwegian Research Council within the ENERGIX program is gratefully acknowledged. The authors also thank an anonymous referee and the editor Nicola Secomandi for their suggestions and feedback, which led to a substantial improvement of the exposition of this chapter.

Appendix A. Proofs

The proofs of Propositions 3.2 and 3.3 are in Appendix A.1 and in Appendix A.2, respectively. Appendix A.3 includes the proofs of the lemmas used in Appendix A.2.

A.1. *Proof of Proposition 3.2*

The covariance at lag k is defined by $\text{cov}(L(t+k), L(t)) := \mathbb{E}[L(t+k)L(t)] - \mathbb{E}[L(t+k)]\mathbb{E}[L(t)]$. We start by calculating $\mathbb{E}[L(t+k)L(t)]$ for $k > 0$:

$$
\begin{aligned}
\mathbb{E}[L(t+k)L(t)] = \mathbb{E} & \left[\left(\int_{t+k}^{t+k+1} (\mu - \beta Y(s))ds + \int_{t+k}^{t+k+1} \sqrt{Y(s)}dB(s) \right) \right. \\
& \left. \times \left(\int_{t}^{t+1} (\mu - \beta Y(s))ds + \int_{t}^{t+1} \sqrt{Y(s)}dB(s) \right) \right] \\
= \mathbb{E} & \left[\int_{t+k}^{t+k+1} (\mu - \beta Y(s))ds \int_{t}^{t+1} (\mu - \beta Y(u))du \right] \\
+ \mathbb{E} & \left[\int_{t+k}^{t+k+1} (\mu - \beta Y(s))ds \int_{t}^{t+1} \sqrt{Y(u)}dB(u) \right] \\
+ \mathbb{E} & \left[\int_{t}^{t+1} (\mu - \beta Y(u))du \int_{t+k}^{t+k+1} \sqrt{Y(s)}dB(s) \right] \\
+ \mathbb{E} & \left[\int_{t+k}^{t+k+1} \sqrt{Y(s)}dB(s) \int_{t}^{t+1} \sqrt{Y(u)}dB(u) \right]. \quad \text{(A.1)}
\end{aligned}
$$

Recall that the filtration $\mathcal{F}_t^Y \equiv \{Y(u), u \leq t\}$ is the σ-algebra generated by Y, which reveals all the information of the stochastic volatility up to time t. By Fubini's Theorem and iterated expectations, for $k > 0$ the second term in (A.1) satisfies

$$
\begin{aligned}
\mathbb{E} & \left[\int_{t+k}^{t+k+1} (\mu - \beta Y(s))ds \int_{t}^{t+1} \sqrt{Y(u)}dB(u) \right] \\
= \mathbb{E} & \left[\int_{t+k}^{t+k+1} \left[(\mu - \beta Y(s)) \int_{t}^{t+1} \sqrt{Y(u)}dB(u) \right] ds \right] \\
= \int_{t+k}^{t+k+1} & \mathbb{E} \left(\mathbb{E} \left[(\mu - \beta Y(s)) \int_{t}^{t+1} \sqrt{Y(u)}dB(u) | \mathcal{F}_s^Y \right] \right) ds \\
= \int_{t+k}^{t+k+1} & \mathbb{E} \left((\mu - \beta Y(s))\mathbb{E} \left[\int_{t}^{t+1} \sqrt{Y(u)}dB(u) | \mathcal{F}_s^Y \right] \right) ds \\
= 0, &
\end{aligned}
$$

where the last equality holds because $\mu - \beta Y(s)$ is $\mathcal{F}_s^Y$-measurable and $\mathbb{E}\left[\int_t^{t+1} \sqrt{Y(u)}dB(u)|\mathcal{F}_s^Y\right] = 0$. Similarly, for the third term in (A.1) we obtain

$$\mathbb{E}\left[\int_t^{t+1} (\mu - \beta Y(s))ds \int_{t+k}^{t+k+1} \sqrt{Y(u)}dB(u)\right]$$

$$= \int_t^{t+1} \mathbb{E}\left((\mu - \beta Y(s))\mathbb{E}\left[\int_{t+k}^{t+k+1} \sqrt{Y(u)}dB(u)|\mathcal{F}_s^Y\right]\right) ds$$

$$= 0.$$

By Itô isometry and for T large enough and $k > 0$ we express the last term in (A.1) as

$$\mathbb{E}\left[\int_{t+k}^{t+k+1} \sqrt{Y(s)}dB(s) \int_t^{t+1} \sqrt{Y(u)}dB(u)\right]$$

$$= \mathbb{E}\left[\int_0^T \mathbf{1}(t+k \leq s \leq t+k+1)\sqrt{Y(s)}dB(s)\right.$$

$$\left. \times \int_0^T \mathbf{1}(t \leq s \leq t+1)\sqrt{Y(s)}dB(s)\right]$$

$$= \mathbb{E}\left[\int_0^T \mathbf{1}(t+k \leq s \leq t+k+1)\mathbf{1}(t \leq s \leq t+1)Y(s)ds\right]$$

$$= 0.$$

We rearrange the first term in (A.1) as

$$\mathbb{E}\left[\int_{t+k}^{t+k+1} (\mu - \beta Y(s))ds \int_t^{t+1} (\mu - \beta Y(u))du\right]$$

$$= \mathbb{E}\left[\int_{t+k}^{t+k+1} \int_t^{t+1} (\mu - \beta Y(s))(\mu - \beta Y(u))duds\right]$$

$$= \int_{t+k}^{t+k+1} \int_t^{t+1} \mathbb{E}\left[(\mu - \beta Y(s))(\mu - \beta Y(u))\right] duds,$$

where we use Fubini's theorem in the last step. The integrand in this expression expands to

$$\mathbb{E}\left[(\mu - \beta Y(s))(\mu - \beta Y(u))\right] = \mu^2 - \mu\beta\left(\mathbb{E}\left[Y(s)\right] + \mathbb{E}\left[Y(u)\right]\right)$$

$$+ \beta^2\mathbb{E}\left[Y(s)Y(u)\right].$$

We can write Y in explicit form by applying Itô's formula to the function $f(y,t) = ye^{\gamma t}$:

$$\begin{aligned} df(Y(t),t) &= \gamma Y(t)e^{\gamma t}dt + e^{\gamma t}dY(t) \\ &= \gamma Y(t)e^{\gamma t}dt + e^{\gamma t}(-\gamma(Y(t) - \lambda)dt + \kappa\sqrt{Y(t)}dW(t)) \\ &= \gamma\lambda e^{\gamma t}dt + \kappa e^{\gamma t}\sqrt{Y(t)}dW(t). \end{aligned}$$

Integrating from 0 to t with $Y(t) = y$ at $t = 0$, we obtain

$$Y(t) = ye^{-\gamma t} + \lambda(1 - e^{-\gamma t}) + \kappa\int_0^t e^{\gamma(s-t)}\sqrt{Y(s)}dW(s). \qquad (A.2)$$

Hence, we have

$$\mathbb{E}\left[Y(t)\right] = y_0 e^{-\gamma t} + \lambda\left(1 - e^{-\gamma t}\right). \qquad (A.3)$$

From (A.2) and (A.3) we obtain

$$\begin{aligned} Y(u)Y(s) = &\left(\mathbb{E}\left[Y(u)\right] + \kappa\int_0^u e^{\gamma(v-u)}\sqrt{Y(v)}dW(v)\right) \\ &\times \left(\mathbb{E}\left[Y(s)\right] + \kappa\int_0^s e^{\gamma(v-s)}\sqrt{Y(v)}dW(v)\right). \qquad (A.4) \end{aligned}$$

Multiplying out and taking expectations makes the Brownian integrals vanish. The Itô isometry yields

$$\begin{aligned} \mathbb{E}&\left[\int_0^u e^{\gamma(v-u)}\sqrt{Y(v)}dW(v)\int_0^s e^{\gamma(v-s)}\sqrt{Y(v)}dW(v)\right] \\ &= e^{-\gamma(u+s)}\mathbb{E}\left[\int_0^{\min(s,u)} e^{2\gamma v}Y(v)dv\right] \\ &= e^{-\gamma(u+s)}\int_0^{\min(s,u)} e^{2\gamma v}\mathbb{E}\left[Y(v)\right]dv, \end{aligned}$$

where Fubini's theorem is used in the last step. We obtain

$$\mathbb{E}[Y(u)Y(s)] = \mathbb{E}[Y(u)]\mathbb{E}[Y(s)] + \kappa^2 e^{-\gamma(u+s)}\int_0^{\min(s,u)} e^{2\gamma v}\mathbb{E}\left[Y(v)\right]dv$$

and thus,

$$\begin{aligned} \mathbb{E}\left[(\mu - \beta Y(s))(\mu - \beta Y(u))\right] = &\ \mu^2 - \mu\beta\left(\mathbb{E}\left[Y(s)\right] + \mathbb{E}\left[Y(u)\right]\right) \\ &+ \beta^2\mathbb{E}[Y(u)]\mathbb{E}[Y(s)] \\ &+ \beta^2\kappa^2 e^{-\gamma(u+s)}\int_0^{\min(s,u)} e^{2\gamma v}\mathbb{E}\left[Y(v)\right]dv. \end{aligned}$$

Because $u < s$, for $k > 0$ it follows that

$$\mathbb{E}[L(t)L(t+k)] = \int_{t+k}^{t+k+1} \int_{t}^{t+1} \mu^2 - \mu\beta\left(\mathbb{E}[Y(s)] + \mathbb{E}[Y(u)]\right)$$

$$+ \beta^2 \mathbb{E}[Y(u)]E[Y(s)]\,du\,ds$$

$$+ \beta^2\kappa^2 \int_{t+k}^{t+k+1} \int_{t}^{t+1} \left(e^{-\gamma(u+s)} \int_{0}^{u} e^{2\gamma v}\mathbb{E}[Y(v)]\,dv\right) du\,ds.$$

$$(A.5)$$

To calculate (A.5), we plug in (A.5) the expression (A.3) for the expectation of Y, the expression

$$\mathbb{E}[Y(u)]\mathbb{E}[Y(s)] = e^{-\gamma(s+u)}(y_0 - \lambda)^2 + \lambda(y_0 - \lambda)(e^{-\gamma s} + e^{-\gamma u}) + \lambda^2$$

for $\mathbb{E}[Y(u)]\mathbb{E}[Y(s)]$, and also use

$$e^{-\gamma(u+s)} \int_{0}^{u} e^{2\gamma v}\mathbb{E}[Y(v)]\,dv = \frac{1}{2\gamma}\left[e^{-\gamma(s+u)}(\lambda - 2y_0)\right.$$

$$\left. + 2e^{-\gamma s}(y_0 - \lambda) + \lambda e^{-\gamma(s-u)}\right],$$

obtaining

$$\mathbb{E}[L(t)L(t+k)] = \int_{t+k}^{t+k+1} \int_{t}^{t+1} \mu^2 - \mu\beta y_0(e^{-\gamma s} + e^{-\gamma u}) - 2\mu\beta\lambda$$

$$+ \mu\beta\lambda(e^{-\gamma s} + e^{-\gamma u})du\,ds + \beta^2 \int_{t+k}^{t+k+1} \int_{t}^{t+1} e^{-\gamma(s+u)}(y_0 - \lambda)^2$$

$$+ \lambda(y_0 - \lambda)(e^{-\gamma s} + e^{-\gamma u}) + \lambda^2 du\,ds + \frac{\beta^2\kappa^2}{2\gamma}$$

$$\times \int_{t+k}^{t+k+1} \int_{t}^{t+1} e^{-\gamma(s+u)}(\lambda - 2y_0) + 2e^{-\gamma s}(y_0 - \lambda) + \lambda e^{-\gamma(s-u)}du\,ds$$

$$(A.6)$$

$$= \mu^2 - \mu\beta y_0 \left(\int_{t+k}^{t+k+1} e^{-\gamma s}ds + \int_{t}^{t+1} e^{-\gamma u}du\right)$$

$$- 2\mu\beta\lambda + \mu\beta\lambda \left(\int_{t+k}^{t+k+1} e^{-\gamma s}ds + \int_{t}^{t+1} e^{-\gamma u}du\right)$$

$$+ \beta^2(y_0 - \lambda)^2 \int_{t+k}^{t+k+1} \int_{t}^{t+1} e^{-\gamma(s+u)}du\,ds$$

$$+\lambda(y_0 - \lambda)\beta^2 \left(\int_{t+k}^{t+k+1} e^{-\gamma s}ds + \int_t^{t+1} e^{-\gamma u}du \right) + \lambda^2\beta^2$$

$$+\frac{\beta^2\kappa^2}{2\gamma} \left[(\lambda - 2y_0) \int_{t+k}^{t+k+1} \int_t^{t+1} e^{-\gamma(s+u)}duds \right.$$

$$\left. +2(y_0 - \lambda) \int_{t+k}^{t+k+1} e^{-\gamma s}ds + \lambda \int_{t+k}^{t+k+1} \int_t^{t+1} e^{-\gamma(s-u)}duds \right]$$

for $\min(s, u) = u$, with the integrals in (A.6) calculated as explained below.

A.2.   *Calculation of the integrals in (A.6)*

For any $s > 0$ we have

$$\int_{t+k}^{t+k+1} e^{-\gamma s}ds = \left(1 - e^{-\gamma}\right) \frac{1}{\gamma}e^{-\gamma(t+k)}, \qquad (A.7)$$

$$\int_{t+k}^{t+k+1} \int_t^{t+1} e^{-\gamma(s+u)}duds = \frac{1 - 2e^{-\gamma} + e^{-2\gamma}}{\gamma^2}e^{-\gamma(2t+k)}, \qquad (A.8)$$

$$\int_{t+k}^{t+k+1} \int_t^{t+1} e^{-\gamma(s-u)}duds = \frac{1}{\gamma^2}(e^{\gamma} + e^{-\gamma} - 2)e^{-\gamma k}. \qquad (A.9)$$

Out of terms (A.7)–(A.9), in the limit (A.9) is the only contributing term. Hence, with stationarity we obtain

$$\mathbb{E}[L(t)L(t+k)] = (\mu - \lambda\beta)^2 + \frac{\beta^2\kappa^2\lambda}{2\gamma^3}e^{-\gamma k}(e^{\gamma} + e^{-\gamma} - 2).$$

The stationary covariance becomes

$$\mathrm{cov}(L(t+k), L(t)) = \frac{\beta^2\kappa^2\lambda}{2\gamma^3}e^{-\gamma k}(e^{\gamma} + e^{-\gamma} - 2)$$

because $\mathbb{E}[L(t)] = \mathbb{E}[L(t+k)] = \mu - \lambda\beta$ with stationarity. Clearly, this quantity tends to zero as k becomes large. The stationary autocorrelation thus becomes

$$\mathrm{AutoCorr}(L(t+k), L(t)) \equiv \frac{\mathrm{cov}(L(t+k), L(t))}{\sqrt{\mathrm{var}(L(t+k))}\sqrt{\mathrm{var}(L(t))}}$$

$$= \frac{\beta^2\kappa^2}{(\beta^2\kappa + 2\gamma)\gamma^2}e^{-\gamma k}(e^{\gamma} + e^{-\gamma} - 2).$$

A.3. *Proof of Proposition 3.3*

We begin by stating some intermediate results and lemmas. The lemmas are technical and their detailed proofs can be found in Appendix A.3. Define the processes X and Z as

$$X(s) := \int_t^s \Phi_1(u)du + \int_t^s \Psi_1(u)dB(u), \qquad (A.10)$$

$$Z(s) := \int_t^s \Phi_2(u)du + \int_t^s \Psi_2(u)dB(u), \qquad (A.11)$$

where the terms $\Phi_1(u)$, $\Psi_1(u)$, $\Phi_2(u)$, and $\Psi_2(u)$ are defined as

$$\Phi_1(u) := \mathbf{1}(t \le u \le t+1)(\mu - \beta Y(u)), \qquad (A.12)$$

$$\Psi_1(u) := \mathbf{1}(t \le u \le t+1)\sqrt{Y(u)},$$

$$\Phi_2(u) := \mathbf{1}(t+k \le u \le t+k+1)(\mu - \beta Y(u)),$$

$$\Psi_2(u) := \mathbf{1}(t+k \le u \le t+k+1)\sqrt{Y(u)}.$$

Applying Itô formula to $f(x,z) = x^2 z^2$ we obtain

$$\begin{aligned}
df(X(u), Z(u)) = & \left[2X(u)Z^2(u)\Phi_1(u) + 2X^2(u)Z(u)\Phi_2(u)\right. \\
& \left. + Z^2\Psi_1^2(u) + 2X(u)Z(u)\Psi_1(u)\Psi_2(u) + X^2(u)\Psi_2^2(u)\right] du \\
& + \left[2X(u)Z^2(u)\Psi_1(u) + 2X^2(u)Z(u)\Psi_2(u)\right] dB(u).
\end{aligned}$$

Taking expectation yields

$$\begin{aligned}
\mathbb{E}[X^2(s)Z^2(s)] = \mathbb{E}&\left[\int_t^s \left(2X(u)Z^2(u)\Phi_1(u) + 2X^2(u)Z(u)\Phi_2(u)\right.\right. \\
& + Z^2\Psi_1^2(u) + 2X(u)Z(u)\Psi_1(u)\Psi_2(u) \\
& \left.\left. + X^2(u)\Psi_2^2(u)\right) du\right].
\end{aligned} \qquad (A.13)$$

Consider the covariance

$$\text{cov}(L^2(t+k), L^2(t)) = \mathbb{E}[L^2(t+k)L^2(t)] - \mathbb{E}[L^2(t+k)]\mathbb{E}[L^2(t)].$$

To find an expression for this quantity we make frequent use of Fubini's Theorem, the tower property, and the Markov property of the process Y. Furthermore, we end up with expressions involving conditional expectations of powers of Y. We now derive formulas to calculate conditional expectations, which also simplify the notational exposition. By the Markov property we have for $t < s$

$$\mathbb{E}\left[Y^n(s)|\mathcal{F}_t^Y\right] = \mathbb{E}\left[(Y^{t,y})^n(s)\right]_{y=Y(t)}, \tag{A.14}$$

where $\mathbb{E}\left[(Y^{t,y})^n(s)\right]_{y=Y(t)}$ is the expectation of the process Y^n starting at $y = Y(t)$ at time t for an integer $n = 1, 2$ indicating the n-th power of Y. The n-th moment is given by

$$\mathbb{E}\left[Y^n(s)\right] = \mathbb{E}[(Y^{0,y_0})^n(s)]_{y_0=Y(0)}.$$

We have the following result.

Lemma 3.1. *The conditional expectation for the process Y defined in* (A.2) *is given by*

$$\mathbb{E}[(Y^{t,y})^n(s)]_{y=Y(t)} = Y^n(t)e^{-n\gamma(s-t)}$$

$$+n\left(\lambda\gamma + \frac{1}{2}(n-1)\kappa^2\right)\int_t^s e^{-n\gamma(s-u)}\mathbb{E}[(Y^{t,y})^{n-1}(u)]_{y=Y(t)}du.$$

The explicit expressions for $\mathbb{E}[(Y^{t,y})^n(s)]_{y=Y(t)}$ for $n = 1, 2, 3, 4$ are given by (A.26)-(A.32) in Appendix A.3.

Let $x \in \mathbb{R}_+$ and define

$$C_k := k\left(\lambda\gamma + \frac{1}{2}(k-1)\kappa^2\right), \quad k = 1, 2, \ldots \tag{A.15}$$

and

$$F_\theta^n(x) := \sum_{m=0}^n f_m^n(\theta)x^m, \tag{A.16}$$

where

$$f_m^n(\theta) := \frac{(1-e^{-\gamma\theta})^{(n-m)}e^{-m\gamma\theta}}{(n-m)!\gamma^{n-m}} \prod_{k=0}^{n-m} C_k \tag{A.17}$$

and $C_0 := 1$. Since $\gamma \geq 0$ clearly the function $f_m^n(\theta)$ is finite for all m, n and $\theta \geq 0$. Hence, the function $F_\theta^n(x)$ is finite.

Lemma 3.2. *Let $Y(0) = y_0$ and $s > u > v > t \geq 0$. Then*

$$\mathbb{E}[Y^n(s)|\mathcal{F}_t^Y] = F_{s-t}^n(Y(t)). \tag{A.18}$$

In particular,

$$\mathbb{E}[Y^n(s)|\mathcal{F}_0^Y] := \mathbb{E}[Y^n(s)] = F_s^n(y_0). \tag{A.19}$$

Also,

$$\mathbb{E}\left[F_{s-t}^n(Y(t))\right] = f_0^n(s-t) + \sum_{m=1}^{n} f_m^n(s-t) \sum_{i=0}^{m} f_i^m(t)y_0^i, \tag{A.20}$$

$$\mathbb{E}\left[Y^k(v)F_{s-u}^n(Y(u))\right] = f_0^n(s-u) \sum_{c=0}^{k} f_c^k(v)y_0^c$$

$$+ \sum_{m=1}^{n} f_m^n(s-u) \sum_{i=0}^{m} f_i^m(u-v) \sum_{j=0}^{k+i} f_j^{k+i}(v)y_0^j, \tag{A.21}$$

$$\mathbb{E}\left[Y^l(u)Y^k(v)F_{s-u}^n(Y(u))\right] = \sum_{m=0}^{n} f_m^n(s-u)$$

$$\times \sum_{i=0}^{m+l} f_i^{m+l}(u-v) \sum_{j=0}^{k+i} f_j^{k+i}(v)y_0^j, \tag{A.22}$$

and

$$\mathbb{E}\left[Y^k(u)F_{s-u}^n(Y(u))\right] = \sum_{m=0}^{n} f_m^n(s-u) \sum_{i=0}^{m+k} f_i^{m+k}(u)y_0^i. \tag{A.23}$$

Furthermore, all the expectations above are finite for all m, n, k, l, and $s > u > v > t \geq 0$.

Lemma 3.3. *The expectation $\mathbb{E}[L^2(t)L^2(t+k)]$ is given by*

$$\mathbb{E}[L^2(t)L^2(t+k)] = D_0(t,k)\mathbb{E}[L^2(t)] + D_1(t,k)\mathbb{E}[L^2(t)Y(t+1)]$$

$$+D_2(t,k)\mathbb{E}[L^2(t)Y^2(t+1)]$$

for the finite deterministic functions $D_0(t,k)$, $D_1(t,k)$, and $D_2(t,k)$ given by (A.37)–(A.39) in Appendix A.3.

Lemma 3.4. *The expectation $\mathbb{E}[L^2(t)Y^n(t+1)]$ is given by*

$$\mathbb{E}[L^2(t)Y^n(t+1)]$$

$$= 2 \int_t^{t+1} \int_t^u \left[\mu^2 \mathbb{E}\left[F_{t+1-u}^n(Y(u))\right] \right.$$

$$-\mu\beta\mathbb{E}\left[(Y(v)+Y(u))F_{t+1-u}^n(Y(u))\right]$$

$$+\beta^2\mathbb{E}\left[Y(u)Y(v)F_{t+1-u}^n(Y(u))\right]\Bigg]dvdu$$

$$+\int_t^{t+1}\mathbb{E}\left[Y(u)F_{t+1-u}^n(Y(u))\right]du,$$

for $n > 0$. Furthermore, $\mathbb{E}[L^2(t)Y^n(t+1)] \leq \infty$.

We now have the necessary tools to prove Proposition 3.3. The stationary autocorrelation of the squared logreturns is given by

$$\lim_{t\to\infty}\text{AutoCorr}(L^2(t),L^2(t+k))$$

$$=\lim_{t\to\infty}\frac{\mathbb{E}[L^2(t)L^2(t+k)]-\mathbb{E}[L^2(t)]\mathbb{E}[L^2(t+k)]}{\sqrt{\text{var}(L^2(t+k))}\sqrt{\text{var}(L^2(t))}}.$$

Because the expectations and the functions $D_n(t,k)$ are finite, it follows that $\mathbb{E}[L^2(t)L^2(t+k)]$ is finite. Furthermore, since L has finite moments of all orders we can write

$$\lim_{t\to\infty}\text{AutoCorr}(L^2(t),L^2(t+k))$$

$$=\frac{\lim_{t\to\infty}\mathbb{E}[L^2(t)L^2(t+k)]-\lim_{t\to\infty}\mathbb{E}[L^2(t)]\lim_{t\to\infty}\mathbb{E}[L^2(t+k)]}{\sqrt{\lim_{t\to\infty}\mathbb{E}[L^4(t+k)]-(\lim_{t\to\infty}\mathbb{E}[L^2(t+k)])^2}\sqrt{\lim_{t\to\infty}\mathbb{E}[L^4(t)]-(\lim_{t\to\infty}\mathbb{E}[L^2(t)])^2}}.$$

For all $n \geq 0$ we have

$$\lim_{t\to\infty}\mathbb{E}[L^n(t+k)]=\lim_{t\to\infty}\mathbb{E}[L^n(t)]=(-i)^n\frac{\partial^n\phi}{\partial u^n}(0)=:\mathbb{E}[L^n],$$

where $\phi(\cdot)$ is the stationary characteristic function for L defined in (3.15). It follows that $\mathbb{E}[L^n]$ is a constant that only depends on the parameters of the distribution of L. Thus, it holds that

$$\lim_{t\to\infty}\text{AutoCorr}(L^2(t),L^2(t+k))=\frac{\lim_{t\to\infty}\mathbb{E}[L^2(t)L^2(t+k)]-(\mathbb{E}[L^2])^2}{\mathbb{E}[L^4]-(\mathbb{E}[L^2])^2}.$$

Combining Lemmas 3.3 and 3.4 yields

$$\mathbb{E}[L^2(t)L^2(t+k)]=D_0(t,k)\mathbb{E}[L^2(t)]$$

$$+2D_1(t,k)\left(\int_t^{t+1}\int_t^u\left[\mu^2\mathbb{E}\left[F_{t+1-u}^1(Y(u))\right]\right.\right.$$

$$- \mu\beta\mathbb{E}\left[(Y(v) + Y(u))F_{t+1-u}^1(Y(u))\right]$$

$$+ \left.\beta^2\mathbb{E}\left[Y(u)Y(v)F_{t+1-u}^1(Y(u))\right]\right]dvdu$$

$$+ \left. \frac{1}{2}\int_t^{t+1}\mathbb{E}\left[Y(u)F_{t+1-u}^1(Y(u))\right]du\right)$$

$$+ 2D_2(t,k)\left(\int_t^{t+1}\int_t^u\left[\mu^2\mathbb{E}\left[F_{t+1-u}^2(Y(u))\right]\right.\right.$$

$$- \mu\beta\mathbb{E}\left[(Y(v) + Y(u))F_{t+1-u}^2(Y(u))\right]$$

$$+ \left.\beta^2\mathbb{E}\left[Y(u)Y(v)F_{t+1-u}^2(Y(u))\right]\right]dvdu$$

$$+ \frac{1}{2}\int_t^{t+1}\mathbb{E}\left[Y(u)F_{t+1-u}^2(Y(u))\right]du\right). \qquad (A.24)$$

Applying Lemma 3.2 and the expressions for $D_n(t,k)$ given by (A.37)–(A.39) in Appendix A.3, the expectation (A.24) can be calculated by elementary calculus. Passing to the limit yields

$$\lim_{t\to\infty}\mathbb{E}[L^2(t), L^2(t+k)] = \tilde{A}_0 + \tilde{A}_1\mathrm{e}^{-\gamma k} + \tilde{A}_2\mathrm{e}^{-2\gamma k},$$

for constants $\tilde{A}_1$, $\tilde{A}_2$, and $\tilde{A}_3$ that depend on the parameters of the distribution of L. Hence, it holds that

$$\lim_{t\to\infty}\mathrm{AutoCorr}(L^2(t), L^2(t+k)) = A_0 + A_1\mathrm{e}^{-\gamma k} + A_2\mathrm{e}^{-2\gamma k}.$$

The calculation of the squared autocorrelation function is straightforward via (A.24).

A.4. *Proofs of Lemmas in Appendix A.2*

Proof of Lemma 3.1

Define $\xi(t) := Y^n(t)$. By Itô's formula we obtain

$$d\xi(t) = nY^{n-1}(-\gamma(Y(t) - \lambda))dt + nY(t)^{n-1}\kappa\sqrt{Y(t)}dW(t)$$

$$+ \frac{1}{2}n(n-1)Y^{n-2}(t)\kappa^2Y(t)dt$$

$$= \left[-n\gamma Y^n(t) + Y^{n-1}(t)\left(n\lambda\gamma + \frac{1}{2}n(n-1)\kappa^2\right)\right]dt$$

$$+ nY(t)^{n-1}\kappa\sqrt{Y(t)}dW(t). \qquad (A.25)$$

We now find an explicit solution for $\xi \equiv Y^n$. Applying Itô's formula to the function $f(\xi(t), t) := \xi(t)e^{n\gamma t}$ yields

$$df(\xi(u), u) = n\gamma\xi e^{n\gamma u} du + e^{n\gamma u} d\xi(u)$$

$$= \left[nY^{n-1}(u)e^{n\gamma u} \left(\lambda\gamma + \frac{1}{2}(n-1)\kappa^2 \right) \right] du$$

$$+ nY(u)^{n-1}\kappa\sqrt{Y(u)}e^{n\gamma u}dW(u).$$

Integrating from t to s gives

$$Y^n(s) = Y^n(t)e^{-n\gamma(s-t)} + n\left(\lambda\gamma + \frac{1}{2}(n-1)\kappa^2 \right) \int_t^s e^{-n\gamma(s-u)}Y^{n-1}(u)du$$

$$+ n\kappa \int_t^s e^{-n\gamma(s-u)}Y^{n-1}(u)\sqrt{Y(u)}dW(u).$$

Taking expectations and using Fubini's Theorem we obtain

$$\mathbb{E}[Y^{n,t,y}(s)]_{y=Y(t)} = Y^n(t)e^{-n\gamma(s-t)}$$

$$+ n\left(\lambda\gamma + \frac{1}{2}(n-1)\kappa^2 \right)$$

$$\cdot \int_t^s e^{-n\gamma(s-u)}\mathbb{E}[Y^{n-1,t,y}(u)]_{y=Y(t)}du.$$

This step completes the proof of Lemma 3.1.

The explicit expression for $\mathbb{E}[Y^{n,t,y}(s)]_{y=Y(t)}$ for $n = 1, 2, 3, 4$ is calculated as follows:

(1) $n = 1$:

$$\mathbb{E}[Y^{t,y}(s)]_{y=Y(t)} = Y(t)e^{-\gamma(s-t)} + C_1 \int_t^s e^{-\gamma(s-u)}du$$

$$= Y(t)e^{-\gamma(s-t)} + \frac{C_1}{\gamma} \left(1 - e^{-\gamma(s-t)} \right)$$

$$=: Y(t)f_1^1(s-t) + f_0^1(s-t). \qquad (A.26)$$

In particular,

$$\mathbb{E}[Y(s)] = y_0 e^{-\gamma(s)} + \frac{C_1}{\gamma} \left(1 - e^{-\gamma(s)} \right)$$

$$=: Y(s)f_1^1(s) + f_0^1(s). \qquad (A.27)$$

(2) $n = 2$:

$$\mathbb{E}[Y^{2,t,y}(s)]_{y=Y(t)} = Y^2(t)e^{-2\gamma(s-t)}$$

$$+ (2\lambda\gamma + \kappa^2) \int_t^s e^{-2\gamma(s-u)}\mathbb{E}[Y^{t,y}(u)]_{y=Y(t)}du$$

$$= e^{-2\gamma s} \left[Y^2(t)e^{2\gamma t} + C_2 \int_t^s e^{2\gamma u} \right.$$

$$\left. \times \left(e^{-\gamma u} \left[Y(t)e^{\gamma t} + \frac{C_1}{\gamma}(e^{\gamma u} - e^{\gamma t}) \right] \right) du \right]$$

$$= Y^2(t)e^{-2\gamma(s-t)} + Y(t)\frac{C_2}{\gamma}(1 - e^{-\gamma(s-t)})e^{-\gamma(s-t)}$$

$$+ \frac{C_1 C_2}{2\gamma^2}(1 - e^{-\gamma(s-t)})^2$$

$$=: Y^2(t)f_2^2(s-t) + Y(t)f_1^2(s-t) + f_0^2(s-t).$$

$$\tag{A.28}$$

In particular,

$$\mathbb{E}[Y^2(s)] = y_0^2 e^{-2\gamma s} + y_0 C_2(1 - e^{-\gamma s})e^{-\gamma s} + \frac{C_1 C_2}{2\gamma^2}(1 - e^{-\gamma s})^2$$

$$=: Y^2(s)f_2^2(s) + Y(s)f_1^2(s) + f_0^2(s). \tag{A.29}$$

(3) $n = 3$:

$$\mathbb{E}[Y^{3,t,y}(s)]_{y=Y(t)} = Y^3(t)e^{-3\gamma(s-t)}$$

$$+ 3\left(\lambda\gamma + \kappa^2\right) \int_t^s e^{-3\gamma(s-u)} \mathbb{E}[Y^{2,t,y}(u)]_{y=Y(t)} du$$

$$= e^{-3\gamma s} \left[Y^3(t)e^{3\gamma t} + C_3 \int_t^s e^{3\gamma u} \right.$$

$$\left. \times \left(e^{-2\gamma u} \left[Y^2(t)e^{2\gamma t} + Y(t)e^{\gamma t}\frac{C_2}{\gamma}(e^{\gamma u} - e^{\gamma t}) \right. \right. \right.$$

$$\left. \left. \left. + \frac{C_1 C_2}{2\gamma^2}(e^{2\gamma u} - 2e^{\gamma(u+t)} + e^{2\gamma t}) \right] \right) du \right]$$

$$= Y^3(t)e^{-3\gamma(s-t)} + Y^2(t)\frac{C_3}{\gamma}(1 - e^{-\gamma(s-t)})e^{-2\gamma(s-t)}$$

$$+ Y(t)\frac{C_2 C_3}{2\gamma^2}(1 - e^{-\gamma(s-t)})^2 e^{-\gamma(s-t)}$$

$$+ \frac{C_1 C_2 C_3}{6\gamma^3}(1 - e^{-\gamma(s-t)})^3$$

$$=: Y^3(t)f_3^3(s-t) + Y^2(t)f_2^3(s-t)$$

$$+ Y(t)f_1^3(s-t) + f_0^3(s-t). \tag{A.30}$$

In particular,

$$\mathbb{E}[Y^3(s)] = y_0^3 e^{-3\gamma s} + y_0^2 \frac{C_3}{\gamma}(1 - e^{-\gamma s})e^{-2\gamma s}$$

$$+ y_0 \frac{C_2 C_3}{2\gamma^2}(1 - e^{-\gamma s})^2 e^{-\gamma s} + \frac{C_1 C_2 C_3}{6\gamma^3}(1 - e^{-\gamma s})^3$$

$$=: Y^3(s)f_3^3(s) + Y^2(s)f_2^3(s) + Y(s)f_1^3(s) + f_0^3(s). \quad \text{(A.31)}$$

(4) $n = 4$:

$$\mathbb{E}[Y^{4,t,y}(s)]_{y=Y(t)} = Y^4(t)e^{-4\gamma(s-t)}$$

$$+ 2\left(2\lambda\gamma + 3\kappa^2\right)\int_t^s e^{-4\gamma(s-u)}\mathbb{E}[Y^{3,t,y}(u)]_{y=Y(t)}du$$

$$= e^{-4\gamma s}\left[Y^4(t)e^{4\gamma t)} + C_4 \int_t^s e^{4\gamma u}e^{-3\gamma u}Y^3(t)e^{3\gamma t}du\right.$$

$$+ C_4 \int_t^s e^{4\gamma u}e^{-3\gamma u}Y^2(t)e^{2\gamma t}\frac{C_3}{\gamma}(e^{\gamma u} - e^{\gamma t})du$$

$$+ C_4 \int_t^s e^{4\gamma u}e^{-3\gamma u}\frac{C_2 C_3}{2\gamma^2}Y(t)e^{\gamma t}$$

$$\times (e^{2\gamma u} - 2e^{\gamma(u+t)} + e^{2\gamma t})du$$

$$+ C_4 \int_t^s e^{4\gamma u}e^{-3\gamma u}\frac{C_1 C_2 C_3}{6\gamma^3}$$

$$\left.\times \left(e^{3\gamma u} - 3e^{\gamma(2u+t)} + 3e^{\gamma(u+2t)} + e^{\gamma t}\right)du\right]$$

$$= Y^4(t)e^{-4\gamma(s-t)} + Y^3(t)\frac{C_4}{\gamma}(1 - e^{-\gamma(s-t)})e^{-3\gamma(s-t)}$$

$$+ Y^2(t)\frac{C_3 C_4}{2\gamma^2}(1 - e^{-\gamma(s-t)})^2 e^{-2\gamma(s-t)}$$

$$+ Y(t)\frac{C_2 C_3 C_4}{6\gamma^3}(1 - e^{-\gamma(s-t)})^3 e^{-\gamma(s-t)}$$

$$+ \frac{C_1 C_2 C_3 C_4}{24\gamma^4}(1 - e^{-\gamma(s-t)})^4$$

$$=: Y^4(t)f_4^4(s-t) + Y^3(t)f_3^4(s-t)$$
$$+ Y^2(t)f_2^4(s-t) + Y(t)f_1^4(s-t)$$
$$+ f_0^4(s-t). \tag{A.32}$$

In particular,

$$\mathbb{E}[Y^4(s)] = y_0^4 e^{-4\gamma s} + y_0^3 \frac{C_4}{\gamma}(1 - e^{-\gamma s})e^{-3\gamma s}$$

$$+ y_0^2 \frac{C_3 C_4}{2\gamma^2}(1 - e^{-\gamma s})^2 e^{-2\gamma s}$$

$$+ y_0 \frac{C_2 C_3 C_4}{6\gamma^3}(1 - e^{-\gamma s})^3 e^{-\gamma s}$$

$$+ \frac{C_1 C_2 C_3 C_4}{24\gamma^4}(1 - e^{-\gamma s})^4$$

$$=: Y^4(s)f_4^4(s) + Y^3(s)f_3^4(s) + Y^2(s)f_2^4(s)$$

$$+ Y(s)f_1^4(s) + f_0^4(s). \tag{A.33}$$

Proof of Lemma 3.2

Because F_{s-t}^n is finite, expression (A.18) is well defined. Clearly, the first part of the lemma holds for $n = 1, 2, 3, and\ 4$ from the calculations given above. The result for a general $n > 0$ follows directly by induction, establishing (A.18). For the formulas we have, using (A.18),

$$\mathbb{E}\left[\mathbb{E}[Y^n(s)|\mathcal{F}_t^Y]\right] = \sum_{m=0}^{n} f_m^n(s-t)\mathbb{E}[Y^m(t)]$$

$$= f_0^n(s-t) + \sum_{m=1}^{n} f_m^n(s-t)\mathbb{E}[Y^m(t)].$$

Since $m > 0$ in the second term, we can apply the first part of the lemma again:

$$\mathbb{E}[Y^m(t)] = F_{t-0}^m(Y(0)) = \sum_{i=0}^{m} f_i^m(t)y_0^i.$$

Hence, we have

$$\mathbb{E}\left[\mathbb{E}[Y^n(s)|\mathcal{F}_t^Y]\right] = f_0^n(s-t) + \sum_{m=1}^{n} f_m^n(s-t) \sum_{i=0}^{m} f_i^m(t)y_0^i,$$

which proves (A.20). The remaining formulas are now obtained. Let $s > u > v > 0$ and $k > 0$. We have

$$\mathbb{E}\left[Y^k(v)F_{s-u}^n(Y(u))\right]$$

$$= \mathbb{E}\left[Y^k(v) \sum_{m=0}^{n} f_m^n(s-u)Y^m(u)\right]$$

$$= \sum_{m=0}^{n} f_m^n(s-u)\mathbb{E}\left[Y^k(v)Y^m(u)\right]$$

$$= \sum_{m=0}^{n} f_m^n(s-u)\mathbb{E}\left[Y^k(v)\mathbb{E}[Y^m(u)|\mathcal{F}_v^Y]\right]$$

$$= f_0^n(s-u)\mathbb{E}[Y^k(v)] + \sum_{m=1}^{n} f_m^n(s-u)\mathbb{E}\left[Y^k(v)\mathbb{E}[Y^m(u)|\mathcal{F}_v^Y]\right]$$

$$= f_0^n(s-u)F_v^k(Y(0)) + \sum_{m=1}^{n} f_m^n(s-u)\mathbb{E}\left[Y^k(v)F_{u-v}^m(Y(v))\right]$$

$$= f_0^n(s-u)\sum_{c=0}^{k} f_c^k(v)y_0^c + \sum_{m=1}^{n} f_m^n(s-u)\mathbb{E}\left[Y^k(v)\sum_{i=0}^{m} f_i^m(u-v)Y^i(v)\right]$$

$$= f_0^n(s-u)\sum_{c=0}^{k} f_c^k(v)y_0^c + \sum_{m=1}^{n} f_m^n(s-u)\sum_{i=0}^{m} f_i^m(u-v)\mathbb{E}\left[Y^{k+i}(v)\right]$$

$$= f_0^n(s-u)\sum_{c=0}^{k} f_c^k(v)y_0^c + \sum_{m=1}^{n} f_m^n(s-u)\sum_{i=0}^{m} f_i^m(u-v)\sum_{j=0}^{k+i} f_j^{k+i}(v)y_0^j.$$

Similarly, for $l > 0$ it follows that

$$\mathbb{E}\left[Y^l(u)Y^k(v)F_{s-u}^n(Y(u))\right] = \sum_{m=0}^{n} f_m^n(s-u)\sum_{i=0}^{m+l} f_i^{m+l}(u-v)\sum_{j=0}^{k+i} f_j^{k+i}(v)y_0^j$$

and

$$\mathbb{E}\left[Y^k(u)F_{s-u}^n(Y(u))\right] = \sum_{m=0}^{n} f_m^n(s-u)\sum_{i=0}^{m+k} f_i^{m+k}(u)y_0^i,$$

proving (A.22) and (A.23). The finiteness of these formulas follows from the fact that $f_m^n(\theta)$, for $\theta \geq 0$, is finite.

Proof of Lemma 3.3

Take $\theta \geq t + k + 1$. Then, by definition of L, we obtain from (A.13) and (A.12)

$$\mathbb{E}[L^2(t)L^2(t+k)] = \mathbb{E}[X^2(\theta)Z^2(\theta)]$$

$$= 2 \int_t^{t+1} \mathbb{E}\left[X(u)Z^2(u)(\mu - \beta Y(u))\right] du$$

$$+ 2 \int_{t+k}^{t+k+1} \mathbb{E}\left[X^2(u)Z(u)(\mu - \beta Y(u))\right] du$$

$$+ \int_t^{t+1} \mathbb{E}\left[Y(u)Z^2(u)\right] du + 4 \cdot 0$$

$$+ \int_{t+k}^{t+k+1} \mathbb{E}\left[Y(u)X^2(u)\right] du$$

$$= 2 \int_{t+k}^{t+k+1} \mathbb{E}\left[X^2(u)Z(u)(\mu - \beta Y(u))\right] du$$

$$+ \int_{t+k}^{t+k+1} \mathbb{E}\left[Y(u)X^2(u)\right] du,$$

where the last equality follows since $Z(u) = 0$ for $u \in [t, t+1]$ by definition of Z in equation (A.11). For $s \in [t+k, t+k+1]$ we have

$$\mathbb{E}[L^2(t)L^2(t+k)] = 2 \int_{t+k}^{t+k+1} \mathbb{E}\left[X^2(s)Z(s)(\mu - \beta Y(s))\right] ds$$

$$+ \int_{t+k}^{t+k+1} \mathbb{E}\left[Y(s)X^2(s)\right] ds. \qquad (A.34)$$

We now calculate the last expectation. By the definition of (A.12) it follows that $X(s)$, defined in (A.10), is $\mathcal{F}_{t+1}$-measurable. Thus,

$$\mathbb{E}\left[Y(s)X^2(s)\right] = \mathbb{E}\left[X^2\mathbb{E}\left[Y(s)|\mathcal{F}_{t+1}\right]\right]$$

$$= f_1^1(s - t - 1)\mathbb{E}[X^2(s)Y(t+1)]$$

$$+ \lambda(1 - f_1^1(s - t - 1)\mathbb{E}[X^2(s)]), \qquad (A.35)$$

where the last equality follows from (A.14) and (A.26). By the tower property and because $X(s)$ is $\mathcal{F}_{t+1}$-measurable for $s \in [t+k, t+k+1]$, we express the first term in (A.34) as

$$\mathbb{E}\left[X^2(s)Z(s)(\mu - \beta Y(s))\right] = \mathbb{E}\left[X^2(s)\mathbb{E}\left[Z(s)(\mu - \beta Y(s))|\mathcal{F}_{t+1}\right]\right].$$

The conditional expectation $\mathbb{E}\left[Z(s)(\mu - \beta Y(s))|\mathcal{F}_{t+1}\right]$ is calculated as

$$\mathbb{E}\left[Z(s)(\mu - \beta Y(s))|\mathcal{F}_{t+1}\right]$$

$$= \mathbb{E}\left[(\mu - \beta Y(s))\left(\int_{t+k}^{s}(\mu - \beta Y(u))du + \int_{t+k}^{s}\sqrt{Y(u)}dB(u)\right)|\mathcal{F}_{t+1}\right]$$

$$= \int_{t+k}^{s}\mathbb{E}\left[(\mu - \beta Y(u))\mathbb{E}\left[(\mu - \beta Y(s))|\mathcal{F}_u\right]|\mathcal{F}_{t+1}\right]du$$

$$+ \mathbb{E}\left[(\mu - \beta Y(s))\mathbb{E}\left[\int_{t+k}^{s}\sqrt{Y(u)}dB(u)|\mathcal{F}_{t+1}\vee\mathcal{F}^Y\right]|\mathcal{F}_{t+1}\right].$$

The last conditional expectation is zero. By using (A.26) and (A.28), we rearrange the remaining part of this expression as

$$\mathbb{E}\left[Z(s)(\mu - \beta Y(s))|\mathcal{F}_{t+1}\right]$$

$$= \int_{t+k}^{s}\mathbb{E}\left[(\mu - \beta Y(u))\left(\mu - \beta f_1^1(s-u)Y(u)\right)\right.$$

$$\left. - \beta\lambda(1 - f_1^1(s-u))\right)|\mathcal{F}_{t+1}\right]du$$

$$= \int_{t+k}^{s}\mathbb{E}\left[\mu^2 - \mu\beta\lambda(1 - f_1^1(s-u)) + \beta^2 f_1^1(s-u)Y^2(u)\right.$$

$$\left. + Y(u)\left(\beta^2\lambda(1 - f_1^1(s-u)) - \mu\beta f_1^1(s-u) - \mu\beta\right)|\mathcal{F}_{t+1}\right]du$$

$$= \mu^2(s-t-k) - \int_{t+k}^{s}\mu\beta\lambda(1 - f_1^1(s-u))du$$

$$+ \beta^2\int_{t+k}^{s}f_1^1(s-u)\left[Y^2(t+1)f_2^2(s-t-1) + Y(t+1)f_1^2(u-t-1)\right.$$

$$\left. + f_0^2(u-t-1)\right]du$$

$$+ \int_{t+k}^{s}\left[(\beta^2\lambda(1 - f_1^1(s-u)) - \mu\beta f_1^1(s-u) - \mu\beta)\right.$$

$$\left. \times\left(f_1^1(u-t-1)Y(t+1) + \lambda(1 - f_1^1(u-t-1))\right)\right]du.$$

The expectation $\mathbb{E}\left[X^2(s)Z(s)(\mu - \beta Y(s))\right]$ can be rearranged as

$$\mathbb{E}\left[X^2(s)Z(s)(\mu - \beta Y(s))\right]$$

$$= \mathbb{E}\left[X^2(s)\left(\mu^2(s - t - k) - \int_{t+k}^{s} \mu\beta\lambda(1 - f_1^1(s - u))du\right)\right.$$

$$+ \beta^2 \int_{t+k}^{s} X^2(s)f_1^1(s - u)$$

$$\times \left[Y^2(t+1)f_2^2(u - t - 1) + Y(t+1)f_1^2(u - t - 1)\right.$$

$$\left. + f_0^2(u - t - 1)\right] du$$

$$+ \int_{t+k}^{s} X^2(s)\left(\beta^2\lambda(1 - f_1^1(s - u)) - \mu\beta f_1^1(s - u) - \mu\beta\right)$$

$$\left. \times \left[f_1^1(u - t - 1)Y(t+1) + \lambda(1 - f_1^1(u - t - 1))\right] du\right].$$

Applying Fubini's Theorem yields

$$\mathbb{E}\left[X^2(s)Z(s)(\mu - \beta Y(s))\right]$$

$$= \mathbb{E}[X^2(s)]\left(\mu^2(s - t - k) - \int_{t+k}^{s} \mu\beta\lambda(1 - f_1^1(s - u))du\right)$$

$$+ \beta^2 \int_{t+k}^{s} f_1^1(s - u)\mathbb{E}[X^2(s)Y^2(t+1)]f_2^2(u - t - 1)du$$

$$+ \beta^2 \int_{t+k}^{s} f_1^1(s - u)\left[\mathbb{E}[X^2(s)Y(t+1)]f_1^2(u - t - 1)\right.$$

$$\left. + \mathbb{E}[X^2(s)]f_0^2(u - t - 1)\right] du$$

$$+ \int_{t+k}^{s} \left(\beta^2\lambda(1 - f_1^1(s - u)) - \mu\beta f_1^1(s - u) - \mu\beta\right)$$

$$\times \left[f_1^1(u - t - 1)\mathbb{E}[X^2(s)Y(t+1)]\right.$$

$$\left. + \mathbb{E}[X^2(s)]\lambda(1 - f_1^1(u - t - 1))\right] du, \tag{A.36}$$

because, for $s \in [t + k, t + k + 1]$, $\mathbb{E}[X^2(s)Y^n(t+1)]$ is independent of s by definition of X. From the expressions (A.36) and (A.35) we obtain

$$\mathbb{E}[L^2(t)L^2(t + k)]$$

$$= 2\mathbb{E}[X^2(s)]\left(\int_{t+k}^{t+k+1} \left[\mu^2(s - t - k) + \frac{1}{2}f_0^1(s - t - 1)\right.\right.$$

$$+ \int_{t+k}^{s} \beta^2 f_0^2(u-t-1) + (\beta^2 f_0^1(s-u) - \mu\beta f_1^1(s-u) - \mu\beta)$$

$$\times f_0^1(u-t-1)du \Big] ds) + 2\mathbb{E}[X^2(s)Y(t+1)]$$

$$\times \left(\int_{t+k}^{t+k+1} \left[\frac{1}{2} f_1^1(s-t-1) + \int_{t+k}^{s} \beta^2 f_1^2(u-t-1) \right. \right.$$

$$+ (\beta^2 f_0^1(s-u) - \mu\beta f_1^1(s-u) - \mu\beta) f_1^1(u-t-1)du \Big] ds)$$

$$+ 2\mathbb{E}[X^2(s)Y^2(t+1)] \left(\int_{t+k}^{t+k+1} \int_{t+k}^{s} \beta^2 f_2^2(t+1,u) f_1^1(s-u)duds \right)$$

$$\equiv D_0(t,k)\mathbb{E}[X^2(s)] + D_1(t,k)\mathbb{E}[X^2(s)Y(t+1)]$$

$$+ D_2(t,k)\mathbb{E}[X^2(s)Y^2(t+1)]$$

$$\equiv D_0(t,k)\mathbb{E}[L^2(t)] + D_1(t,k)\mathbb{E}[L^2(t)Y(t+1)]$$

$$+ D_2(t,k)\mathbb{E}[L^2(t)Y^2(t+1)],$$

where the last two steps hold by the definition of X and the definitions of the following deterministic functions of time t and the time lag k:

$$D_0(t,k) := 2 \int_{t+k}^{t+k+1} \left[\mu^2(s-t-k) + \frac{1}{2} f_0^1(s-t-1) \right.$$

$$+ \int_{t+k}^{s} \beta^2 f_0^2(u-t-1)$$

$$+ (\beta^2 f_0^1(s-u) - \mu\beta f_1^1(s-u) - \mu\beta) f_0^1(u-t-1)du \Big] ds.$$

$$\text{(A.37)}$$

$$D_1(t,k) := 2 \int_{t+k}^{t+k+1} \left[\frac{1}{2} f_1^1(s-t-1) + \int_{t+k}^{s} \beta^2 f_1^2(u-t-1) \right.$$

$$+ (\beta^2 f_0^1(s-u) - \mu\beta f_1^1(s-u) - \mu\beta) f_1^1(u-t-1)du \Big] ds.$$

$$\text{(A.38)}$$

$$D_2(t,k) := 2 \int_{t+k}^{t+k+1} \int_{t+k}^{s} \beta^2 f_2^2(t+1,u) f_1^1(s-u)duds. \qquad \text{(A.39)}$$

Since each term $f_m^n(\cdot)$ in (A.37)–(A.39) is finite, each function $D_n(t,k)$, with $n = 0, 1, 2$, is well defined. The claimed results follows.

Proof of Lemma 3.4

For $n > 0$ we have

$$\mathbb{E}[L^2(t)Y^n(t+1)] = \mathbb{E}[X^2(s)Y^n(t+1)]$$

$$= \mathbb{E}\left[Y^n(t+1)\left(\int_t^{t+1}(\mu - \beta Y(u))du + \int_t^{t+1}\sqrt{Y(u)}dB(u)\right)^2\right]$$

$$= \mathbb{E}\left[Y^n(t+1)\left(\int_t^{t+1}(\mu - \beta Y(u))du\right)^2\right]$$

$$+2\mathbb{E}\left[Y^n(t+1)\int_t^{t+1}(\mu - \beta Y(u))du\int_t^{t+1}\sqrt{Y(u)}dB(u)\right]$$

$$+\mathbb{E}\left[Y^n(t+1)\left(\int_t^{t+1}\sqrt{Y(u)}dB(u)\right)^2\right]$$

$$= 2\int_t^{t+1}\int_t^u \mathbb{E}\left[(\mu - \beta Y(u))(\mu - \beta Y(v))\mathbb{E}\left[Y^n(t+1)|\,\mathcal{F}_u^Y\right]\right]dvdu$$

$$+2\mathbb{E}\left[Y^n(t+1)\int_t^{t+1}(\mu - \beta Y(u))du\mathbb{E}\left[\int_t^{t+1}\sqrt{Y(u)}dB(u)|\mathcal{F}_{t+1}^Y\right]\right]$$

$$+\mathbb{E}\left[\mathbb{E}\left[Y^n(t+1)\left(\int_t^{t+1}\sqrt{Y(u)}dB(u)\right)^2|\mathcal{F}_{t+1}^Y\right]\right]$$

$$= 2\int_t^{t+1}\int_t^u \mathbb{E}\left[(\mu - \beta Y(u))(\mu - \beta Y(v))\mathbb{E}\left[Y^n(t+1)|\,\mathcal{F}_u^Y\right]\right]dvdu$$

$$+\int_t^{t+1}\mathbb{E}\left[Y(u)\mathbb{E}\left[Y^n(t+1)|\mathcal{F}_u^Y\right]\right]du.$$

Applying Lemma 3.2 we obtain

$$\mathbb{E}[L^2(t)Y^n(t+1)] = 2\int_t^{t+1}\int_t^u \mathbb{E}\left[(\mu^2 - \mu\beta(Y(v) + Y(u))\right.$$

$$+\beta^2 Y(u)Y(v))F_{t+1-u}^n(Y(u))\big]\,dvdu$$

$$+ \int_t^{t+1} \mathbb{E}\left[Y(u)F_{t+1-u}^n(Y(u))\right] du$$

$$= 2 \int_t^{t+1} \int_t^u \left[\mu^2 \mathbb{E}\left[F_{t+1-u}^n(Y(u))\right] \right.$$

$$- \mu\beta\mathbb{E}\left[(Y(v) + Y(u))F_{t+1-u}^n(Y(u))\right]$$

$$\left. + \beta^2 \mathbb{E}\left[Y(u)Y(v)F_{t+1-u}^n(Y(u))\right] \right] dvdu$$

$$+ \int_t^{t+1} \mathbb{E}\left[Y(u)F_{t+1-u}^n(Y(u))\right] du.$$

By Lemma 3.2, $\mathbb{E}[L^2(t)Y^n(t+1)]$ is finite.

References

[1] A. K. Dixit and R. S. Pindyck, *Investment Under Uncertainty*. Princeton University Press, Princeton, NJ, USA (1994).

[2] L. Trigeorgis, *Real Options: Managerial Flexibility and Strategy in Resource Allocation*. The MIT Press, Cambridge, MA, USA (1996).

[3] M. Burger, B. Graeber, and G. Schindlmayr, *Managing Energy Risk: An Integrated View on Power and Other Energy Markets*. John Wiley & Sons Ltd, Chichester, England, UK (2014).

[4] L. Clewlow and C. Strickland, *Energy Derivatives: Pricing and Risk Management*. Lacima Publications, London, England, UK (2000).

[5] A. Eydeland and K. Wolyniec, *Energy and Power Risk Management: New Developments in Modeling, Pricing, and Hedging*. John Wiley & Sons Inc., Hoboken, NJ, USA (2003).

[6] H. Geman, *Commodities and Commodity Derivatives: Modeling and Pricing for Agriculturals, Metals and Energy*. John Wiley & Sons Ltd, Chichester, England, UK (2005).

[7] N. Secomandi and D. J. Seppi, Real options and merchant operations of energy and other commodities, *Foundations and Trends in Technology, Information and Operations Management*. **6**(3–4), 161–331 (2014).

[8] F. E. Benth, J. S. Benth, and S. Koekebakker, *Stochastic Modelling of Electricity and Related Markets*. World Scientific Publishing, Singapore (2008).

[9] O. E. Barndorff-Nielsen, Normal inverse Gaussian distributions and stochastic volatility modelling, *Scandinavian Journal of Statistics*. **24**(1), 1–13 (1997).

[10] O. E. Barndorff-Nielsen and N. Shephard, Non-Gaussian Ornstein-Uhlenbeck-based models and some of their uses in financial economics, *Journal of the Royal Statistical Society. Series B (Statistical Methodology)*. **63** (2), 167–241 (2001).

[11] S. L. Heston, A closed-form solution for options with stochastic volatility with applications to bond and currency options, *Review of Financial Studies.* **6**(2), 327–343 (1993).

[12] J. C. Cox, J. E. Ingersoll, Jr., and S. A. Ross, A theory of the term structure of interest rates, *Econometrica.* **53**(2), 385–407 (1985).

[13] E. Benz and S. Trück, Modeling the price dynamics of CO_2 emission allowances, *Energy Economics.* **31**(1), 4–15 (2009).

[14] J. Seifert, M. Uhrig-Homburg, and M. Wagner, Dynamic behavior of CO_2 spot prices, *Journal of Environmental Economics and Management.* **56**(2), 180–194 (2008).

[15] M. S. Paolella and L. Taschini, An econometric analysis of emission allowance prices, *Journal of Banking & Finance.* **32**(10), 2022–2032 (2008).

[16] G. Daskalakis, D. Psychoyios, and R. N. Markellos, Modeling CO_2 emission allowance prices and derivatives: Evidence from the European trading scheme, *Journal of Banking & Finance.* **33**(7), 1230–1241 (2009).

[17] Z.-H. Feng, L.-L. Zou, and Y.-M. Wei. Carbon price volatility: Evidence from EU ETS. Working Paper 4, Center for Energy and Environmental Policy Research, Beijing Institute of Technology, Beijing, China (2009).

[18] R. Cont. Volatility clustering in financial markets: Empirical facts and agent-based models. In (eds). G. Teyssière and A. P. Kirman, *Long Memory in Economics*, pp. 289–309. Springer, Berlin, Germany (2007).

[19] F. E. Benth, The stochastic volatility model of Barndorff-Nielsen and Shephard in commodity markets, *Mathematical Finance.* **21**(4), 595–625 (2011).

[20] A. A. Drăgulescu and V. M. Yakovenko, Probability distribution of returns in the Heston model with stochastic volatility, *Quantitative Finance.* **2**(6), 443–453 (2002).

[21] D. B. Madan and E. Seneta, The variance Gamma (V.G.) model for share market returns, *The Journal of Business.* **63**(4), 511–524 (1990).

[22] D. B. Madan, P. P. Carr, and E. C. Chang, The variance Gamma process and option pricing, *European Finance Review.* **2**(1), 79–105 (1998).

[23] E. Seneta, Fitting the variance-Gamma model to financial data, *Journal of Applied Probability.* **41**, 177–187 (2004).

[24] S. Zhang and X. Zhang, Exact simulation of IG-OU processes, *Methodology and Computing in Applied Probability.* **10**(3), 337–355 (2008).

Chapter 4

Optimal Exploitation of a Mineral Resource under Stochastic Market Prices

René Caldentey[*,‡], Rafael Epstein[†,§], and Denis Sauré[†,¶]

[*]*Booth School of Business, The University of Chicago, 5807 S Woodlawn Avenue, Chicago, IL 60637.*
[†]*Department of Industrial Engineering, University of Chile, República 701, Santiago, Chile.*

[‡]*Rene.Caldentey@ChicagoBooth.edu*
[§]*repstein@dii.uchile.cl*
[¶]*dsaure@dii.uchile.cl*

In this chapter, we study the operation and optimal exploitation of a mining project. We model the project as a collection of minimal extraction units or blocks, each with its own mineral composition and extraction costs. The decision maker's problem is to maximize the economic value of the project by controlling the sequence and time of extraction, as well as investing in costly capacity expansions. We use a *real options* approach based on contingent claim analysis and risk-neutral valuation to solve the problem for a fixed extraction sequence, taking as an input the stochastic process that regulates the time dynamics of futures prices. Our solution method works in two steps. First, we consider a fixed production capacity and use approximate dynamic programming to compute upper and lower bounds on the value function in terms of the spot price and mineralogical characteristics of the blocks. We use these bounds to obtain an operating policy that is asymptotically optimal as the spot price grows large. In the second step, we extend this asymptotic approximation to handle capacity expansion decisions. Our numerical computations suggest that the proposed policy is near optimal. Finally, we test our methodology in a setting based on data from a real project at Codelco (the world's largest copper producer).

4.1. Introduction

In this, chapter we develop a real options model for optimizing the long-term exploitation of multi-sector mining projects.This research is part of an ongoing project with Codelco — the World's largest copper producer — and its main theme has been the development of a long-term decision support system for production and capacity expansion plans.

Chile is the world's largest copper producer with an annual production reaching 5.7 million tons in 2013, followed by China with 1.7, and Peru with 1.2 [1]. Chile also holds 28% of the world's copper reserves, of which 17% is held by state-owned Codelco.Unsurprisingly, copper is one of Chile's most important industries, accounting for approximately 20% and 50% of the country's GDP and total exports, respectively. For countries like Chile, ensuring an efficient management of their natural resources is a strategic matter. Most of the complexity associated with such a task is due to the combination of two factors: (*i*) large-scale operations involving multiple inter-temporal decisions and (*ii*) an uncertain production and market environment. In the copper industry, production uncertainty relates to factors such as heterogeneity of the mineral composition and equipment breakdowns, while marketplace uncertainty is driven by demand volatility and the stochastic evolution of market prices.

Decision-support systems based on large-scale optimization models have been successfully implemented in the copper sector (see e.g., [2] for a recent example in the Chilean copper industry), as well as in other natural resource industries (e.g., [3] in the forest industry, or [4,5] in the crude oil industry). By using these systems, managers evaluate alternative operational policies striving to select those that maximize the short-term and long-term profitability of their businesses. Most of these models, however, operate under deterministic input, based on average estimates of market prices and demand. As a consequence, non-adaptive operational and investment strategies, based on the so-called *discounted cashflow valuation* methodology, are predominately used by these companies, despite their failure to capture the decision maker's ability to dynamically react to a stochastically changing environment (e.g., see [6]). As a result, companies operate under suboptimal extraction and investment plans.

The real option approach overcomes these limitations of the discounted cashflow criteria by explicitly incorporating the dynamic nature of the decision-making process and the stochastic behavior of output prices and cash flows. Early research on the subject dates back to the '80s. One of the earliest example is the work of Mc Donald and Siegel [7] who study the optimal operation of a project under stochastic revenues and production costs when a shut-down option is available. For a comprehensive exposition on the real options approach we refer the reader to [8–10].

In the context of natural resource management, there is an extensive real options literature that focuses on operational decisions such as determining optimal extraction policies or evaluating the options of temporarily closing-up, re-opening, or abandoning a specific project (e.g., [11–18]). An important aspect of this literature is the way in which risk over commodities' spot prices is incorporated in the valuation process. Specifically, the existence of a well-established futures market allows the use of risk-neutral (or arbitrage-free) valuation techniques similar to those used for valuing financial derivatives (e.g., [19, 20]). An early example of this risk-neutral approach is the work of Brennan and Schwartz [21] who consider optimal extraction policies for a non-renewable natural resource. Other examples are [22–25].

Our work builds on Brennan and Schwartz [21] in the way we model the stochastic evolution of spot prices and in the resulting risk-neutral valuation approach. On the other hand, our work distinguishes itself from previous formulations in the way we model the extraction process. Most of this previous research either favors mathematical tractability by simplifying the production process, or considers realistic but intractable production models that can only be solved numerically. In this chapter, we develop a real options model that addresses some of the limitations of previous approaches, preserving tractability. Specifically, and consistent with current practice in the industry (see, e.g., [2]), we model the mining project as a collection of minimal extraction blocks with different mineral composition and extraction costs. As a result, a production plan must specify an extraction sequence (that is, the order in which blocks will be extracted and processed) as well as the timing of such an extraction. We also model the option to invest in capacity expansions over time. Finally, we use real data from a Chilean mining project to illustrate the application of our methodology.

It is important to note that our model does not capture some relevant features of the operations of a mining project. Most notoriously, we do not incorporate the switching costs of temporarily idling the project or of shutting it down permanently. However, these omissions are not particularly severe for large mining companies such as Codelco that can reallocate resources when a particular project is suspended. Another limitation of our model is its focus on calculating the economic value of a prespecified sequence of blocks as opposed to determining such an optimal sequence. Two reasons support this modeling feature. First, the problem of determining an optimal dynamic (adaptive) extraction sequence is a stochastic sequencing problem in a directed network, which is difficult to solve exactly due to the curse of dimensionality. In this regard, we view this research as a necessary building block for tackling the more general stochastic network formulation. Second, our experience at Codelco suggests that in practice mining companies are interested in a relatively small set of predetermined extraction sequences. Hence, managers of these firms evaluate each of these extraction sequences and determine the one that maximizes the economic value of the mining projects.

Because of our characterization of the production process and the incorporation of stochastic market prices, our research contributes to narrow the gap between the academic literature and current practice in the copper industry. For instance, most market-leading mine planning optimization softwares (e.g., Whittle, Chronos, MineMax, and NPV Scheduler; see, e.g., [26]) operate with deterministic price paths that cannot capture market risk. Also, it is worth highlighting that, although we focus on copper mining operations, our model and results can be extended to the production of other non-renewable natural resources, such as crude oil, natural gas, and other types of mineral deposits.

The rest of this chapter is organized as follows. Section 4.2 provides a description of the exact model. In Sec. 4.3, we assume that production capacity is fixed and we derive general properties of an optimal operating policy. We then derive a family of approximations to the optimal value of the project that include valid lower and upper bounds as special cases. We use these bounds to propose two simple extraction policies and to derive an approximate operating policy that is asymptotically optimal as the spot price and/or production capacity grow large. We perform a set of numerical experiments to assess the quality of our proposed approximations. In Sec. 4.4 we extend the results of Sec. 4.3 to include capacity expansion decisions. Section 4.5 presents an application of our methodology to obtain an extraction policy for *El Diablo Regimiento*, a 230 million ton project at Codelco. Conclusions and future research are discussed in Sec. 4.6. Appendix A includes proofs.

4.2.   Model Description

We begin this section with a brief description of the mining operational process and then consider the dynamics of the spot copper prices. Subsequently, we describe our mathematical formulation of the production process. Finally, we discuss the risk-neutral valuation approach that we use to formulate the optimization problem as a dynamic programming problem.

4.2.1.   *Mining Operations Description*

Mining operations can be seen as a sequence of stages involving geological, extraction, concentration, and refining activities. Geological activities are necessary for the discovery and characterization of new deposits. They are of great importance at the early stages of exploration and design of the mine, and are continuously required through the lifespan of a mining project for updating the geological characteristics of the mineral. Extraction activities are required to feed the concentration plants, and their structure depends on whether they are performed on an open pit mine or on an underground mine.

For an open pit operation, mineral is extracted using controlled explosions on the surface of the resource. After a blast, mineral is carried out of the pit by large trucks. In underground mines, extraction is typically conducted at specific locations (extractions points) where the material is removed using a combination of controlled explosions and gravity. In both settings, as mine sectors are located at different heights, possibly overlapping each other, upper sectors must be extracted first for the extraction to be feasible and safe. Further discussion on extracting methods can be found in [27].

The grade (percentage of copper) of the extracted material is variable, but typically below 2.0%. The material with grade over a pre-determined cut-off threshold goes through a sequence of size-reducing processes (both mechanical and chemical), concentration and refinement, which output ore with 99.9% grade that is sold as a commodity in the marketplace. Material

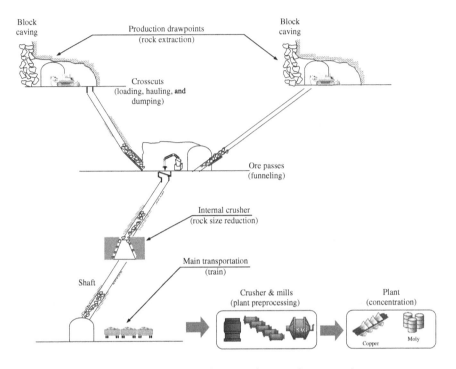

Fig. 4.1   Mining process for an underground copper mine.

with grade below the threshold is either left *in situ* in the case of underground mines, or sent to dump deposits in the case of open pit mines.
Cut-off grade strategies are typically defined in the early stages of the planning process using an approximate "opportunity" cost of the mineral (see,
e.g., [28]).

Figure 4.1 shows schematically the entire mining operations process
for the underground case. Further discussion on exploration and geological
activities can be found in [23], while the concentration and refining operations are discussed in detail in [29]. A description of the entire process can
be found in [30].

4.2.2.   *Spot Prices*

Copper's spot price is a critical ingredient in the valuation of a mining project, as it modulates project revenues, influencing extraction plans
and capacity expansion, among other decisions. In addition, the inherently

stochastic behavior of the spot price complicates the optimization and the evaluation of a project.

Traditionally, the early real options literature modeled commodity spot prices using Geometric Brownian Motions (GBMs). Empirical evidence, analytical tractability, the unpredictability of the price path, and the early applications of GBM in mathematical finance (e.g., [19, 31, 32]) are some of the main reasons behind this choice. However, it has been recognized (e.g., [25, 33]) that many commodity prices exhibit a mean reverting trend that captures the natural market-equilibrium tendency of these prices to revert towards a level that reflects production costs and companies' flexibility to adjust production capacity (i.e., open/close projects) to balance demand and supply in response to changing market conditions. For example, the following mean-reverting process is proposed by Schwartz [34]

$$\mathrm{d}S_t = \kappa \left(\mu - \ln(S_t) \right) S_t \, \mathrm{d}t + \sigma \, S_t \, \mathrm{d}B_t$$

to model the spot price S_t of a commodity, where B_t a standard Brownian Motion. (In what follows, we assume that all relevant stochastic processes are embedded in a filtered probability space $(\Omega, \mathcal{F}, \mathcal{F}_t, \mathbb{P})$.) The speed of adjustment, κ, represents the degree of mean reversion to the long-run adjusted mean μ while σ measures the volatility of the price process. In a series of papers [24, 33, 34], Schwartz propose three variations of a mean-reverting stochastic model driven by one, two and three factors. These models are empirically validated for copper, gold, and crude oil.

Despite being economically sound, mean-reverting processes do not systematically dominate GBM models when it comes to statistically fitting the empirical data of commodity prices. Dixit and Pindyck [8] test the GBM versus a mean-reverting hypothesis using copper prices for the last 200 years and conclude that the mean reversion hypothesis should be accepted. However, they also claim that the GBM hypothesis cannot be rejected if only 30–40 years of data is included (see Fig. 4.2). Similar conclusions are reported in [35] for 10 different natural resources, including copper. More recently, Geman [36, 37] analyzes energy commodity prices (oil and natural gas) and concludes that depending on the time period the GBM model offers a better fit than a mean-reverting one.

In what follows, for clarity of exposition and mathematical tractability, we adopt the GBM framework, *à la* Brennan and Schwartz [21], to model the stochastic evolution of the copper's spot price. We refer the interested reader to [38, Chapter 3] and to the recent monograph [39] for further discussion

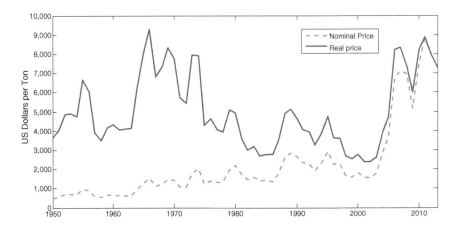

Fig. 4.2   Copper spot price evolution since 1950.
Source: London Metal Exchange.

on the modeling of commodity prices and their economic implications for project valuation.

4.2.3.   *Production Model*

We adopt a continuous-time model to represent the operation of the mine, and assume that exploration stages have been already completed. Hence, the decision maker is mainly concerned with determining an optimal extraction and capacity expansion plan for a fixed mining project with known mineral content and quality.

Consistent with current industry practice, we represent the mine as a collection of mineral *blocks*, each having specific geological properties. These blocks represent the minimal extraction units so that production decisions are made at the block level. Executing a mining plan results in an extraction sequence for these blocks. However, not all sequences are feasible due to technical or safety reasons. For instance, different sectors of the mine are located at different elevations, usually overlapping with each other. Due to safety reasons, extraction from upper sectors must be finished before extraction from lower sectors can start. While the problem of identifying an optimal sequence is an important and challenging one, in this chapter we assume a fixed and feasible extraction sequence is given and focus exclusively on determining the timing of the extraction and how production capacity should be expanded. We note, however, that fixing the sequence of extraction is not a serious limitation as it is often the case in practice that the decision maker only wants to evaluate a few predetermined sequences. In Proposition 4.4 below we propose an efficient method to compare alternative extraction sequences. We also discuss a concrete example of this scenario-based valuation approach in Sec. 4.5.

From a mathematical standpoint, we model the mining sector as a collection of N blocks. Without loss of generality, and for notational convenience, we use a backward indexing of these blocks $\{N, \ldots, 1\}$ so that block N is the first block to be extracted and block 1 is the last one. We define Q_j and L_j to be the amount of material and average grade (percent of copper), respectively, available in block $j = 1, \ldots, N$.

A production policy has two basic components: (i) the time at which each block starts being extracted, and (ii) the available processing capacities at these extraction epochs. We denote by $\mathcal{T} := (\tau_1, \ldots, \tau_N)$ the sequence of extraction times of the blocks. That is, τ_j is time at which block j starts being extracted. (We define $\tau_{N+1} := 0$.) Given the extraction times $\mathcal{T}$, we denote by $\mathcal{K} := (K_1, \ldots, K_N)$ the vector of production capacities.[a] The j-th component of this vector, K_j, is the available production capacity at time $t = \tau_j$ when block j starts extraction. For completeness, we define K_{N+1} to be the initial level of capacity.

For simplicity, we assume that the decision maker does not increase production capacity during the extraction of a block, and expansion decisions are only made in between block extractions.In addition, we assume that all the available capacity is used during the extraction of a block. That is, the decision maker will always run the operation at 100% utilization (recall we assume that mining capacity is binding). While these assumptions provide mathematical tractability, they are not particularly restrictive from a theoretical standpoint, as one can always reduce the size of the blocks by increasing their number (N). (We can show that a "bang–bang" extraction policy is optimal when blocks are infinitesimally small.) Furthermore, in practice these decisions involve production disruptions that usually cannot occur in the middle of the extraction of a block.

Given a production policy $(\mathcal{T}, \mathcal{K})$, we define $T := (T_1, \ldots, T_N)$ where $T_j := Q_j / K_j$ is the time it takes to extract and process block j. Finally, we say a production policy $(\mathcal{T}, \mathcal{K})$ is feasible if it satisfies the sequencing

---

[a]For simplicity we assume that the production capacity refers to a binding *mining capacity*, rather than to treating and marketing capacity [28].

conditions

$$\tau_j \geq \tau_{j+1} + T_{j+1} \quad \text{and} \quad K_j \geq K_{j+1}, \quad \text{for all} \quad j = 1, \ldots, N,$$

where we define $T_{N+1} := 0$. Other constraints such as imposing a fixed planning horizon $\bar{T}$ or a maximum production capacity $\bar{K}$, that is,

$$\tau_1 + T_1 \leq \bar{T} \quad \text{and} \quad K_1 \leq \bar{K}$$

can also be included. In this chapter, we assume an infinite horizon $\bar{T} = \infty$.

4.2.4. *Project Valuation and Optimality Conditions*

The long-term planning problem consists on finding an investment and operational policy that maximizes the net present value of the mineral resources. From the decision maker's perspective, this long-term value maximization amounts to selecting an optimal production policy $(\mathcal{T}, \mathcal{K})$ as described in the previous section.

Determining the value of the project to be maximized is, in general, a difficult task. In practice, most mining companies consider the average discounted value of the cashflows of the project as the appropriate objective function to use. However, this approach imposes some serious challenges in terms of selecting the appropriate discount factor, or equivalently, the correct probability measure to compute expectations. Fortunately, these complications can be circumvented by exploiting the existence of a futures market for copper, so that a no-arbitrage condition allows the use of a replicating-portfolio argument to compute the market value of the mining project.[b] For more details, the reader is referred to [21] for an application of this approach in the context of a natural resource exploitation and to [40] for the general theory. In what follows, we briefly summarize the main step behind this risk-neutral valuation approach.

We can view the stream of cashflows as a derivative of the underlying copper spot price S_t, for which a futures market is available. Using a no-arbitrage argument and under a complete market assumption, it follows that the economic value of the project cashflows can be obtained

---

[b]Copper futures and options contracts are traded on a daily basis at the London Metal Exchange (LME) with maturities ranging from 3 to 63 months. These derivatives offer buyers and sellers the opportunity to hedge their risk exposure due to spot-price fluctuations.

using a *contingent claim* approach. To this end, let S_t be the spot price of copper which we assume evolves according to a GBM (see Sec. 4.2.2 for details)

$$dS_t = \mu\, S_t\, dt + \sigma\, S_t\, dB_t, \tag{4.1}$$

where σ is the instantaneous spot-price volatility, which we assume is known and constant, and μ is the drift of the spot price that could be stochastic. Following Brennan and Schwartz [21], we assume the existence of a constant *convenience yield* rate ρ on the commodity, which captures the benefit associated with physically holding the commodity instead of holding a contract for future delivery. Our constant convenience yield assumption is certainly restrictive and it is mainly imposed for mathematical tractability. For alternative and more realistic models of this convenience yield we refer the interested reader to [24, 34, 41, 42] and references therein. We also refer the reader to the recent monograph [39] for a discussion of the merit of the classical interpretation of the concept of convenience yield as a pseudo-dividend and to the chapter by Evans and Guthrie [43] in this volume for a different interpretation of this concept.

Let $\mathbb{Q}$ be a probability measure (equivalent to $\mathbb{P}$) under which the spot price, S_t, discounted at the risk-free rate, r, net of the convenience yield, ρ, is a $\mathbb{Q}$-martingale, that is,

$$\mathbb{E}^{\mathbb{Q}}\left[e^{-(r-\rho)\,t}\, S_t \mid S_\tau\right] = e^{-(r-\rho)\,\tau}\, S_\tau, \quad \text{for } \tau \le t. \tag{4.2}$$

Assuming that the spot price follows the GBM dynamics in equation (4.1), this Equivalent Martingale Measure (EMM) $\mathbb{Q}$ exists and is unique. We can compute this EMM by means of a Girsanov transformation (see [40, Chapter 5]). Define the *market price of risk* to be

$$\lambda_t := \frac{\mu - (r - \rho)}{\sigma},$$

so that the *Radon–Nikodym derivative* of $\mathbb{Q}$ with respect to $\mathbb{P}$ is given by

$$\frac{d\mathbb{Q}}{d\mathbb{P}} = \exp\left(-\int_0^\infty \lambda_t\, dB_t - \frac{1}{2}\int_0^\infty \lambda_t^2\, dt\right).$$

It is not hard to show that the spot-price process S_t satisfies

$$dS_t = (r - \rho)\, S_t\, dt + \sigma\, S_t\, d\tilde{B}_t, \tag{4.3}$$

where $\tilde{B}$ is a Brownian motion under $\mathbb{Q}$ that satisfies $d\tilde{B}_t = dB_t + \lambda_t \, dt$. Solving equation (4.3) leads to

$$S_t = S_0 \exp\left(\left(r - \rho - \frac{\sigma^2}{2}\right) t + \sigma \tilde{B}_t\right),$$

where S_0 represents the spot price at time $t = 0$.

Under the risk-neutral valuation approach, the economic value of the project for a given production policy is equal to the expected value (under $\mathbb{Q}$) of the project cashflows discounted at the risk-free rate. In our operational context, these cashflows are the difference between the revenues generated by the commercialization of the final product in the spot market minus production and capacity investment costs. Following the standard practice at Codelco, we assume that all production is immediately sold in the market, that is, the company does not hold any inventory of the final product.

Let us consider the j-th block in the extraction sequence. The extraction of this block j starts at time τ_j at a constant extraction rate K_j and finishes at time $\tau_j + T_j$. We let $W_j(S, K)$ denote the expected cashflows generated by this block discounted to time τ_j, conditional on $S_{\tau_j} = S$ and $K_j = K$. That is, $W_j(S, K)$ is defined as

$$\mathbb{E}^{\mathbb{Q}}\left[\int_0^{T_j(K_j)} e^{-rt} \left(L_j \, K_j \, S_{\tau_j+t} - A_j \, K_j\right) dt \,\bigg|\, S_{\tau_j} = S, \, K_j = K\right],$$

where $L_j \, K_j$ is the rate at which copper is produced and A_j is the marginal production cost for block j. For simplicity, we assume that the marginal cost A_j is constant but depends on j. This assumption allows us to model mining operations in which production costs tend to increase as extraction progresses, which might be attributed to the fact that the distance from the extraction points to the processing plant increases over time. (In practice, however, processing costs might depend on additional factors, such as the spot price, as they should impact cut-off policies.) Using (4.2) we can show that $W_j(S, K) = R_j(K) \, S - C_j(K)$ where

$$R_j(K) := L_j \left(\frac{1 - e^{-\rho \, T_j(K)}}{\rho}\right) K,$$

$$C_j(K) := A_j \left(\frac{1 - e^{-r \, T_j(K)}}{r}\right) K.$$

The decision maker selects a production policy that maximizes the expected cumulative discounted payoff. That is, the decision maker solves

$$\sup_{\mathcal{T},\mathcal{K}} \mathbb{E}^{\mathbb{Q}} \left[\sum_{j=1}^{N} e^{-r\,\tau_j} \left[R_j(K_j)\, S_{\tau_j} - C_j(K_j) - \gamma\, (K_j - K_{j+1}) \right] \right], \qquad (4.4)$$

where $\gamma > 0$ is the marginal cost of capacity expansion. We denote by F^* the optimal value of the objective function in (4.4).

A few remarks about (4.4) are in order. First, the term $e^{-r\,\tau_j}\, \gamma\, (K_j - K_{j+1})$ assumes that any capacity expansion takes place at the same time τ_j when the extraction of block j starts. However, while the decision maker might have the ability to build capacity at any point in time in the interval $[\tau_{j+1} + T_{j+1}, \tau_j]$, because capacity expansions are costly, it is in the decision maker's best interest to postpone this action as much as possible. Second, formulation (4.4) also assumes capacity expansions are instantaneous; otherwise, we would need to add a time lag between the time expansion begins and the time the additional capacity becomes available. Third, in (4.4) we assume that the cost of expansion is linear, whereas in practice it might exhibit a nonlinear behavior.

We can reformulate (4.4) using dynamic programming. The state space of this dynamic program represents the possible states of the project at the time extraction of a block is completed. A state is the triplet (S, j, K), where S is the spot price, j is the index of the block to be extracted next and K is the available production capacity. We denote by $F_j(S, K)$ the expected optimal discounted profit to go in state (S, j, K).

The state (S, j, K) is sufficient in our model because of the Markovian dynamics of the spot price and because we are assuming that capacity and production rates are fixed during the extraction of a block. Therefore, in order to derive an optimal production policy it is enough to evaluate the value function only at those time epochs when extraction of a block is completed. In fact, suppose we look at the system exactly at the time extraction of block $j - 1$ is completed. Let (S, j, K) be the state of the system at such time. The decision maker must select the time τ_j when to start extracting block j. This time τ_j is a stopping time with respect to the filtration generated by S_t, $\mathcal{F}_t$. Finally, at this extraction time the decision maker must also decide if capacity should be expanded from the current level K to a new level K_j, with $K \leq K_j \leq \bar{K}$. (Recall that $\bar{K}$ is an upper bound on the maximum level of capacity that can be installed.) We can thus write the following recursion for the value function $F_j(S,K)$:

$$F_j(S,K) = \sup_{\tau_j, K_j} \mathbb{E}^{\mathbb{Q}}\left[e^{-r\tau_j}\left(R_j(K_j)S_{\tau_j} - C_j(K_j) - \gamma(K_j - K)\right.\right.$$

$$\left.\left. + e^{-rT_j}F_{j-1}(S_{\tau_j+T_j}, K_i)\right)\Big|S_0 = S\right] \quad (4.5a)$$

subject to

the dynamics of the spot price, S_t, (4.3), $\qquad$ (4.5b)

τ_j is an $\mathcal{F}_t$ stopping time, $\qquad$ (4.5c)

$$T_j = \frac{Q_j}{K_j}, \quad K \le K_j \le \bar{K}, \qquad (4.5d)$$

and the boundary condition $F_0(S,K) = 0$ for all S, K. (4.5e)

The dynamic program (4.5) is in general difficult to solve, so in the sequel we approximate its solution in two steps. First, in Sec. 4.3 we study the optimal timing of extraction for a fixed capacity K. Then, in Sec. 4.4 we relax this assumption and derive near-optimal capacity expansion decisions.

4.2.5. *Notation and Conventions*

Notation plays an important role in the ensuing material. Hence, we introduce here some general notation and conventions that we use throughout the rest of this chapter.

We say that a function $f(S)$ is *asymptotically equal* to a function $g(S)$, which we denote by

$$f(S) \stackrel{S\to\infty}{\longrightarrow} g(S),$$

if $\lim_{S\to\infty}|f(S) - g(S)| = 0$. The first and second derivatives of a smooth function $f(S)$ with respect to S are denoted by $f'(S)$ and $f''(S)$, respectively.

We let $\mathcal{C}^k(\mathbb{R}_+)$ be the set of real-valued continuous functions on $\mathbb{R}_+$ having derivatives of order $k \ge 0$. We also define the set $\mathcal{C}_+^2$, which plays a key role in our characterization of the value function, as follows:

$$\left\{f \in \mathcal{C}^1(\mathbb{R}_+) \;:\; \exists \text{ a scalar } \theta_f \text{ and a finite set } N_f \subseteq \mathbb{R}_+ \text{ such that}\right.$$

$$\left.|f'(S)| \le \theta_f \;\forall S \in \mathbb{R}_+ \text{ and } f''(S) \text{ exists } \forall S \in \mathbb{R}_+ \setminus N_f\right\}.$$

In this definition θ_f and N_f can depend on f. Consider two arbitrary vectors $X = (X_j)$ and $\alpha = (\alpha_j)$, we define

$$X_{k,j}^+ := \sum_{h=k+1}^{j} X_h,$$

$$\alpha_{k,j}^{\times} := \prod_{h=k+1}^{j} \alpha_h,$$

$$(\alpha^{\times} X)_{k,j}^+ := \sum_{h=k+1}^{j} \alpha_{h,j}^{\times} X_h.$$

We use the specialized notation $X_j^+ := X_{0,j}^+$, $\alpha_j^{\times} := \alpha_{0,j}^{\times}$, and $(\alpha^{\times} X)_j^+ := (\alpha^{\times} X)_{0,j}^+$. In the usage of summations and multiplications we adopt the convention $\sum_{h=k}^{j} X_h = 0$ and $\prod_{h=k}^{j} X_h = 1$ if $j < k$.

For $j \leq N$, we define the average production cost as $\mathbb{C}_j(K) := C_j(K)/R_j(K)$. We also define the quantities

$$\mathcal{R}_{k,j}(K) := \sum_{h=k+1}^{j} e^{-\rho\, T_{h,j}^+(K)} R_h(K),$$

$$\mathcal{C}_{k,j}(K) := \sum_{h=k+1}^{j} e^{-r\, T_{h,j}^+(K)} C_h(K),$$

$$\mathcal{R}_j(K) := \mathcal{R}_{0,j}(K),$$

$$\mathcal{C}_j(K) := \mathcal{C}_{0,j}(K),$$

which we interpret as follows. Suppose there are j blocks left, the spot price is S and the capacity is K. Then, if the decision maker decides to extract the j blocks (starting with block j and finishing with block 1) without changing capacity or stopping at any time then the discounted expected payoff of this non-idling policy would be

$$\mathcal{W}_j(S, K) := \mathcal{R}_j(K)\, S - \mathcal{C}_j(K).$$

4.3. Optimal Production Plan with Fixed Capacity

In this section, we solve formulation (4.5) under the assumption that capacity expansions are not allowed and we let K be this fixed capacity.

(Thus, for convenience, we drop dependencies on K in this section.) We will relax this assumption in Sec. 4.4. In this setting, we derive analytically upper and lower bounds, as well as two asymptotic approximations, for the corresponding value function. Part of the analysis in this section follows closely and extends the results in [8, §5.2].

Let $F_j(S)$ be the maximum expected discounted profit when there are j blocks left and the spot price is S. We solve for the sequence of value functions $\{F_j(S), j = 1, \ldots, N\}$ using forward induction on j. That is, starting with the boundary condition $F_0(S) := 0$, we can sequentially compute $F_1(S)$, $F_2(S)$, ..., $F_N(S)$ solving (4.5). To this end, suppose that we have already computed the value function $F_{j-1}(S)$ and let us solve for $F_j(S)$. For this, let us define the auxiliary function

$$G_j(S) := W_j(S) + e^{-r\,T_j}\,\mathbb{E}^{\mathbb{Q}}[F_{j-1}(S_{T_j})|S_0 = S].$$

With this definition, problem (4.5) is equivalent to

$$F_j(S) = \sup_{\tau \geq 0} \mathbb{E}^{\mathbb{Q}}\left[e^{-r\,\tau}\,G_j(S_\tau)\,\Big|\,S_0 = S\right], \tag{4.6}$$

where the supremum is taken over the set of stopping times τ with respect to $\mathcal{F}_t$ (the filtration generated by S_t) which represents the time when block j should start being produced. To solve this optimal stopping problem, we impose optimality conditions in the form of a set of partial differential inequalities (quasi-variational inequalities or QVI) that characterize the optimal stopping time. To this end, let us define the operator $\mathcal{A}$ that applies on functions $F \in \mathcal{C}_+^2$ as follows (see Sec. 4.2.5 for definitions):

$$\mathcal{A}F(S) := \frac{1}{2}\sigma^2 S^2\,F''(S) + (r - \rho)\,S\,F'(S) - rF(S),$$

for all $S \in \mathbb{R}_+ \setminus N_F$.

Definition 4.1. (QVI) The function $F \in \mathcal{C}_+^2$ satisfies the quasi-variational inequalities for model (4.6) if the following three conditions are satisfied:

$$\mathcal{A}F(S) \leq 0, \text{ for all } S \in \mathbb{R}_+ \setminus N_F,$$

$$F(S) - G_j(S) \geq 0, \text{ for all } S \geq 0, \tag{4.7}$$

$$(F(S) - G_j(S))\,\mathcal{A}F(S) = 0, \text{ for all } S \in \mathbb{R}_+ \setminus N_F.$$

As one would expect, a solution to these QVI conditions partitions the state space $S \geq 0$ into two regions: A *continuation* region in which the optimal policy is to delay production, and an *intervention* region in which production should start immediately. These regions are defined as

$$\text{Continuation: } \mathcal{D} := \big\{ S \geq 0 : F(S) > G_j(S) \text{ and } \mathcal{A}F(S) = 0 \big\},$$

$$\text{Intervention: } \mathcal{I} := \big\{ S \geq 0 : F(S) = G_j(S) \text{ and } \mathcal{A}F(S) \leq 0 \big\}.$$

For every solution of the QVI we can associate a stopping time τ as in the following definition.

Definition 4.2. Let $F \in \mathcal{C}_+^2$ be a solution of the QVI in (4.7). We define the QVI-control τ as

$$\tau := \inf \big\{ t \geq 0 : F(S_t) = G_j(S_t) \big\}.$$

We are now ready to formalize the *verification* theorem that provides the connection between the QVI conditions and the original optimization problem in (4.6).

Theorem 4.1. (VERIFICATION) *Let $F \in \mathcal{C}_+^2$ be a non-negative solution of the QVI in (4.7). Then, it holds that*

$$F(S) \geq F_j(S), \text{ for every } S \geq 0.$$

In addition, if the continuation region $\mathcal{D}$ is bounded and there exists a QVI-control τ associated with F, that is, $\mathbb{E}^{\mathbb{Q}}[\tau] < \infty$, then it is optimal and $F(S) = F_j(S)$.

According to this result, we can tackle the problem of determining the value function $F_j(S)$ by solving the QVI conditions. This task is in general difficult given the *free boundary* nature of these conditions (that is, part of the problem is to determine the intervention and continuation regions). We approach this problem using an "educated guess." Intuitively, we expect that if the spot price is sufficiently large then immediate production should be an optimal decision. If this intuition is correct, then we expect that there exists a single threshold value S_j^* such that $\mathcal{D} = \{0 \leq S < S_j^*\}$ and $\mathcal{I} = \{S \geq S_j^*\}$. In what follows, we solve the QVI conditions imposing this additional condition, and then use Theorem 4.1 to verify that our proposed solution is indeed optimal.

Based on our previous discussion, the QVI conditions imply that

$$0 = \mathcal{A}F_j(S), \text{ for all } S < S_j^*,$$

$$F_j(S) = G_j(S), \text{ for all } S \geq S_j^*. \tag{4.8}$$

Equation (4.8) corresponds to the Hamilton–Jacobi Bellman (HJB) equation, and the second is known as a *value-matching* condition. In addition, we expect the two following conditions to hold:

$$F_j(0) = 0,$$
$$F_j'(S_j^*) = G_j'(S_j^*).$$

The first condition simply states that if the price process reaches the absorbing state $S = 0$ then the value of the mining project is zero. The second condition guarantees that $F_j(S)$ is differentiable at the threshold price $S = S_j^*$ (that is, it is a *smooth-pasting* condition). This condition is necessary to ensure that $F_j(S) \in \mathcal{C}_+^2$.

Equation (4.8) is a second-order homogeneous ordinary differential equation. Because of its special structure, its general solution can be expressed as a linear combination of any two independent solutions. The function S^β satisfies equation (4.8) provided that β is a root of the quadratic equation

$$\frac{1}{2}\sigma^2 \beta(\beta - 1) + (r - \rho)\beta - r = 0.$$

The two roots are

$$\beta := \frac{1}{2} - (r - \rho)/\sigma^2 + \sqrt{1/4 + [(r - \rho)/\sigma^2]^2 + (r + \rho)/\sigma^2} > 1,$$

$$\tilde{\beta} := \frac{1}{2} - (r - \rho)/\sigma^2 - \sqrt{1/4 + [(r - \rho)/\sigma^2]^2 + (r + \rho)/\sigma^2} < 0.$$

The general solution to equation (4.8) can be written as

$$F_j(S) = M_j\, S^\beta + \tilde{M}_j\, S^{\tilde{\beta}},$$

for two constants M_j and $\tilde{M}_j$. However, the boundary condition at $S = 0$ implies that $\tilde{M}_j = 0$. Our candidate solution $F_j(S)$ is thus given by

$$F_j(S) = \begin{cases} M_j\, S^\beta, & \text{if } S < S_j^*, \\ G_j(S), & \text{otherwise.} \end{cases} \qquad (4.9)$$

We are now ready to state the main result of this section.

Theorem 4.2. *For every block j, there exists a pair of non-negative scalars (M_j, S_j^*) such that the value function $F_j(S)$ in (4.6) is given by (4.9). The values of M_j and S_j^* are*

$$M_j := \min\left\{M \geq 0 : M\, S^\beta \geq G_j(S) \text{ for all } S \geq 0\right\},$$

$$S_j^* := \min\left\{S \geq 0 : M_j\, (S)^\beta = G_j(S)\right\}.$$

Moreover, the value function $F_j(S)$ is increasing and convex in $S \geq 0$.

The proof of Theorem 4.2, which can be found in [44], shows that the characterization above implies that M_j and S_j^* satisfy the value matching and smooth-pasting conditions

$$M_j \, (S_j^*)^\beta = G_j(S_j^*), \tag{4.10}$$

$$\beta \, M_j \, (S_j^*)^{\beta-1} = G_j'(S_j^*). \tag{4.11}$$

For $j = 1$, condition (4.9) reduces to

$$F_1(S) = \begin{cases} M_1 \, S^\beta, & \text{if } S < S_1^*, \\ R_1 \, S - C_1, & \text{if } S \geq S_1^*, \end{cases} \tag{4.12}$$

and the value-matching and smooth-pasting conditions (4.10) and (4.11) become

$$M_1 \, (S_1^*)^\beta = R_1 \, S_1^* - C_1,$$

$$M_1 \, \beta \, (S_1^*)^{\beta-1} = R_1,$$

which lead to

$$S_1^* = \frac{\beta \, C_1}{(\beta - 1) \, R_1} = \frac{\beta}{\beta - 1} \, \mathbb{C}_1, \tag{4.13}$$

$$M_1 = \frac{C_1}{\beta - 1} \, (S_1^*)^{-\beta}. \tag{4.14}$$

Recall from Sec. 4.2.5 that $\mathbb{C}_1$ is the average per unit extraction cost for block 1. Hence, the choice of S_1^* above guarantees a per unit net margin of $1/(\beta - 1)$.

Unfortunately, extending the previous analysis to compute $F_j(S)$ for an arbitrary j is difficult because of the expectation $\mathbb{E}^\mathbb{Q}[F_{j-1}(S_{T_j})|S_0 = S]$ in the definition of $G_j(S)$ and the fact that there is no simple characterization of $F_j(S)$ for $j \geq 2$. Nevertheless, we have been able to establish a useful asymptotic property of $F_j(S)$ (see Sec. 4.2.5 for notation).

Proposition 4.1. *The value function $F_j(S)$ is asymptotically equal to* $\mathcal{W}_j(S)$, *that is,*

$$F_j(S) \overset{S \to \infty}{\longrightarrow} \mathcal{W}_j(S) = \mathcal{R}_j \, S - \mathcal{C}_j.$$

Proposition 4.1 highlights some important properties of the value function but it does not provide tight estimates of $F_j(S)$ unless S is large. For small values of S we could use numerical methods to solve the recursion in (4.9) and obtain an approximation of the value function. Instead of following this numerical approach, we derive some closed-form approximations for $F_j(S)$ that provide insight about the structure of this solution and its dependence on the model parameters. First, we develop a family of approximations for $F_j(S)$, which include valid lower and upper bounds as special cases. Then, we use asymptotic analysis to extend these bounds. We conclude this section with some numerical computations that compare the performance of these bounds.

4.3.1. *Upper Bound*

To obtain an upper bound on the value of $F_j(S)$ we assume that the extraction of block $j-1$ can start even if the extraction of block j is not fully completed but simply started. We use a superscripted 'U' to distinguish those quantities that are derived using this approximation. For example, $F_j^{\mathrm{U}}(S)$ denotes the value function resulting from this approximation. Because $F_j^{\mathrm{U}}(S)$ is the solution of a less restricted problem it follows that $F_j(S) \leq F_j^{\mathrm{U}}(S)$.

Similar to the original optimization in (4.6), the bound $F_j^{\mathrm{U}}(S)$ satisfies the following recursion

$$F_j^{\mathrm{U}}(S) = \sup_{\tau \geq 0} \mathbb{E}^{\mathbb{Q}}[e^{-r\tau} W_j(S_\tau) + e^{-r\tau} F_{j-1}^{\mathrm{U}}(S_\tau) \,\big|\, S_0 = S],$$

with $F_0^{\mathrm{U}}(S) = 0$ for all $S \geq 0$. It is not hard to see that $F_j^{\mathrm{U}}(S)$ satisfies the HJB equation (4.8) inside the continuation region. Therefore, it follows that

$$F_j^{\mathrm{U}}(S) = \begin{cases} M_j^{\mathrm{U}} S^\beta, & \text{if } S \leq S_j^{\mathrm{U}}, \\ R_j S - C_j + F_{j-1}^{\mathrm{U}}(S), & \text{otherwise.} \end{cases} \tag{4.15}$$

We can use backward induction to compute recursively M_j^{U} and S_j^{U}, starting at block 1. We postpone this analysis to Sec. 4.3.3 where we derive an algorithm that performs this task efficiently.

4.3.2. *Lower Bound*

We can obtain a lower bound on the value of $F_j(S)$ using the convexity of the value function and Jensen's inequality. We use a superscripted 'L' to denote quantities that are derived using this approximation.

Consider again the optimal stopping time problem for $F_j(S)$ in (4.6):

$$F_j(S) = \sup_{\tau \geq 0} \mathbb{E}^{\mathbb{Q}}[e^{-r\tau} W_j(S_\tau) + e^{-r(\tau+T_j)} F_{j-1}(S_{\tau+T_j}) \,\big|\, S_0 = S].$$

Suppose there exists a convex function $F_{j-1}^{\mathrm{L}}(S)$ such that $F_{j-1}^{\mathrm{L}}(S) \leq F_{j-1}(S)$ for all $S \geq 0$. We then have

$$F_j(S) \geq \sup_{\tau \geq 0} \mathbb{E}^{\mathbb{Q}}[e^{-r\tau} W_j(S_\tau) + e^{-r(\tau+T_j)} F_{j-1}^{\mathrm{L}}(S_{\tau+T_j}) \, \big| \, S_0 = S].$$

For an arbitrary stopping time τ let $\mathfrak{F}_\tau$ be the σ-algebra generated by τ. Then, using iterated (conditional) expectation, the convexity of $F_{j-1}^{\mathrm{L}}(S)$ and condition (4.2) we obtain

$$\mathbb{E}^{\mathbb{Q}}[e^{-r(\tau+T_j)} F_{j-1}^{\mathrm{L}}(S_{\tau+T_j}) | S_0 = S]$$

$$= \mathbb{E}^{\mathbb{Q}}[e^{-r(\tau+T_j)} \mathbb{E}^{\mathbb{Q}}[F_{j-1}^{\mathrm{L}}(S_{\tau+T_j}) | \mathfrak{F}_\tau] | S_0 = S]$$

$$\geq \mathbb{E}^{\mathbb{Q}}[e^{-r(\tau+T_j)} F_{j-1}^{\mathrm{L}}(\mathbb{E}^{\mathbb{Q}}[S_{\tau+T_j} | \mathfrak{F}_\tau]) | S_0 = S]$$

$$= \mathbb{E}^{\mathbb{Q}}[e^{-r(\tau+T_j)} F_{j-1}^{\mathrm{L}}(e^{(r-\rho) T_j} S_\tau) | S_0 = S]$$

and so

$$F_j(S) \geq \sup_{\tau \geq 0} \mathbb{E}^{\mathbb{Q}}[e^{-r\tau} W_j(S_\tau) + e^{-r(\tau+T_j)} F_{j-1}^{\mathrm{L}}(e^{(r-\rho) T_j} S_\tau) | S_0 = S].$$

From this bound, we derive the following recursion for $F_j^{\mathrm{L}}(S)$:

$$F_j^{\mathrm{L}}(S) = \sup_{\tau \geq 0} \mathbb{E}^{\mathbb{Q}}[e^{-r\tau} W_j(S_\tau) + e^{-r(\tau+T_j)} F_{j-1}^{\mathrm{L}}(e^{(r-\rho) T_j} S_\tau) \, \big| \, S_0 = S],$$

with $F_0^{\mathrm{L}}(S) := 0$ for all $S \geq 0$. Using arguments similar to the ones used to derive (4.9), we can show that

$$F_j^{\mathrm{L}}(S) = \begin{cases} M_j^{\mathrm{L}} S^\beta, & \text{if } S \leq S_j^{\mathrm{L}}, \\ R_j S - C_j + e^{-r T_j} F_{j-1}^{\mathrm{L}}(e^{(r-\rho) T_j} S), & \text{otherwise,} \end{cases} \quad (4.16)$$

where M_j^L and S_j^L satisfy value-matching and smooth-pasting conditions, and that $F_j^{\mathrm{L}}(S) \leq F_j(S)$ for all $S \geq 0$ and j.

In the following section, we provide a general method to compute $F_j^{\mathrm{L}}(S)$ and verify that it is indeed a convex function as required (see Corollary 4.1 below). Our approach is based on a general family of approximations that includes $F_j^{\mathrm{U}}(S)$ and $F_j^{\mathrm{L}}(S)$ as special cases.

4.3.3. (α, η)-Approximations

The recursions that define the upper bound $F_j^{\mathrm{U}}(S)$ in (4.15) and the lower bound $F_j^{\mathrm{L}}(S)$ in (4.16) share a similar structure that can be exploited to derive a unified approximation method.

Definition 4.3. Let $\alpha = (\alpha_j)$ and $\eta = (\eta_j)$ be two positive vectors. We say that a set of continuous and differentiable functions $\{\mathcal{F}_j(S), j = 0, \ldots, N\}$ is an (α, η)-approximation of the value functions in (4.9) if $\mathcal{F}_0(S) = 0$ for all $S \geq 0$ and

$$\mathcal{F}_j(S) = \begin{cases} \mathcal{M}_j \, S^\beta, & \text{if } S \leq \mathcal{S}_j, \\ R_j \, S - C_j + \alpha_j \, \mathcal{F}_{j-1}(\eta_j \, S), & \text{otherwise,} \end{cases} \quad j = 1, \ldots, N. \quad (4.17)$$

Because $\mathcal{F}_j(S)$ is continuous and differentiable, the values of $\mathcal{S}_j$ and $\mathcal{M}_j$ are implicitly determined imposing value matching and smooth pasting conditions similar to those in (4.10)–(4.11).

This family of approximations generalizes our upper and lower bounds. Indeed, it follows from (4.15) that the upper bound $F_j^{\mathrm{U}}(S)$ is a special case of (4.17) with $\alpha_j = \eta_j = 1$. Similarly, we can recover the lower bound $F_j^{\mathrm{L}}(S)$ if we chose $\alpha_j = \exp(-r\,T_j)$ and $\eta_j = \exp((r - \rho)\,T_j)$.

In what follows, we derive an efficient algorithm that solves (4.17) for an arbitrary (α, η)-approximation. In order to obtain some intuition on how the algorithm works, let us first consider the special case of two blocks, that is, $N = 2$.

Using backward induction, we first compute $\mathcal{F}_1(S)$. In this case, the solution to (4.17) is identical to the solution in (4.12) –(4.14). That is, we have

$$\mathcal{F}_1(S) = \begin{cases} \mathcal{M}_1 \, S^\beta, & \text{if } S \leq \mathcal{S}_1, \\ R_1 \, S - C_1, & \text{if } S \geq \mathcal{S}_1, \end{cases} \quad (4.18)$$

where $\mathcal{S}_1 = [\beta/(\beta - 1)]\mathbb{C}_1$ and $\mathcal{M}_1 = [C_1/(\beta - 1)](\mathcal{S}_1)^{-\beta}$.

Based on this solution, we can solve for $\mathcal{F}_2(S)$. As before, we compute the value of $\mathcal{M}_2$ and $\mathcal{S}_2$ using the value matching and smooth pasting conditions

$$\mathcal{M}_2 \, (\mathcal{S}_2)^\beta = R_2 \, \mathcal{S}_2 - C_2 + \alpha_2 \, \mathcal{F}_1(\eta_2 \, \mathcal{S}_2),$$

$$\beta \mathcal{M}_2(\mathcal{S}_2)^{\beta-1} = R_2 + \alpha_2 \, \eta_2 \, \mathcal{F}_1'(\eta_2 \, \mathcal{S}_2).$$

We identify two possible cases depending on the value of $\mathcal{F}_1(\eta_2 \, \mathcal{S}_2)$. Suppose first that $\mathcal{S}_1 \geq \eta_2 \, \mathcal{S}_2$, then $F_1(\eta_2 \, \mathcal{S}_2) = \mathcal{M}_1 \, (\eta_2 \, \mathcal{S}_2)^\beta$ and the value-matching and smooth-pasting conditions imply that

$$\mathcal{S}_2 = \left(\frac{\beta}{\beta-1}\right)\mathbb{C}_2,$$

$$\mathcal{M}_2 = \alpha_2\,\eta_2^\beta\,\mathcal{M}_1 + \left(\frac{\mathbb{C}_2}{\beta-1}\right)(\mathcal{S}_2)^{-\beta}.$$

The corresponding value of $\mathcal{F}_2(S)$ has three pieces:

$$\mathcal{F}_2(S) = \begin{cases} \mathcal{M}_2\,S^\beta, & \text{if } S, \leq \mathcal{S}_2, \\ R_2\,S - C_2 + \alpha_2\,\eta_2^\beta\,S^\beta\,\mathcal{M}_1, & \text{if } \mathcal{S}_2 \leq S \leq \mathcal{S}_1/\eta_2, \\ (R_2 + \alpha_2\,\eta_2\,R_1)\,S - (C_2 + \alpha_2\,C_1), & \text{if } S \geq \mathcal{S}_1/\eta_2. \end{cases}$$

The requirement $\mathcal{S}_1 \geq \eta_2\,\mathcal{S}_2$ is equivalent to $\mathbb{C}_1 \geq \eta_2\,\mathbb{C}_2$.

Let us now consider the case where $\mathcal{S}_1 < \eta_2\,\mathcal{S}_2$. It follows that $\mathcal{F}_1(\eta_2\,\mathcal{S}_2) = R_1\,\eta_2\,\mathcal{S}_2 - C_1$ and the value-matching and smooth-pasting conditions lead to

$$\mathcal{S}_2 = \left(\frac{\beta}{\beta-1}\right)\frac{C_2 + \alpha_2\,C_1}{R_2 + \alpha_2\,\eta_2\,R_1},$$

$$\mathcal{M}_2 = \left(\frac{C_2 + \alpha_2\,C_1}{\beta-1}\right)(\mathcal{S}_2)^{-\beta},$$

and

$$\mathcal{F}_2(S) = \begin{cases} \mathcal{M}_2\,S^\beta, & \text{if } S \leq \mathcal{S}_2, \\ (R_2 + \alpha_2\,\eta_2\,R_1)\,S - (C_2 + \alpha_2\,C_1), & \text{if } S \geq \mathcal{S}_2. \end{cases} \tag{4.19}$$

In this case, one can show that the condition $\mathcal{S}_1 < \eta_2\,\mathcal{S}_2$ is equivalent to $\mathbb{C}_1 < \eta_2\,\mathbb{C}_2$, which is consistent with the previous case.

The actual value of $\mathcal{F}_2(S)$ depends on the relationship between $\mathbb{C}_1$ and $\eta_2\,\mathbb{C}_2$. Interestingly, for the case $\mathbb{C}_1 < \eta_2\,\mathbb{C}_2$ the value of $\mathcal{F}_2(S)$ in (4.19) is analogous to the value of $\mathcal{F}_1(S)$ in (4.18). Indeed, in this case we can combine the two blocks into a single one so that the solution in (4.19) is equivalent to a single-block project with modified extraction cost $C_2 + \alpha_2\,C_1$ and modified mineral content $R_2 + \alpha_2\,\eta_2\,R_1$. To obtain some intuition about why the two blocks are "pooled" together, let us consider the lower bound approximation. In this case, the condition $\mathcal{S}_1 < \eta_2\,\mathcal{S}_2$ is equivalent to $S_1^{\mathrm{L}} < \exp((r - \rho)\,T_2)\,S_2^{\mathrm{L}} = \mathbb{E}^{\mathbb{Q}}[S_{T_2}|S_0 = S_2^{\mathrm{L}}]$. In other words, blocks 1 and 2 are combined when the threshold price for block 1 is below the expected value of the spot price at the time when extraction of block 2 is completed.

Hence, in expectation, the extraction of blocks 1 and 2 is performed without interruption and so we can view these two blocks as a single one.

The following proposition extends the previous two-block analysis to the case of an arbitrary number of blocks. Embedded in this proposition is an algorithm that takes as input a j-block project with characteristics $\{(C_k, R_k, \alpha_k, \eta_k),\ k = 1, \ldots, j\}$ and produces a $\tilde{\jmath}$-block project with characteristics $\{(\widetilde{C}_k, \widetilde{R}_k, \widetilde{\alpha}_k, \widetilde{\eta}_k),\ k = 1, \ldots, \tilde{\jmath}\}$ and $\tilde{\jmath} \le j$. The algorithm aggregates blocks using the same criteria discussed above. The resulting sequence $\{(\widetilde{C}_k, \widetilde{R}_k, \widetilde{\alpha}_k, \widetilde{\eta}_k),\ k = 1, \ldots, \tilde{\jmath}\}$ satisfies some properties that greatly simplify the computation of $\mathcal{F}_j(S)$. (See Sec. 4.2.5 for notation.)

Proposition 4.2. *Consider a project with j blocks with characteristics* $\{(C_k, R_k, \alpha_k, \eta_k),\ k = 1, \ldots, j\}$ *and use the following algorithm to create an artificial sequence of (possibly aggregated) blocks:*

ALGORITHM:

Step 0 (Initialization) : Set $\widetilde{C}_k = C_k$, $\widetilde{R}_k = R_k$, $\widetilde{\alpha}_k = \alpha_k$ *and* $\widetilde{\eta}_k = \eta_k$, $k = 1, \ldots, j$ *and* $\tilde{\jmath} = j$.

Step 1: Compute the auxiliary variables

$$\widetilde{\theta}_k := \widetilde{\alpha}_k \widetilde{\eta}_k,$$

$$\widetilde{\mathbb{C}}_k := \frac{\widetilde{C}_k}{\widetilde{R}_k},$$

$$\widetilde{\mathbb{C}}_{k,l} := \frac{\left(\widetilde{\alpha}^{\times} \widetilde{C}\right)^{+}_{k-1,l}}{\left(\widetilde{\theta}^{\times} \widetilde{R}\right)^{+}_{k-1,l}},$$

for all $k, l = 1, \ldots, \tilde{\jmath}$ *and* $k \le l$.

Step 2: Find $\tilde{k} = \min\{2 \le k \le \tilde{\jmath} : \widetilde{\mathbb{C}}_{k-1} < \widetilde{\eta}_k \widetilde{\mathbb{C}}_k\}$. *If such* $\tilde{k}$ *does not exist then stop.*

Step 3: Find $\tilde{h} = \max\{1 \le h \le \tilde{k}-1 : \widetilde{\eta}^{\times}_{h,\tilde{k}} \widetilde{\mathbb{C}}_{h+1,\tilde{k}} \le \widetilde{\mathbb{C}}_h\}$. *If such* $\tilde{h}$ *does not exist then set* $\tilde{h} = 0$.

Step 4: Define $\xi = \tilde{k} - \tilde{h} - 1$ *and introduce the following transformation:* $\tilde{\jmath} = \tilde{\jmath} - \xi$ *and*

$$(\widetilde{R}_k, \widetilde{C}_k, \widetilde{\alpha}_k, \widetilde{\eta}_k) = \begin{cases} (\widetilde{R}_k,\ \widetilde{C}_k,\ \widetilde{\alpha}_k,\ \widetilde{\eta}_k), & \text{if } k \le \tilde{h}, \\ \left(\left(\widetilde{\theta}^{\times} \widetilde{R}\right)^{+}_{\tilde{h},\tilde{k}},\ \left(\widetilde{\alpha}^{\times} \widetilde{C}\right)^{+}_{\tilde{h},\tilde{k}},\ \widetilde{\alpha}^{\times}_{\tilde{h},\tilde{k}},\ \widetilde{\eta}^{\times}_{\tilde{h},\tilde{k}}\right), & \text{if } k = \tilde{h} + 1, \\ (\widetilde{R}_{k+\xi},\ \widetilde{C}_{k+\xi},\ \widetilde{\alpha}_{k+\xi},\ \widetilde{\eta}_{k+\xi}), & \text{if } \tilde{h} + 2 \le k \le \tilde{\jmath}. \end{cases}$$

(In this step we have created a new block $\tilde{h} + 1$ *by aggregating all the blocks from* $\tilde{h} + 1$ *to* $\tilde{k}$, *hence the total number of blocks has decreased by* ξ.)

Step 5 : *Go to step* 1.

After the algorithm stops, no further block aggregation is possible. The output of the algorithm is a modified project that has $\tilde{\jmath}$ blocks. The k-th block in this new sequence has mineral content $\tilde{R}_k$ and extraction cost $\tilde{C}_k$. For this modified sequence of (possibly aggregated) blocks we define

$$\tilde{\mathcal{S}}_k := \left(\frac{\beta}{\beta - 1} \right) \tilde{\mathbb{C}}_k, \tag{4.20}$$

$$\widetilde{\mathcal{M}}_k := \tilde{\alpha}_k \, \tilde{\eta}_k^{\beta} \, \widetilde{\mathcal{M}}_{k-1} + \left(\frac{\tilde{C}_k}{\beta - 1} \right) (\tilde{\mathcal{S}}_k)^{-\beta}, \tag{4.21}$$

with $k \leq \tilde{\jmath}$ and $\widetilde{\mathcal{M}}_0 = 0$.

Finally, for block j in the original configuration we have that $\mathcal{S}_j = \tilde{\mathcal{S}}_{\tilde{\jmath}}$ and

$$\mathcal{F}_j(S) = \left(\tilde{\theta}^{\times} \tilde{R} \right)_{h,\tilde{\jmath}}^{+} S - \left(\tilde{\alpha}^{\times} \tilde{C} \right)_{h,\tilde{\jmath}}^{+} + \widetilde{\mathcal{M}}_h \, \tilde{\alpha}_{h,\tilde{\jmath}}^{\times} \left(\tilde{\eta}_{h,\tilde{\jmath}}^{\times} \right)^{\beta} S^{\beta}, \tag{4.22}$$

where $h = \max \left\{ 0 \leq k \leq \tilde{\jmath} \,|\, \tilde{\mathcal{S}}_k \geq \tilde{\eta}_{h,\tilde{\jmath}}^{\times} S \right\}$ and $\tilde{\mathcal{S}}_0 = \infty$.

Corollary 4.1, which follows from Proposition 4.2, characterizes the function $\mathcal{F}_j(\cdot)$.

Corollary 4.1. *The function $\mathcal{F}_j(S)$ in equation (4.22) is convex in S.*

Example 4.1 illustrates the mechanics of the algorithm in Proposition 4.2.

Example 4.1. Focus on a six-block mining sector with the characteristics given in Table 4.1. Consider an interest rate $r = 0.12$ and a convenience yield $\rho = 0.06$. We specialize the result in Proposition 4.2 to the case of the lower bound $F^{\mathrm{L}}(S)$. To do so, set $\alpha_k = \exp(-rT_k)$ and $\eta_k = \exp[(r - \rho)T_k]$ for $k \leq 6$. In the first iteration of the

Table 4.1 Characteristics of the mining sector considered in Example 4.1.

Block	R_k	C_k	T_k	$\mathbb{C}_k$
1	0.25	14	1.2	56
2	0.3	9	1.6	30
3	0.4	16	1	40
4	0.32	10	2	31.25
5	0.35	12.25	0.7	35
6	0.4	18	0.9	45

AFTER ITERATION 1				
Block Number		$\widetilde{R}_k$	$\widetilde{C}_k$	$\widetilde{T}_k$
New	Original			
1	1	0.25	14	1.2
2	2, 3	0.68	24	2.6
3	4	0.32	10	2
4	5	0.35	12.25	0.7
5	6	0.4	18	0.9

AFTER ITERATION 2				
Block Number		$\widetilde{R}_k$	$\widetilde{C}_k$	$\widetilde{T}_k$
New	Original			
1	1	0.25	14	1.2
2	2, 3, 4	0.93	29.5	4.6
3	5	0.35	12.25	0.7
4	6	0.4	18	0.9

Fig. 4.3   Values of $\widetilde{R}_k$ and $\widetilde{C}_k$ after the first and second iterations of the algorithm.

AFTER ITERATION 3				
Block Number		$\widetilde{R}_k$	$\widetilde{C}_k$	$\widetilde{T}_k$
New	Original			
1	1	0.25	14	1.2
2	2, 3, 4, 5	1.25	39.43	5.3
3	6	0.4	18	0.9

AFTER ITERATION 4				
Block Number		$\widetilde{R}_k$	$\widetilde{C}_k$	$\widetilde{T}_k$
New	Original			
1	1	0.25	14	1.2
2	2, 3, 4, 5, 6	1.58	53.39	6.2

Fig. 4.4   Values of $\widetilde{R}_k$ and $\widetilde{C}_k$ after the third and fourth iterations of the algorithm.

algorithm we find (step 2) that $\tilde{k} = 3$. We then compute $\widetilde{\mathbb{C}}_{2,3} \cdot \exp [(r - \rho) \cdot T_{2,3}^+] = 41.07 < \widetilde{\mathbb{C}}_1$ and $\widetilde{\mathbb{C}}_{3,3} \cdot \exp[(r - \rho) \cdot T_{3,3}^+] = 40 > \widetilde{\mathbb{C}}_2$ and conclude (step 3) that $\tilde{h} = 1$. From step 4, we obtain $\xi = 1$ and the new number of blocks is $\tilde{\jmath} = 5$ (blocks 2 and 3 are pooled together). Figures 4.3–4.4 summarize the values of $\widetilde{R}_k$ and $\widetilde{C}_k$ after the first, second, third, and fourth iterations of the algorithm. In order to update the values of $\tilde{\alpha}_k$ and $\tilde{\eta}_k$ it is sufficient to update the values of the processing time $\widetilde{T}_k$.

The algorithm stops after four iterations. In the final configuration the mining project consists of only two blocks: The initial block 1 and a new block 2 that aggregates the original blocks 2 to 6. From equations (4.20)–(4.21), we derive the threshold price for block 6 in the original block configuration:

$$\widetilde{S}_6 = \left(\frac{\beta}{\beta - 1} \right) \left(\frac{53.39}{1.58} \right) = \frac{33.79\,\beta}{\beta - 1}.$$

The interpretation of this price is as follows: As soon as the spot price exceeds $\widetilde{S}_6$ the extraction of block 6 should start.

The algorithm in Proposition 4.2 provides a simple method to reduce the size of the mining project by appropriately aggregating blocks and then computing the value function and threshold prices for the modified block configuration. In practice, blocks cannot be pooled together and must be extracted one at a time. The modified sequence of blocks is thus of limited practical use for extraction purposes. Nevertheless, we propose the following simple feasible extraction policy based on the solution proposed by Proposition 4.2:

Extraction policy based on the approximation $\mathcal{F}_j(S)$:

(1) Consider a sector with j blocks. Using the algorithm in Proposition 4.2, aggregate blocks to obtain a new block configuration with $\tilde{\jmath} \leq j$ blocks.
(2) For this artificial configuration compute the threshold price $\widetilde{S}_{\tilde{\jmath}}$ using equations (4.20) and (4.21).
(3) For the original block configuration with j blocks start extracting block j as soon as the spot price exceeds $\widetilde{S}_{\tilde{\jmath}}$ with $\widetilde{S}_{\tilde{\jmath}} = \mathcal{S}_j$, which is the optimal threshold price for the approximation $\mathcal{F}_j(S)$.
(4) Once the extraction of block j is completed, iterate this sequence of steps for the remaining $j - 1$ blocks.

This extraction policy uses the artificial configuration of blocks proposed by Proposition 4.2 only to compute the threshold price that determines when the first block (in the original sequence) should start being processed. For instance, the results in Example 4.1 suggest that block 6 should start being processed as soon as the spot price satisfies $S_t \geq 33.79$ $\beta/(\beta - 1)$.

We now briefly discuss how the extraction sequence is chosen in practice. When a mining project is designed, its extraction sequence is implicitly built. For example, in underground mines, a common design rule is to select the initial extraction front near blocks with higher grade. The idea behind this (greedy) rule is to extract the better material first at the lowest marginal cost. This simple rule has two important consequences from the point of view of our solution. First, the quality of the ore tends to be a decreasing function of the extraction front. Hence, the parameter R_k is usually increasing in k (recall that we index blocks backward with block 1 being the last block in the sequence). Second, as the operation advances through the extraction fronts, it is executed farther away from the initial front and the extracted materials must be moved a longer distance. This additional transportation increases the marginal extraction cost, that is, C_k is generally decreasing in k. Hence, we expect $\mathbb{C}_k = C_k/R_k$ to be a decreasing function of k under this greedy design. According to step 2 in the algorithm in Proposition 4.2 there is no block aggregation if $\mathbb{C}_{k-1} \geq \eta_k \mathbb{C}_k$. Hence, we can roughly state that there should be no block aggregation under this greedy design rule if η_k is not "much larger" than 1. This condition holds trivially for the case of the upper bound ($\eta_k = 1$). For the lower bound, $\eta_k = \exp[(r - \rho)T_k]$ and so we expect no block aggregation if the interest rate and/or the processing times are small.

4.3.4. *Asymptotic Approximations*

We now characterize the limiting behavior of the upper and lower bounds as the spot price goes to infinity and use it to propose two simple approximations for the value function.

Figure 4.5 (left panel) plots the value function $F_j(S)$ (numerically computed), the upper bound $F_j^U(S)$ and the lower bound $F_j^L(S)$ as a function of S using the data in Example 4.1.

Both bounds perform well for small values of S, however, as S becomes large the lower bound performs substantially better. The upper bound has an optimality gap $F_j^U(S) - F_j(S)$ that increases monotonically with S. This behavior is in part due to the fact that the upper bound assumes that it is possible to extract all blocks simultaneously, which is an option that is more valuable when S is large. Furthermore, we can show that for S sufficiently large the upper and lower bounds are linear functions of S. The dashed lines in Fig. 4.5 (left panel) represent these linear asymptotes. The

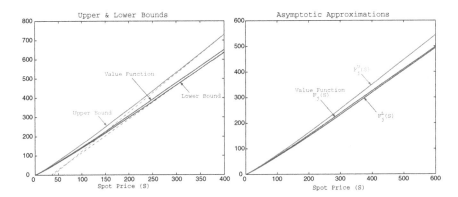

Fig. 4.5   LEFT PANEL: Value function $F_j(S)$, upper bound $F_j^U(S)$ and lower bound $F_j^L(S)$ as a function of the spot price S (in cUS\$/lb) using the data in Example 4.1. The dashed lines correspond to linear asymptotes for the upper and lower bound approximations. RIGHT PANEL: Asymptotic approximations of the value function based on equations (4.24) and (4.25).

following corollary follows directly from Proposition 4.2 (see Sec. 4.2.5 for notation).

Corollary 4.2. *Consider a project with j blocks and let $\mathcal{F}_j(S)$ be the approximation in (4.17) for some pair (α_k, η_k), $k = 1, \ldots, j$. Let $(\widetilde{R}_k, \widetilde{C}_k, \widetilde{S}_k, \widetilde{M}_k, \widetilde{\alpha}_k, \widetilde{\eta}_k, \widetilde{\theta}_k)$, $k = 1, \ldots, \tilde{j}$ be the characteristics of the resulting mining project produced by the algorithm in Proposition 4.2. Then, for S sufficiently large the approximation $\mathcal{F}_{\tilde{j}}(S)$ is a linear function of S. In particular, for all $S \geq \widetilde{S}_1 / \widetilde{\eta}_{\tilde{j}}^{\times}$ it holds that*

$$\mathcal{F}_{\tilde{j}}(S) = \left(\theta^{\times} R\right)_{\tilde{j}}^{+} S - \left(\alpha^{\times} C\right)_{\tilde{j}}^{+}. \tag{4.23}$$

For the special case of the upper bound $F_j^{U}(S)$, we have $\alpha_k = \eta_k = 1$ so that

$$F_{\tilde{j}}^{U}(S) = R_{\tilde{j}}^{+} S - C_{\tilde{j}}^{+}$$

for all $S \geq \widetilde{S}_1$. Similarly, if we set $\alpha_k = \exp(-rT_k)$ and $\eta_k = \exp[(r - \rho)T_k]$ we recover the lower bound $F_j^{L}(S)$ and equation (4.23) reduces to

$$F_{\tilde{j}}^{L}(S) = \mathcal{R}_{\tilde{j}} S - \mathcal{C}_{\tilde{j}}$$

for all $S \geq \widetilde{S}_1 \exp[-(r - \rho)T_{1,\tilde{j}}^{+}]$.

The function $F_j^{L}(\cdot)$ has exactly the same linear asymptote derived for $F_j(\cdot)$ in Proposition 4.1. This observation explains the quality of the lower bound $F_j^{L}(S)$ depicted in Fig. 4.5 (left panel) as S grows large.

Corollary 4.2 also suggests a simple approximation for $F_j(S)$ based on the stated linear asymptotes. Recall from condition (4.9) that $F_j(S)$ satisfies

$$F_j(S) = \begin{cases} M_j S^{\beta_1}, & \text{if } S \leq S_j^{*}, \\ W_j(S) + e^{-r T_j} \mathbb{E}^{\mathbb{Q}}[F_{j-1}(S_{T_j}) | S_0 = S], & \text{if } S \geq S_j^{*}, \end{cases}$$

with $F_0(S) = 0$. As we mentioned earlier, the difficult part of solving this recursion is computing the expectation $\mathbb{E}^{\mathbb{Q}}[F_{j-1}(S_{T_j}) | S_0 = S]$. Because this expectation is evaluated for values of S greater than the threshold S_j^{*}, we can obtain a simple (asymptotic) approximation if we replace $F_{j-1}(S)$ by one of the linear asymptotes derived in Corollary 4.2.

Using the upper bound asymptote $F_{j-1}^{U}(S) = R_{\tilde{j}}^{+} S - C_{\tilde{j}}^{+}$ and the martingale property (4.2) we find $\mathbb{E}^{\mathbb{Q}}[R_{\tilde{j}}^{+} S - C_{\tilde{j}}^{+} | S_0 = S] = R_{\tilde{j}}^{+} \exp[(r - \rho) T_j]$

$S - C_j^+$. Thus, we can approximate $F_j(S)$ by

$$\widehat{F}_j^{\mathrm{U}}(S) := \begin{cases} \widehat{M}_j^{\mathrm{U}}\, S^{\beta_1}, & \text{if } S \le \widehat{S}_j^{\mathrm{U}}, \\ \left(R_j + e^{-\rho\, T_j}\, R_{j-1}^+\right) S - \left(C_j + e^{-r\, T_j}\, C_{j-1}^+\right), & \text{if } S \ge \widehat{S}_j^{\mathrm{U}}. \end{cases}$$

$$(4.24)$$

(We use a hat '∧' to denote quantities that are derived using the asymptotic approximation.) Using the value matching and smooth pasting conditions we obtain

$$\widehat{S}_j^{\mathrm{U}} = \frac{\beta \left(C_j + e^{-r\, T_j}\, C_{j-1}^+\right)}{(\beta - 1)\left(R_j + e^{-\rho\, T_j}\, R_{j-1}^+\right)},$$

$$\widehat{M}_j^{\mathrm{U}} = \left(\frac{C_j + e^{-r\, T_j}\, C_{j-1}^+}{\beta - 1}\right)\left(\widehat{S}_j^{\mathrm{U}}\right)^{-\beta}.$$

Following exactly the same steps, we can obtain an alternative approximation for $F_j(S)$ based on the lower bound asymptote in Corollary 4.2:

$$\widehat{F}_j^{\mathrm{L}}(S) := \begin{cases} \widehat{M}_j^{\mathrm{L}}\, S^{\beta}, & \text{if } S \le \widehat{S}_j^{\mathrm{L}}, \\ \mathcal{R}_j\, S - \mathcal{C}_j, & \text{if } S \ge \widehat{S}_j^{\mathrm{L}}, \end{cases}$$

$$(4.25)$$

with

$$\widehat{S}_j^{\mathrm{L}} = \frac{\beta\, \mathcal{C}_j}{(\beta - 1)\, \mathcal{R}_j},$$

$$\widehat{M}_j^{\mathrm{L}} = \left(\frac{\mathcal{C}_j}{\beta - 1}\right)\left(\widehat{S}_j^{\mathrm{L}}\right)^{-\beta}.$$

Figure 4.5 (right panel) plots the values of $\widehat{F}_j^{\mathrm{U}}(S)$ and $\widehat{F}_j^{\mathrm{L}}(S)$ as well as the value function $F_j(S)$ (numerically computed). As we can see, $\widehat{F}_j^{\mathrm{L}}(S)$ performs quite well over the entire range of prices. This behavior is in part due to the fact that by construction $\widehat{F}_j^{\mathrm{L}}(S)$ has exactly the same linear behavior of $F_j(S)$ and $F_j^{\mathrm{L}}(S)$ as S goes to infinity.

To support the conclusions drawn from Fig. 4.5, we compare numerically the performance of the upper bound $F_j^{\mathrm{U}}(S)$, the lower bound $F_j^{\mathrm{L}}(S)$ and the asymptotic approximations $\widehat{F}_j^{\mathrm{U}}(S)$ and $\widehat{F}_j^{\mathrm{L}}(S)$. We measure this performance as the average relative error of these approximations across a large range of initial spot prices for different values of the model parameters. More specifically, if $\mathcal{F}_j(S)$ is an arbitrary approximation for the value function $F_j(S)$ then we measure the performance of this approximation by

$$\mathcal{P}(\mathcal{F}_j) := \frac{1}{S_{\max} - S_{\min}} \int_{S_{\min}}^{S_{\max}} \frac{|\mathcal{F}_j(S) - F_j(S)|}{F_j(S)} \, dS.$$

We choose the interval of spot prices $[S_{\min}, S_{\max}]$ large enough so that it includes almost the entire range of the historical copper spot prices. In particular, we chose $S_{\min} = 1.3\text{K}$ [US\$/Ton] and $S_{\max} = 13\text{K}$ [US\$/Ton].

Tables 4.2 and 4.3 present the value of $\mathcal{P}(\mathcal{F}_j)$ for the four approximations using the data of Example 4.1. We vary the squared volatility of the spot price σ^2 in Table 4.2 and the interest rate r and the extraction capacity

Table 4.2   Performance measure $\mathcal{P}(\mathcal{F}_j)$ for the approximations F^{U}, F^{L}, $\widehat{F}^{\text{U}}$, and $\widehat{F}^{\text{L}}$ as a function of the spot-price volatility σ^2.

σ^2	F^{U}	F^{L}	$\widehat{F}^{\text{U}}$	$\widehat{F}^{\text{L}}$
0.5	0.20	0.08	0.13	0.03
1.0	0.20	0.08	0.13	0.04
1.5	0.21	0.07	0.13	0.04
2.0	0.21	0.06	0.14	0.03
2.5	0.22	0.06	0.14	0.03
3.0	0.22	0.05	0.15	0.03
3.5	0.23	0.04	0.15	0.02
4.0	0.23	0.03	0.16	0.02
4.5	0.24	0.02	0.16	0.01
5.0	0.24	0.02	0.16	0.01
Av.	22.0%	5.1%	14.4%	2.6%

Table 4.3   Performance measure $\mathcal{P}(\mathcal{F}_j)$ for the approximations F^{U}, F^{L}, $\widehat{F}^{\text{U}}$, and $\widehat{F}^{\text{L}}$ as a function of the discount factor r and the extraction capacity K.

r	F^{U}	F^{L}	$\widehat{F}^{\text{U}}$	$\widehat{F}^{\text{L}}$	K	F^{U}	F^{L}	$\widehat{F}^{\text{U}}$	$\widehat{F}^{\text{L}}$
0.1	0.20	0.09	0.13	0.04	1.0	0.20	0.08	0.13	0.04
0.2	0.19	0.05	0.13	0.02	2.0	0.09	0.06	0.06	0.03
0.3	0.19	0.02	0.13	0.01	3.0	0.06	0.04	0.03	0.02
0.4	0.19	0.01	0.14	0.01	4.0	0.04	0.04	0.02	0.02
0.5	0.19	0.00	0.14	0.00	5.0	0.03	0.03	0.02	0.02
0.6	0.19	0.01	0.15	0.00	6.0	0.03	0.03	0.01	0.01
0.7	0.19	0.01	0.15	0.00	7.0	0.02	0.02	0.01	0.01
0.8	0.19	0.01	0.15	0.00	8.0	0.02	0.02	0.01	0.01
0.9	0.19	0.01	0.16	0.01	9.0	0.02	0.02	0.01	0.01
1.0	0.20	0.01	0.16	0.01	10.0	0.02	0.02	0.01	0.01
Av.	19.2%	2.1%	14.2%	1.0%	Av.	5.2%	3.5%	3.0%	1.7%

K in Table 4.3. In all three cases, we can see that F_j^{L} and $\widehat{F}_j^{\mathrm{L}}$ have a significantly better performance than F_j^{U} and $\widehat{F}_j^{\mathrm{U}}$. This finding is consistent with our previous discussion based on Fig. 4.5. In addition, the asymptotic approximation $\widehat{F}^{\mathrm{L}}$ has the best performance across all instances with an average error between 1% and 3%.

In terms of the sensitivity of these results, we can see that the squared volatility of the spot price, σ^2, has a different impact on these approximations. Both $\mathcal{P}(F^{\mathrm{U}})$ and $\mathcal{P}(\widehat{F}^{\mathrm{U}})$ increase with σ^2 while the opposite is true for $\mathcal{P}(F^{\mathrm{L}})$ and $\mathcal{P}(\widehat{F}^{\mathrm{L}})$. The results in the bottom-left panel in Table 4.2 suggest that the interest rate r does not have a significant effect on the approximations. Finally, the extraction capacity K affects these four approximations in a similar way, that is, they are all monotonically decreasing with K. This behavior is a consequence of the following result.

Proposition 4.3. *Let $F_j(S, K)$, $F_j^{\mathrm{U}}(S, K)$ and $F_j^{\mathrm{L}}(S, K)$ be the value function and upper and lower bounds, respectively, for block j when the spot price is S and the extraction capacity is K. Then, in the limit as K goes to infinity the upper and lower bound approximations converge to the true value function. That is, it holds that*

$$\lim_{K \to \infty} F_j^{\mathrm{U}}(S, K) = \lim_{K \to \infty} F_j^{\mathrm{L}}(S, K) = \lim_{K \to \infty} F_j(S, K)$$

for all $S \geq 0$. Hence, in the limit as K goes to infinity we have $\mathcal{P}(\widetilde{F}) = \mathcal{P}(\widehat{F}) = 0$.

We make a simple observation that is particularly useful when selecting an optimal sequence of extraction. Suppose we have a mining sector with j blocks and we want to compare two possible sequences of extraction π^1 and π^2. Based on Proposition 4.1, the expected discounted value of the project under sequence π^i is asymptotically equal to $\mathcal{R}_j^{\pi^i} S - \mathcal{C}_j^{\pi^i}$, $i = 1, 2$. Hence, for S sufficiently large the best sequence is the one that maximizes the value of $\mathcal{R}_j^{\pi^i}$. For moderate value of S, on the other hand, the comparison is not straightforward. However, we extend this condition in Proposition 4.4 using the asymptotic approximation $\widehat{F}^{\mathrm{L}}(S)$ instead of the real value function $F(S)$ to perform the comparison between π^1 and π^2.

Proposition 4.4. *Consider two possible sequences of extraction π^1 and π^2 for a mining project with j blocks. Let $\widehat{F}_i^{\mathrm{L}}(S) = \mathcal{R}_j^{\pi^i} S - \mathcal{C}_j^{\pi^i}$ be the (lower bound) asymptotic approximation for the value function if sequence π^i is used, $i = 1, 2$. Then it holds that $\widehat{F}_1^{\mathrm{L}}(S) \geq \widehat{F}_2^{\mathrm{L}}(S)$ for all $S \geq 0$ if and only* *if the following two conditions are satisfied:*

$$\mathcal{R}_j^{\pi^1} \geq \mathcal{R}_j^{\pi^2},$$

$$\left(\frac{\mathcal{R}_j^{\pi^1}}{\mathcal{R}_j^{\pi^2}}\right)^{\beta} \geq \left(\frac{\mathcal{C}_j^{\pi^1}}{\mathcal{C}_j^{\pi^2}}\right)^{\beta-1}.$$

4.4. Capacity Expansions

The set of approximations for the value function derived in Sec. 4.3 assume a fixed processing capacity K. In this section, we relax this assumption and show how to extend some of these approximations to include capacity expansion decisions. In particular, we only discuss how to extend the lower bound asymptote $\widehat{F}_j^{\text{L}}(S)$ because it has the best numerical performance.

Using the notation introduced in Sec. 4.2, we let quantities depend on K, when appropriate. For example, recall that $F_j(S, K)$ denotes the value function for a single-sector project when there are j blocks left, the spot price is S and the processing capacity is K. We find convenient to define $\bar{F}_j(S) := F_j(S, \bar{K})$, $\bar{W}_j(S) := W_j(S, \bar{K})$, $\bar{R}_j := R_j(\bar{K})$, $\bar{C}_j := C_j(\bar{K})$, and $\bar{T}_j := T_j(\bar{K})$, where $\bar{K}$ is the upper bound on the maximum level of capacity.

For a given S and K we define the auxiliary function

$$G_j(S, K) := \sup_{K \leq \tilde{K} \leq \bar{K}} W_j(S, \tilde{K}) + e^{-r\,T_j(\tilde{K})}\, \mathbb{E}^{\mathbb{Q}}[F_{j-1}(S_{T_j(\tilde{K})}, \tilde{K})|S_0 = S]$$

$$-\gamma\,(\tilde{K} - K), \tag{4.26}$$

and let $K_j^*(S, K)$ be the value of $\tilde{K}$ at which the maximum is attained. This function computes the optimal expected payoff if the state of the system is (S, K) and the decision maker is forced to start production immediately. In this case, and similar to (4.6), the dynamic programming recursion takes the form

$$F_j(S, K) = \sup_{\tau \geq 0} \mathbb{E}^{\mathbb{Q}}[e^{-r\tau} G_j(S_\tau, K)|S_0 = S],$$

where $F_0(S, K) := 0$. Using arguments similar to the ones used to derive equation (4.9) from equation (4.6), we can show that there exist two functions $M_j(K)$ and $S_j^*(K)$ such that

$$F_j(S, K) = \begin{cases} M_j(K)\,S^{\beta}, & \text{if } S \leq S_j^*(K), \\ G_j(S, K), & \text{if } S \geq S_j^*(K). \end{cases} \tag{4.27}$$

The functions $M_j(K)$ and $S_j^*(K)$ are determined using the smooth-pasting and value-matching conditions

$$\beta\, G_j(S_j^*(K), K) = G_j'(S_j^*(K), K)\, S_j^*(K),$$

$$M^j(K) = G_j(S_j^*(K), K)\, \left(S_j^*(K)\right)^{-\beta},$$

where G_j' denotes the derivative of G_j with respect to its first parameter. Most of the difficulty of computing the value function $F_j(S, K)$ in (4.27) reduces to determining the auxiliary function $G_j(S, K)$. Equation (4.27) suggests that we only need to compute the value of $G_j(S, K)$ for S greater than the threshold $S_j^*(K)$. As in Sec. 4.3 we use an asymptotic approximation as a proxy for $G_j(S, K)$ in this range.

Proposition 4.5, which follows directly from Proposition 4.1, characterizes the asymptotic behavior of both the optimal capacity $K_j^*(S, K)$ and the function $G_j(S, K)$.

Proposition 4.5. *In the limit as S goes to infinity, the optimal capacity $K_j^*(S, K)$ converges to the upper bound $\bar{K}$ and the function $G_j(S, K)$ converges to a linear function of the price. In particular,*

$$G_j(S, K) \overset{S \to \infty}{\longrightarrow} \bar{\mathcal{R}}_j\, S - \bar{\mathcal{C}}_j - \gamma\,(\bar{K} - K),$$

where

$$\bar{\mathcal{R}}_j := \sum_{k=1}^{j} \bar{R}_k\, e^{-\rho\, \bar{T}_{k,j}^+},$$

$$\bar{\mathcal{C}}_j := \sum_{k=1}^{j} \bar{C}_k\, e^{-r\, \bar{T}_{k,j}^+}.$$

If we use the linear asymptotic behavior of $G_j(S, K)$ in (4.27), we obtain the following approximations of $S_j^*(K)$ and $M_j(K)$:

$$S_j^*(K) \approx \left(\frac{\beta}{\beta - 1}\right) \left(\frac{\bar{\mathcal{C}}_j + \gamma\,(\bar{K} - K)}{\bar{\mathcal{R}}_j}\right), \qquad (4.28)$$

$$M_j(K) \approx \left(\frac{\bar{\mathcal{R}}_j}{\beta}\right)^{\beta} \left(\frac{\beta - 1}{\bar{\mathcal{C}}_j + \gamma\,(\bar{K} - K)}\right)^{\beta - 1}. \qquad (4.29)$$

According to these solutions, the threshold price $S_j^*(K)$ is a linear and decreasing function of K. That is, when capacity is large a small spot price is enough to induce the decision maker to start production.

To complete our approximation when capacity expansion is possible, we need to approximate $K_j^*(S, K)$, that is, specify how capacity should be expanded over time. The optimization in (4.26) is in general difficult to perform. However, because $F_j(S, K)$ equals $G_j(S, K)$ for S sufficiently large, we can exploit one more time the asymptotic approximation in Proposition 4.5 to obtain $K_j^*(S, K) \approx \max_K \mathcal{K}_j(S)$, where

$$\mathcal{K}_j(S) := \underset{0 \leq \tilde{K} \leq \bar{K}}{\arg\max} \left\{ \mathcal{R}(\tilde{K}) S - \mathcal{C}(\tilde{K}) - \gamma \tilde{K} \right\}. \tag{4.30}$$

The function $\mathcal{K}_j(S)$ provides the optimal capacity expansion decision if there is no installed capacity and the spot price is S (it is an increasing function of S). Define $\bar{S}_j := \inf\{S \geq 0 : \mathcal{K}_j(S) = \bar{K}\}$. The price $\bar{S}_j$ is the threshold price above which it is always optimal to expand capacity to its maximum possible level $\bar{K}$ independently of the current capacity level.

The chart in the left panel of Fig. 4.6 plots the values of $\mathcal{K}_j(S)$ for $j = 1, \ldots, 6$ using the data in Example 4.1. As expected, the inequalities $\mathcal{K}_1(S) \leq \mathcal{K}_2(S) \leq \cdots \leq \mathcal{K}_6(S)$ hold for all S. This ordering reflects the fact that additional capacity is more valuable when the mining project has more blocks. This monotonicity also implies that $\bar{S}_6 \leq \bar{S}_5 \leq \cdots \leq \bar{S}_1$.

Based on the thresholds $S_j^*(K)$ and $\mathcal{K}_j(S)$ we can divide the state space $\{(S, K) : 0 \leq K \leq \bar{K} \text{ and } S \geq 0\}$ in three subregions depicted in the right panel of Fig. 4.6. In Region I $:= \{(S, K) : 0 \leq S \leq S_j^*(K), K \leq \bar{K}\}$ the spot price is very low and one is better off by idling production until the price

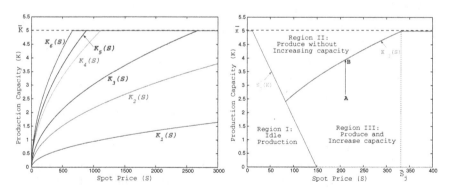

Fig. 4.6 LEFT PANEL: Capacity expansion function $\mathcal{K}_j(S)$ for $j = 1, \ldots, 6$ using the data in Example 4.1, $\gamma = 10$, and a maximum capacity $\bar{K} = 5$. RIGHT PANEL: Optimal production and capacity expansion decisions based on the switching curves $S_j^*(K)$ and $\mathcal{K}_j(S)$ using the data of Example 4.1, $\gamma = 5$ and $\bar{K} = 5$. Both panels display spot prices in cUS$/lb.

reaches the threshold $S_j^*(K)$. On the other hand, in Region II := $\{(S, K) : S_j^*(K) \leq S, \mathcal{K}_j(S) \leq K \leq \bar{K}\}$ the spot price and capacity are both high and production should start but no capacity expansion is required. Finally, in Region III := $\{(S, K) \in \mathcal{S} : S_j^*(K) \leq S$ and $0 \leq K \leq \mathcal{K}_j(S)\}$ the spot price is high but production capacity is low. In this region, one should expand capacity from K to $\mathcal{K}_j(S)$ and produce. For example, if the system is in point A in Fig. 4.6 then capacity should be expanded to point B and then production should start.

The negative slope of $S_j^*(K)$ implies that the opportunity cost of idling production increases as capacity increases. In other words, a large mining project will tend to operate almost independently of the price, whereas a small project will turn production on and off as the spot price oscillates. On the other hand, the positive slope of $\mathcal{K}_j(S)$ reflects the intuitive fact that capacity becomes more valuable as the spot price increases.

4.5. Case Study

In this section, we use the methodology proposed in the previous sections to estimate the economic value of a mining project at *El Teniente*. This mine is located in the central region of Chile, 3,000 meters above the sea level. It is the largest underground copper mine in the world. With a processing capacity of almost 50 million tons/year, it produced more than 450,000 metric tons of refined copper in 2013. This mine has multiple active sectors and is in continuous expansion. One of these sectors is *El Diablo Regimiento*, which started production in 2005 and is scheduled to complete its operations around 2020. Because of its unusual spatial distribution, several extraction sequences have been considered, each one requiring a different economic evaluation. The project is currently in its third phase (out of five). Mining operators are under continued pressure to evaluate substantial changes to production plans within limited amounts of time.

We focus on describing how to tackle the sequencing problem for *El Diablo Regimiento*. Based on the original extraction sequence, we divide the almost 230 million tons of material in this sector into 10 blocks. Figure 4.7 shows schematically the spatial distribution of these blocks.

Table 4.4 summarizes the mineral content, grade, and extraction time for the ten blocks of *El Diablo Regimiento*. Based on the spatial distribution of the blocks, we evaluate six extraction sequences (shown in Table 4.5),

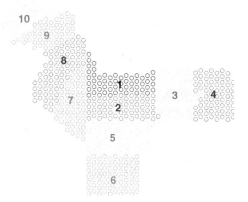

Fig. 4.7   Block spatial distribution at *El Diablo Regimiento*.

Table 4.4   Mineral content Q_j, copper grade L_j, and extraction time T_j for the 10 blocks of *El Diablo Regimiento*.

Block	Q_j (Million Tons)	L_j (%)	T_j (Years)
1	21.415	0.827	2.93
2	21.268	0.915	2.91
3	29.526	0.823	4.04
4	28.351	0.881	3.88
5	24.854	0.845	3.40
6	23.931	0.848	3.28
7	21.476	0.768	2.94
8	26.110	0.727	3.58
9	14.913	0.694	2.04
10	13.126	0.776	1.80

Table 4.5   Six feasible extraction sequences.

Sequence	Order
N1	1-2-3-4-5-6-7-8-9-10
N2	10-9-8-7-1-2-5-3-4-6
N3	4-3-2-1-7-8-9-10-5-6
N4	6-5-2-1-3-4-7-8-9-10
N5	1-2-7-8-9-10-5-6-3-4
N6	1-2-5-3-7-8-6-4-9-10

where sequence $N1$ is the one considered in the original design at *El Teniente*. The first block of each of these sequences is the first one to be extracted. This set of sequences represents only a small fraction of the total number of possible extraction sequences.

Because production costs depend on the actual sequence of extraction, we do not have a fixed extraction cost for each block. For the purpose of the computational experiments reported in this section, we use a simplified method to approximate these extraction costs. If we let $\pi = (\pi_1, \pi_2, \ldots, \pi_{10})$ be any of the six sequences that we consider, then the marginal extraction cost (in cUS\$/lb) for the j-th block in this sequence π is[c]

$$A_j^\pi = 0.4857 + 0.0162 \cdot d_{1j},$$

where d_{ij} denotes the distance between blocks i and j (see Table 4.6). In other words, we approximate the marginal extraction cost of a block as an affine function of the distance from the block to the initial extraction front, with the caveat that additional factors might have to be considered in practice.

We consider a fixed production capacity of 7.3 million tons/year for this sector. For this exercise, we set additional parameters as follows: A recovery factor of 85% (this value further penalizes L_i and represents the loss in recovery of mineral during the concentration and refinement processes), $r = 12\%$, $\sigma = 0.5$, and $\rho = 6\%$ (Casassus and Collin [42] report an average value of the instantaneous convenience yield for copper of 6.3%).

Table 4.6   Distance (in meters) d_{ij} between blocks i and j at *El Diablo Regimiento.*

d_{ij}	1	2	3	4	5	6	7	8	9	10
1	0	90	190	321	191	314	159	189	275	367
2	90	0	102	234	174	295	157	240	350	438
3	190	102	0	133	233	336	182	299	424	507
4	321	234	133	0	343	425	272	399	532	607
5	191	174	233	343	0	124	327	380	454	547
6	314	295	336	425	124	0	450	503	569	661
7	159	157	182	272	327	450	0	128	263	335
8	189	240	299	399	380	503	128	0	136	209
9	275	350	424	532	454	569	263	136	0	93
10	367	438	507	607	547	661	335	209	93	0

---

[c]The intercept and slope were estimated using production costs at *El Teniente* considering the extraction sequence $N1$ and using aggregate.

For each of the six sequences we numerically compute the value function and the asymptotic approximation based on the lower bound in (4.25). Table 4.7 summarizes the results.

The best extraction sequence according to the value function F is given by N1 (the original sequence). This sequence remains the best when using the asymptotic approximation $\widehat{F}^{\text{L}}$. In terms of project value, the right most column in Table 4.7 reports the relative error between F and $\widehat{F}^{\text{L}}$. The values computed using the asymptotic approximations have a relatively small error that ranges from 9% to 0.3%. This error decreases when the spot price S increases, an observation consistent with Proposition 4.1 and Corollary 4.2. The dominance of the sequence N1 is consistent with Proposition 4.4. Indeed, this sequence has the best asymptotic behavior with the highest slope $\mathcal{R}^{N1} = 24.78$ among all the six considered sequences.

We conclude this section discussing how to use the results of Sec. 4.4 to estimate an optimal capacity expansion policy for *El Diablo Regimiento*. Supposing that initially there is no installed capacity, we can use (4.28)–(4.30) to obtain an approximation for the optimal initial capacity. In these computations we use $\gamma = 7.5$ US\$/(ton/year) and $\overline{K} = 20$ million tons/year.

For each of the six considered sequences we compute the asymptotic approximation based on the lower bound in (4.27) and the expansion rule in (4.30). Table 4.8 summarizes the results.

Interestingly, the optimal sequence in this case is N5 as opposed to N1, which is optimal when the capacity is fixed at 7.3 million tons/year. Because sequence N1 is the one considered in the original design of *El Diablo Regimiento*, it seems that management at *El Teniente* has not fully valued the option of increasing capacity. Of course, there are other practical considerations that are not included in our model that might explain this discrepancy. Finally, it is optimal to expand capacity to its maximum level $\overline{K} = 20$ million tons/year if the spot price exceeds 100 cUS\$/lb. This price is rather low compared to the current spot price of about 300 cUS\$/lb, but higher than the prevalent price at the early stages of the planning process (around 2003).

4.6. Conclusions and Future Research

In this chapter, we develop a tractable continuous-time model of a mining operation and propose a methodology to compute near-optimal production and capacity expansion policies.

Table 4.7   Value function for the six extraction sequences in *El Diablo Regimiento*.

| Price | N1 | | N2 | | N3 | | N4 | | N5 | | N6 | | Relative |
S	F	$\widehat{F}^{\mathrm{L}}$	F	$\widehat{F}^{\mathrm{L}}$	F	$\widehat{F}^{\mathrm{L}}$	F	$\widehat{F}^{\mathrm{L}}$	F	$\widehat{F}^{\mathrm{L}}$	F	$\widehat{F}^{\mathrm{L}}$	Error
50	607	552	556	499	598	543	599	541	587	535	602	549	9.1%
100	1367	1251	1255	1130	1350	1232	1352	1227	1325	1213	1356	1245	8.5%
150	2143	2007	1975	1812	2120	1975	2123	1967	2078	1945	2125	1996	6.3%
200	2926	2803	2704	2534	2896	2761	2901	2751	2837	2717	2901	2786	4.2%
250	3721	3614	3446	3295	3684	3567	3691	3562	3608	3505	3689	3590	2.9%
300	4509	4416	4183	4053	4465	4363	4474	4363	4373	4283	4469	4384	2.1%
350	5298	5219	4921	4810	5247	5159	5259	5164	5138	5062	5251	5178	1.5%
400	6097	6030	5670	5577	6040	5965	6054	5975	5914	5849	6043	5982	1.1%
450	6888	6832	6410	6335	6823	6762	6840	6776	6681	6628	6827	6777	0.8%
500	7679	7635	7152	7092	7607	7558	7627	7577	7449	7406	7611	7571	0.6%
550	8480	8446	7902	7859	8401	8364	8423	8388	8226	8194	8404	8375	0.4%
600	9272	9248	8644	8617	9186	9160	9211	9189	8995	8972	9189	9169	0.3%

Notes: Prices in column S are expressed in cUS\$/lb. The F columns represent the numerically computed value function (in million US\$) and the $\widehat{F}^{\mathrm{L}}$ columns represent the asymptotic approximation using the lower bound in (4.25) (in million US\$).

Table 4.8 Optimal capacity K^* (in million tons/year) and expected value F (numerically computed, in million US\$) for the six considered sequences of extraction at *El Diablo Regimiento* as a function of the price S in cUS\$/lb. The value of K^* is computed using the asymptotic approximation $\widehat{F}^L$ and equation (4.30).

Price	N1		N2		N3		N4		N5		N6	
S	K^*	F	K^*	F	K^*	F	K^*	F	K^*	F	K^*	F
30	0.01	66.78	0.01	58.23	0.01	61.82	0.01	58.75	0.01	68.09	0.01	66.69
40	5.1	89.04	0.01	77.64	0.9	82.43	0.01	78.33	4.7	90.79	4.4	88.91
50	7.75	111.29	0.01	97.05	4.65	103.04	0.01	97.91	7.2	113.49	7.4	111.14
60	10.6	133.55	5.2	116.47	7.25	123.65	6.7	117.5	9.95	136.19	10.45	133.37
70	13.9	155.81	7.3	135.88	10.05	144.25	9.4	137.08	13.05	158.89	13.85	155.6
80	17.5	178.07	9.55	155.29	13.25	164.86	12.45	156.66	16.5	181.59	17.6	177.83
90	20	200.33	12.1	174.7	16.85	185.47	15.85	176.25	20	204.28	20	200.06
100	20	222.59	14.95	194.11	20	206.08	19.55	195.83	20	226.98	20	222.29
110	20	244.85	18.1	213.52	20	226.68	20	215.41	20	249.68	20	244.51
120	20	267.11	20	232.93	20	247.29	20	234.99	20	272.38	20	266.74
130	20	289.36	20	252.34	20	267.9	20	254.58	20	295.08	20	288.97
140	20	311.62	20	271.75	20	288.51	20	274.16	20	317.78	20	311.2

On the modeling side, we represent the mining project as a finite collection of mineral blocks. These blocks are distinguished by ore content, mineralogical composition, and extraction costs. In our model, an optimal production policy defines the sequence in which blocks should be extracted and the timing of extraction. Our discrete block representation of the mine is consistent with current practice and deviates from previous research that commonly models mine characteristics (such as ore content, grade and production costs) as continuous variables. In this respect, our model contributes to bridge the gap between the academic research and current practice in the mining industry, representing a first step towards a methodology for optimal sequence selection.

We use a two-step approach o approximate the optimal operating and capacity expansion policy. First, in Sec. 4.3 we fix the sequence and production capacity and solve for the optimal timing of extraction contingent upon the evolution of the spot price. We derive general properties of an optimal policy and show that the value of the project is asymptotically equal to an affine function of the price. Unfortunately, for moderate values of the price we do not obtain a simple characterization of the value function. For this reason, we derive upper and lower bounds on the value function, respectively, and use them to propose two simple extraction policies. In addition, we use these bounds to obtain a pair of asymptotic approximations to the value function. Out of these approximations, the one derived using asymptotic analysis and based on the lower bound (4.25), $\widehat{F}^{\mathrm{L}}(S)$, turns out to be asymptotically equal to the true value function. Moreover, our numerical analysis shows that $\widehat{F}^{\mathrm{L}}(S)$ performs extremely well for a wide range of prices and other parameters with an average error of 2%. We also establish necessary and sufficient conditions to decide when an extraction sequence dominates another one for all values of the spot price.

Second, in Sec. 4.4 we show how to extend the models of Sec. 4.3 to identify efficient capacity expansion policies. Our discussion is based on the asymptotic approximation $\widehat{F}^{\mathrm{L}}(S)$ but the same methodology can be extended to other approximations of the value function. The resulting production/capacity policy is of the threshold type. Specifically, the (spot price, installed capacity) state space is partitioned into three regions (see the right panel in Fig. 4.6). In region I, the spot price is relatively low and its optimal policy is to idle production. In region II, both the price and the capacity are high and production is optimally performed with no increase in capacity. In region III, the spot price is high but capacity is relatively small and it is optimal to increase capacity to a level that depends on the current spot price and then produce accordingly. Our analysis provides a set of simple equations that characterize the threshold functions that separate these three regions. As a general rule, we observe that the option to idle production becomes less valuable as the capacity of a project increases. In other words, large mining projects will tend to operate almost independently of the output price, whereas small projects will switch production on and off as the spot price oscillates.

In Sec. 4.5 we apply our methodology to a real instance of the problem at *El Teniente*. The example that we consider is based on a real project, called *El Diablo Regimiento*. Our analysis shows that the original planned sequence is optimal if production capacity is fixed at its nominal value of 7.3 million tons/year. However, if we allow the production capacity to be optimally chosen then a different sequence maximizes the economic value of *El Diablo Regimiento*.

There are a number of possible extensions to our model. First, an important component of an optimal production policy is the sequence in which blocks are extracted. We do not explicitly address the question of how to dynamically choose this sequence. Instead, we take a scenario-based approach and assume that a set of potential sequences have been already identified. This *open-loop* approach is indeed consistent with how mining projects are evaluated at Codelco, but lacks the flexibility of adjusting the extraction sequence based on the evolution of the spot price. However, dynamically adjusting the sequence of extraction has a combinatorial structure which makes it extremely hard to solve. Extending our methodology to explicitly include dynamic sequencing is a challenging research problem with both theoretical and practical importance.

Second, our model could be extended by more carefully representing the relationship between the spot price and production levels.In our model the spot price is independent of the output of the mining project, a standard assumption in the literature that is reasonable if the producer is a small player with limited market power. However, this assumption is not realistic for a company like Codelco, which produces 10% of the world's copper production. In this situation, we should expect the level of production to impact spot (and futures) prices (see [45]). This type of *large investor* effect has received some attention in the mathematical finance literature (e.g., [46, 47]) but, with few exceptions (e.g., [48, 49], it is poorly studied in the literature on real options.

Acknowledgments

The authors would like to thank Nicola Secomandi and an anonymous referee for their helpful and constructive comments on the initial version of this chapter.

Appendix A. Proofs

A.1. *Proof of Theorem 4.1*

Let $F(S) \in \mathcal{C}_+^2$ be a solution to the QVI conditions in (4.7). Given the assumptions on $F(\cdot)$, we can apply integration by parts followed by Itô's lemma (see [50]) to obtain

$$e^{-r\tau} F(S_\tau) = F(S) + \int_0^\tau e^{-rt} \mathcal{A}F(S_t)\,\mathrm{d}t + \int_0^\tau e^{-rt} F'(S_t)\,\sigma\,S_t\,\mathrm{d}\tilde{B}_t.$$

The first QVI condition $\mathcal{A}F(S) \leq 0$ and the non-negativity of F yield

$$0 \leq e^{-r\tau} F(S_\tau) \leq F(S) + \int_0^\tau e^{-rt} F'(S_t)\,\sigma\,S_t\,\mathrm{d}\tilde{B}_t. \qquad (\mathrm{A.1})$$

The process

$$Y_t := F(S) + \int_0^t e^{-ru} F'(S_u)\,\sigma\,S_u\,\mathrm{d}\tilde{B}_u$$

is thus a non-negative local $\mathbb{Q}$-martingale, and, hence, a $\mathbb{Q}$-supermatingale. Taking expectations with respect to $\mathbb{E}^{\mathbb{Q}}[\cdot]$ in (A.1), we obtain

$$\mathbb{E}^{\mathbb{Q}}[e^{-r\tau} F(S_\tau)] \leq F(S).$$

Furthermore, using the second QVI condition gives

$$\mathbb{E}^{\mathbb{Q}}[e^{-r\tau} G_j(S_\tau)] \leq F(S).$$

Because this inequality holds for any stopping time τ, we conclude $F(S) \geq F_j(S)$. Finally, by Dynkin's formula and the fact that the QVI-control is the first exit time from a bounded set (continuation region $\mathcal{D}$), all the inequalities in this proof become equalities for the QVI-control associated with $F(\cdot)$.

A.2. Proof of Proposition 4.1

We derive an upper and lower bound approximation for $F_j(S)$, from which the result follows.

We obtain a lower bound on $F_j(S)$ if we assume that idling production is impossible when prices are below the production thresholds $\{S_k^*\}$. Under this non-idling restriction it follows that

$$
F_j(S) \geq \mathbb{E}^{\mathbb{Q}} \left[\sum_{k=1}^{j} e^{-r\, T_{k,j}^+} W_j(S_{\mathcal{T}_{k,j}}) \right]
$$

$$
= \sum_{k=1}^{j} e^{-r\, T_{k,j}^+} \left(R_k\, \mathbb{E}^{\mathbb{Q}}[S_{T_{k,j}^+} | S_0 = S] - C_k \right) = \mathcal{R}_j\, S - \mathcal{C}_j. \quad \text{(A.2)}
$$

To obtain an upper bound, we introduce a modified price process $\mathcal{S}_t$ given by

$$
\mathcal{S}_t = S_t + \sum_{k:\mathcal{T}_{k,j}\leq t} \left(S_k^* - \mathcal{S}_{T_{k,j}^+ -} \right)^+,
$$

$$
\mathcal{S}_{0-} = S_0.
$$

Recall that S_k^* is the switching price for block k, that is, the extraction of block k should start as soon as the spot price exceeds this threshold. We define the auxiliary value function $\mathcal{F}_j(S)$, which is the expected payoff for a project with j blocks under the modified price process $\mathcal{S}_t$ and using the switching prices $\{S_k^* : 1 \leq k \leq j\}$ to control production. It is not hard to see that $\mathcal{S}_t \geq S_t$ pathwise. It follows that $F_j(S) \leq \mathcal{F}_j(S)$ for all S. In addition, because of the specific construction of $\mathcal{S}_t$, under $\mathcal{S}_t$ production is never idled; that is, $\mathcal{S}_{T_{k,j}^+} \geq S_k^*$ (a.s.) for all $1 \leq k \leq j$. Therefore, we have

$$
F_j(S) \leq \mathcal{F}_j(S) = \sum_{k=1}^{j} e^{-r\, T_{k,j}^+} (R_k\, \mathbb{E}^{\mathbb{Q}}[\mathcal{S}_{\mathcal{T}_{k,j}} | S_0 = S] - C_k)
$$

$$
= \mathcal{R}_j\, S - \mathcal{C}_j + \sum_{k=1}^{j} e^{-r\, T_{k,j}^+} R_k\, \mathbb{E}^{\mathbb{Q}}[\mathcal{S}_{T_{k,j}^+} - S_{T_{k,j}^+} | S_0 = S].
$$

$$
\text{(A.3)}
$$

Combining (A.2) and (A.3) gives

$$
0 \leq F_j(S) - (\mathcal{R}_j\, S - \mathcal{C}_j) \leq \sum_{k=1}^{j} e^{-r\, T_{k,j}^+} R_k\, \mathbb{E}^{\mathbb{Q}}[\mathcal{S}_{T_{k,j}^+} - S_{T_{k,j}^+} | S_0 = S].
$$

To complete the proof, we need to show that the term on the right of the second inequality vanishes as S increases to infinity. By the definition of $\mathcal{S}_t$

we have

$$\mathbb{E}^{\mathbb{Q}}[\mathcal{S}_{T_{k,j}^+} - S_{T_{k,j}^+} | S_0 = S] = \sum_{n=k}^{j} \mathbb{E}^{\mathbb{Q}}\left[\left(S_k^* - \mathcal{S}_{T_{k,j}^+ -}\right)^+ | S_0 = S\right]$$

$$\leq \sum_{n=k}^{j} S_k^* \, \mathbb{Q}(\mathcal{S}_{T_{k,j}^+ -} \leq S_k^* | S_0 = S)$$

$$\leq \sum_{n=k}^{j} S_k^* \, \mathbb{Q}(\mathcal{S}_{T_{k,j}^+} \leq S_k^* | S_0 = S),$$

where the last inequality uses the (a.s.) facts that $\mathcal{S}_t \geq S_t$ and S_t is continuous. Under measure $\mathbb{Q}$, S_t is log-normal with drift $r - \rho - \sigma^2/2$ and diffusion coefficient σ (see (4.3)). Thus, it is not hard to show that

$$\mathbb{Q}(S_{T_{k,j}^+} \leq S_k^* | S_0 = S) = \mathbb{Q}\left(\tilde{B}_{T_{k,j}^+} \geq \frac{1}{\sigma}\left[\ln\left(\frac{S}{S_k^*}\right) + \left(r - \rho - \frac{\sigma^2}{2}\right) T_{k,j}^+\right]\right),$$

where $\tilde{B}_t$ is a standard $\mathbb{Q}$-Brownian motion. Hence, for $S \geq S_j^m$ $\exp(-\min_k\{(r - \rho - \sigma^2/2) T_{k,j}^+\})$, we can bound the tail probability by (e.g., [51, Theorem XIII-2.1])

$$\mathbb{Q}\left(\tilde{B}_{T_{k,j}^+} \geq \frac{1}{\sigma}\left[\ln\left(\frac{S}{S_k^*}\right) + \left(r - \rho - \frac{\sigma^2}{2}\right) T_{k,j}^+\right]\right)$$

$$\leq \exp\left(-\frac{1}{\sigma^2}\left[\ln\left(\frac{S}{S_k^*}\right) + \left(r - \rho - \frac{\sigma^2}{2}\right) T_{k,j}^+\right]^2\right)$$

$$\leq \exp\left(-\frac{1}{\sigma^2} \min_{1 \leq k \leq j}\left\{\left[\ln\left(\frac{S}{S_j^m}\right) + \left(r - \rho - \frac{\sigma^2}{2}\right) T_{k,j}^+\right]^2\right\}\right).$$

Based on this bound, it is not hard to show that for

$$S \geq S_j^m \exp\left(-\min_k\left\{\left(r - \rho - \frac{\sigma^2}{2}\right) T_{k,j}^+\right\}\right)$$

we have

$$\sum_{k=1}^{j} e^{-r\,T_{k,j}^+} R_k \, \mathbb{E}^{\mathbb{Q}}[\mathcal{S}_{T_{k,j}^+} - \mathcal{S}_{T_{k,j}^+} | S_0 = S]$$

$$\leq S_j^m \, R_j^m \, \frac{j\,(j+1)}{2} \, \exp\left(-\frac{1}{\sigma^2} \min_{1 \leq k \leq j} \left\{ \left[\ln\left(\frac{S}{S_j^m} \right) \right. \right. \right.$$

$$\left. \left. \left. + \left(r - \rho - \frac{\sigma^2}{2} \right) T_{k,j}^+ \right]^2 \right\} \right),$$

which goes to 0 as S goes to infinity.

A.3.   *Proof of Proposition 4.2*

We use the following intermediate result, which can be established using backward induction on k starting from $j - 1$.

Lemma 4.1. *Consider a j-block project with characteristics $(R_k, C_k, \alpha_k, \eta_k)$, $k = 1, \ldots, j$. Suppose that*

$$\frac{C_{k-1}}{R_{k-1}} \geq \eta_k \, \frac{C_k}{R_k}, \quad k = 2, 3, \ldots, j.$$

Then, for any $k \leq j - 1$

$$\eta_{k,j}^{\times} \, \frac{(\alpha^{\times} C)_{k-1,j}^+}{(\theta^{\times} R)_{k-1,j}^+} \leq \frac{C_k}{R_k}, \quad \text{where} \quad \theta = (\theta_k) = (\alpha_k \, \eta_k).$$

We divide the proof of Proposition 4.2 in two parts.

PART I: We first prove the correctness of (4.20)–(4.22). We consider the "modified" sequence of blocks produced by the algorithm and show that these expressions do characterize $\mathcal{S}_j$, $\mathcal{M}_j$, and $\mathcal{F}_j$ for this modified sequence.

We drop the tildes '~' in our notation for convenience. Consider an arbitrary j-block project with characteristics $(R_k, C_k, \alpha_k, \eta_k)$, $k = 1, \ldots, j$ such that

$$\mathbb{C}_{k-1} \geq \eta_k \, \mathbb{C}_k, \quad k = 2, 3, \ldots, j. \tag{A.4}$$

According to step 2 in the algorithm, condition (A.4) ensures that there is no block aggregation, as required.

We now use induction on j to prove that for a j-block project satisfying condition (A.4) the sets of threshold prices $\{\mathcal{S}_k\}_{k=1}^j$ and constants $\{\mathcal{M}_k\}_{k=1}^j$ are given by (4.20) and (4.21), and the approximation $\mathcal{F}_j(S)$ satisfies (4.22), that is,

$$\mathcal{F}_j(S) = \left(\theta^\times R\right)_{h,j}^+ S - \left(\alpha^\times C\right)_{h,j}^+ + \mathcal{M}_h \, \alpha_{h,j}^\times \left(\eta_{h,j}^\times\right)^\beta S^\beta, \qquad (A.5)$$

where $h = \max\left\{0 \le k \le j \,|\, \mathcal{S}_k \ge \eta_{k,j}^\times S\right\}$ and $\mathcal{S}_0 = \infty$.

- For $j = 1$ the claimed result follows directly from (4.18).
- Assume that the claimed result is true for some $j - 1$. That is, the values of $\{\mathcal{S}_k\}_{k=1}^{j-1}$ and $\{\mathcal{M}_k\}_{k=1}^{j-1}$ are given by (4.20) and (4.21) and $\mathcal{F}_{j-1}(S)$ is given by (A.5). Combining condition (A.4) and the value of $\mathcal{S}_k$ ($k = 1, \ldots, j - 1$) in (4.20)–(4.21) we conclude that

$$\mathcal{S}_{k-1} \ge \eta_k \, \mathcal{S}_k, \quad k = 2, 3, \ldots, j - 1. \qquad (A.6)$$

- We now prove the result for j. First, we show that $\mathcal{S}_{j-1} \ge \eta_j \, \mathcal{S}_j$. Suppose, by contradiction, that it is not the case, that is, $\mathcal{S}_{j-1} < \eta_j \, \mathcal{S}_j$. If so, condition (A.6) and the fact that $\mathcal{S}_0 = \infty$ imply that there exists a $\hat{k} \le j - 2$ such that

$$\eta_{\hat{k}+1} \, \mathcal{S}_{\hat{k}+1} < \eta_{\hat{k}+1} \, \eta_{\hat{k}+2} \cdots \eta_j \, \mathcal{S}_j \le \mathcal{S}_{\hat{k}} \Leftrightarrow \eta_{\hat{k}+1} \, \mathcal{S}_{\hat{k}+1} < \eta_{\hat{k},j}^\times \, \mathcal{S}_j \le \mathcal{S}_{\hat{k}}.$$
$$(A.7)$$

By the definition of $\mathcal{S}_j$ and $\mathcal{M}_j$ and the value matching and smooth pasting conditions we obtain

$$\mathcal{M}_j \, \mathcal{S}_j^\beta = \mathcal{R}_j \, \mathcal{S}_j - C_j + \alpha_j \, \mathcal{F}_{j-1}(\eta_j \, \mathcal{S}_j),$$

$$\beta \, \mathcal{M}_j \, \mathcal{S}_j^{\beta-1} = \mathcal{R}_j + \alpha_j \, \eta_j \, \mathcal{F}_{j-1}'(\eta_j \, \mathcal{S}_j).$$

Using the induction hypothesis we can replace $\mathcal{F}_{j-1}(\eta_j \, \mathcal{S}_j)$ using (A.5). The value of the index h used in (A.5) to evaluate $\mathcal{F}_{j-1}(\eta_j \, \mathcal{S}_j)$ is exactly equal to $\hat{k}$ in (A.7). In fact, at $S = \eta_j \, \mathcal{S}_j$, h is equal to $\max\left\{0 \le k \le j - 1 \,|\, \mathcal{S}_k \ge \eta_{k,j-1}^\times (\eta_j \, \mathcal{S}_j)\right\}$ or, equivalently, $\max\left\{0 \le k \le j - 1 \,|\, \mathcal{S}_k \ge \eta_{k,j}^\times \mathcal{S}_j\right\}$. This index is $\hat{k}$ by definition. We thus obtain

$$\mathcal{F}_{j-1}(\eta_j \, \mathcal{S}_j) = \left(\theta^\times R\right)_{\hat{k},j-1}^+ \eta_j \, \mathcal{S}_j - \left(\alpha^\times C\right)_{\hat{k},j-1}^+$$

$$+ \mathcal{M}_{\hat{k}} \, \alpha_{\hat{k},j-1}^\times \left(\eta_{\hat{k},j-1}^\times\right)^\beta (\eta_j \, \mathcal{S}_j)^\beta.$$

After some algebra, the value matching and smooth pasting conditions imply

$$\mathcal{S}_j = \left(\frac{\beta}{\beta-1}\right)\frac{(\alpha^\times C)^+_{\hat{k},j}}{(\theta^\times R)^+_{\hat{k},j}}, \tag{A.8}$$

$$\mathcal{M}_j = \mathcal{M}_{\hat{k}}\,\alpha^\times_{\hat{k},j}\,(\eta^\times_{\hat{k},j})^\beta + \left(\frac{(\alpha^\times C)^+_{\hat{k},j}}{\beta-1}\right)\mathcal{S}_j^\beta. \tag{A.9}$$

However, condition (A.4), the induction hypothesis $\mathcal{S}_{\hat{k}+1} = \beta\,C_{\hat{k}+1}/((\beta-1)\,R_{\hat{k}+1})$ and Lemma 4.1 imply

$$\eta^\times_{\hat{k},j}\mathcal{S}_j = \eta_{\hat{k}+1}\,\eta^\times_{\hat{k}+1,j}\mathcal{S}_j$$

$$= \eta_{\hat{k}+1}\,\eta^\times_{\hat{k}+1,j}\left(\frac{\beta}{\beta-1}\right)\frac{(\alpha^\times C)^+_{\hat{k},j}}{(\theta^\times R)^+_{\hat{k},j}}$$

$$\le \eta_{\hat{k}+1}\left(\frac{\beta}{\beta-1}\right)\frac{C_{\hat{k}+1}}{R_{\hat{k}+1}}$$

$$= \eta_{\hat{k}+1}\,\mathcal{S}_{\hat{k}+1}.$$

This inequality contradicts (A.7) and we conclude that $\mathcal{S}_{j-1} \ge \eta_j\,\mathcal{S}_j$, as claimed. This conclusion implies that $\hat{k} = j - 1$ and we can compute the values of $\mathcal{S}_j$ and $\mathcal{M}_j$ replacing $\hat{k}$ by $j-1$ in (A.8) and (A.9), which leads to

$$\mathcal{S}_j = \left(\frac{\beta}{\beta-1}\right)\frac{C_j}{R_j},$$

$$\mathcal{M}_j = \alpha_j\,\eta_j^\beta\,\mathcal{M}_{j-1} + \left(\frac{C_j}{\beta-1}\right)(\mathcal{S}_j)^{-\beta},$$

proving (4.20) and (4.21) as required. Finally, from the condition $\eta_j\,\mathcal{S}_j \le \mathcal{S}_{j-1}$ and the induction hypothesis it is straightforward to show that $\mathcal{F}_j(S)$ is given by (4.22), which completes the induction. The claimed properties hold by the principle of mathematical induction.

PART II: We prove that for an arbitrary j-block project with characteristics $(R_k, C_k, \alpha_k, \eta_k)$, $k = 1, \ldots, j$, the values of $\mathcal{F}_j(S)$ and $\mathcal{S}_j$ are given by (4.20)–(4.22), respectively. The difference with respect to Part I is that we are not assuming that condition (A.4) is satisfied.

We proceed again using induction on the number of blocks, j.

- For $j = 1$ (4.18) directly implies the claimed result.
- Suppose that the claimed result is true for $j - 1$.
- We show that the claimed result holds for j. The induction hypothesis implies that the value of $\mathcal{F}_{j-1}(S)$ is derived using a modified sequence of blocks that satisfies condition (A.4). Furthermore, all that we need to know about the characteristics of blocks $j - 1$, $j - 2$, ..., 1 to compute $\mathcal{F}_j(S)$ is contained in $\mathcal{F}_{j-1}(S)$. Hence, we can assume without loss of generality that the sequence of blocks $j - 1$, $j - 2$, ..., 1 does satisfy condition (A.4), that is,

$$\frac{C_{k-1}}{R_{k-1}} \geq \eta_k \frac{C_k}{R_k}, \quad k = 2, 3, \ldots, j - 1. \tag{A.10}$$

If this condition is also satisfied for block j then the entire sequence satisfies condition (4.18) and the claimed result follows from Part I. Hence, we assume that block j does not satisfy (A.4), that is,

$$\frac{C_{j-1}}{R_{j-1}} < \eta_j \frac{C_j}{R_j}. \tag{A.11}$$

In the remainder of this proof, we apply the algorithm in Proposition 4.2 to a sequence of blocks satisfying conditions (A.10) and (A.11) and verify that the value of $\mathcal{F}_j(S)$ and $\mathcal{S}_j$ are given by (4.20)–(4.22), respectively.

The inequality in (A.11) and condition (A.10) imply that $\tilde{k} = j$ in Step 2 of the algorithm. We let $\tilde{h}$ be the solution to Step 3 in the algorithm, that is,

$$\tilde{h} = \max\{1 \leq h \leq j - 1 : \eta_{h,j}^\times \mathbb{C}_{h+1,j} \leq \mathbb{C}_h\}.$$

Using these values of $\tilde{k}$ and $\tilde{h}$, Step 4 of the algorithm pools together blocks $\tilde{h} + 1$, $\tilde{h} + 2, \ldots, j$ into a single block. Hence, after this first iteration of the algorithm the resulting sequence of blocks has $\tilde{\jmath} = \tilde{h} + 1$ blocks with characteristics

$$\widetilde{R}_k = R_k, \quad \widetilde{C}_k = C_k, \quad \widetilde{\alpha}_k = \alpha_k, \quad \widetilde{\eta}_k = \eta_k, \quad k = 1, \ldots, \tilde{\jmath} - 1$$

and

$$\widetilde{R}_{\tilde{\jmath}} = (\theta^\times R)_{\tilde{h},j}^+, \quad \widetilde{C}_{\tilde{\jmath}} = (\alpha^\times C)_{\tilde{h},j}^+, \quad \widetilde{\alpha}_{\tilde{\jmath}} = \alpha_{\tilde{h},j}^\times, \quad \widetilde{\eta}_{\tilde{\jmath}} = \eta_{\tilde{h},j}^\times.$$

By (A.10) and the definition of $\tilde{h}$, the resulting sequence satisfies

$$\frac{\widetilde{C}_{k-1}}{\widetilde{R}_{k-1}} \geq \widetilde{\eta}_k \frac{\widetilde{C}_k}{\widetilde{R}_k}, \quad k = 2, 3, \ldots, \tilde{\jmath}.$$

Therefore, the algorithm stops after the first iteration. Using this modified sequence, (4.20) and (4.21) lead to

$$
\mathcal{S}_j = \left(\frac{\beta}{\beta-1}\right) \frac{\tilde{C}_{\bar{j}}}{\tilde{R}_{\bar{j}}} = \left(\frac{\beta}{\beta-1}\right) \frac{(\alpha^\times C)^+_{\bar{h},j}}{(\theta^\times R)^+_{\bar{h},j}}.
$$

To verify the correctness of this solution, we compute $\mathcal{S}_j$ using its definition in (4.17). We have

$$
\mathcal{F}_j(S) = \begin{cases} \mathcal{M}_j\, S^\beta, & \text{if } S \le \mathcal{S}_j, \\ R_j\, S - C_j + \alpha_j\, \mathcal{F}_{j-1}(\eta_j\, S), & \text{otherwise.} \end{cases}
$$

Recall that the value of $\mathcal{F}_{j-1}(S)$ is known by the induction hypothesis and it is given by (4.22). This induction hypothesis and, in particular, condition (A.10) imply

$$
\frac{\mathcal{S}_{k-1}}{\eta^\times_{k-1,j-1}} \ge \frac{\mathcal{S}_k}{\eta^\times_{k,j-1}}, \quad k = 2, \dots, j-1.
$$

Suppose that the value of $\mathcal{S}_j$ satisfies

$$
\frac{\mathcal{S}_{\bar{h}+1}}{\eta^\times_{\bar{h}+1,j-1}} < \eta_j\, \mathcal{S}_j \le \frac{\mathcal{S}_{\bar{h}}}{\eta^\times_{\bar{h},j-1}}, \tag{A.12}
$$

for some $\bar{h} \le j-1$. These inequalities and equation (4.22) imply

$$
\mathcal{F}_{j-1}(\eta_j\, \mathcal{S}_j) = (\theta^\times R)^+_{\bar{h},j-1}\, \eta_j\, \mathcal{S}_j - (\alpha^\times C)^+_{\bar{h},j-1}
$$

$$
+ \mathcal{M}_{\bar{h}}\, \alpha^\times_{\bar{h},j-1} \left(\eta^\times_{\bar{h},j-1}\right)^\beta (\eta_j\, \mathcal{S}_j)^\beta.
$$

Using this condition and the value matching and smooth pasting conditions, after some algebra we obtain

$$
\mathcal{S}_j = \left(\frac{\beta}{\beta-1}\right) \frac{(\alpha^\times C)^+_{\bar{h},j}}{(\theta^\times R)^+_{\bar{h},j}}.
$$

For this solution to be consistent with the inequalities in (A.12) we need

$$
\bar{h} = \max\left\{ 1 \le h \le j-1 : \eta_j \left(\frac{\beta}{\beta-1}\right) \frac{(\alpha^\times C)^+_{h,j}}{(\theta^\times R)^+_{h,j}} \frac{\mathcal{S}_h}{\eta^\times_{h,j-1}} \right\}
$$

$$
= \max\{ 1 \le h \le j-1 : \eta^\times_{h,j}\, \mathbb{C}_{h+1,j} \le \mathbb{C}_h \}.
$$

We thus have $\bar{h} = \tilde{h}$, which proves that the value of $\mathcal{S}_j$ in (4.20) and (4.21) is indeed correct. Given that we now know the value of $\mathcal{S}_j$, it is a matter of simple (but tedious) calculations to verify that the values of $\mathcal{M}_j$ and $\mathcal{F}_j(S)$ are exactly those reported in (4.20)–(4.22). The principle of mathematical induction implies that the claimed properties hold.

A.4. *Proof of Proposition 4.3*

We only provide a sketch of the proof. As $K \to \infty$ one can show that the algorithm in Proposition 4.2 produces exactly the same sequence of aggregated blocks for the upper and lower bound approximations. From this observation, it follows that the upper and lower bounds have the same limit: $\lim_{K\to\infty} F_j^{\mathrm{U}}(S,K) = \lim_{K\to\infty} F_j^{\mathrm{L}}(S,K)$. The claimed result follows because $F_j(S,K)$ is bounded above and below by $F_j^{\mathrm{U}}(S,K)$ and $F_j^{\mathrm{L}}(S,K)$, respectively.

A.5. *Proof of Proposition 4.4*

This proof follows directly from (4.25). Indeed, suppose that $F_1^{\mathrm{L}}(S) \geq F_2^{\mathrm{L}}(S)$ for all S. Then, (4.25) implies that $M_j^{\pi_1} \geq M_j^{\pi_2}$ for S sufficiently small (that is, $S \leq \min\{S_j^{*\pi_1}, S_j^{*\pi_2}\}$, where $S_j^{*\pi_1}$ and $S_j^{*\pi_2}$ are the threshold prices under sequences π_1 and π_2, respectively). This inequality is equivalent to

$$\left(\frac{\mathcal{R}_j^{\pi_1}}{\mathcal{R}_j^{\pi_2}}\right)^{\beta} \geq \left(\frac{\mathcal{C}_j^{\pi_1}}{\mathcal{C}_j^{\pi_2}}\right)^{\beta-1}.$$

Similarly, for S sufficiently large $F_1^{\mathrm{L}}(S) \geq F_2^{\mathrm{L}}(S)$ implies that $\mathcal{R}_j^{\pi_1} \geq \mathcal{R}_j^{\pi_2}$. Conversely, assume that the following conditions are satisfied:

$$\mathcal{R}_j^{\pi_1} \geq \mathcal{R}_j^{\pi_2},$$
$$\left(\frac{\mathcal{R}_j^{\pi_1}}{\mathcal{R}_j^{\pi_2}}\right)^{\beta} \geq \left(\frac{\mathcal{C}_j^{\pi_1}}{\mathcal{C}_j^{\pi_2}}\right)^{\beta-1}.$$

Then, (4.25) immediately implies that $F_1^{\mathrm{L}}(S) \geq F_2^{\mathrm{L}}(S)$ for S sufficiently small or sufficiently large. Finally, the validity of the inequality ($F_1^{\mathrm{L}}(S) \geq F_2^{\mathrm{L}}(S)$) extends to all $S \geq 0$ by the convexity of $F_1^{\mathrm{L}}(S)$ and $F_2^{\mathrm{L}}(S)$.

References

[1] Codelco. Yearbook. Available at: http://www.codelco.com/memoria2013/. Accessed in September 2014.

[2] R. Epstein, M. Goic, A. Weintraub, J. Catalan, P. Santibanez, R. Urrutia, R. Cancino, S. Gaete, A. Aguayo, and F. Caro, Optimizing long-term production plans in underground and open-pit copper mines, *Operations Research*. **60**(1), 4–17 (2012).

[3] R. Epstein, R. Morales, J. Serón, and A. Weintraub, Use of OR systems in the Chilean forest industry, *Interfaces*. **29**(1), 7–29 (1999).

[4] T. Baker and L. Ladson, Successive linear programming at Exxon, *Management Science*. **31**(3), 264–274 (1985).

[5] J. Dyer, R. Lund, J. Larsen, and R. Leone, A decision support system for prioritizing oil and gas exploration activities, *Operations Research*. **38**(3), 386–396 (1990).

[6] S. Myers, Finance theory and financial strategy, *Interfaces*. **14**(1), 126–137 (1984).

[7] R. McDonald and D. Siegel, Investment and the valuation of firms when there is an option to shut down, *International Economic Review*. **26**(2), 331–349 (1985).

[8] A. Dixit and R. Pindyck, *Investment under Uncertainty*. Princeton University Press, Princeton, NJ, USA (1994).

[9] L. Trigeorgis, *Real Options: Managerial Flexibility and Strategy in Resource Allocation*. MIT Press, Cambridge, MA, USA (1996).

[10] H. Smit and L. Trigeorgis, *Strategic Investment: Real Options and Games*. Princeton University Press, Princeton, NJ, USA (2012).

[11] N. Aleksandrov, R. Espinoza, and L. Gyurkó, Optimal oil production and the world supply of oil, *Journal of Economic Dynamics and Control*. **37**(7), 1248–1263 (2013).

[12] J. Cherian, J. Patel, and I. Khripko. Optimal extraction of nonrenewable resources when costs cumulate. In (eds.), M. Brennan and L. Trigeorgis, *Project Flexibility, Agency, and Competition: New Developments in the Theory and Application of Real Options*, pp. 224–253. Oxford University Press, New York, NY, USA (1999).

[13] R. Dimitrakopoulos and S. Sabour, Evaluating mine plans under uncertainty: Can the real options make a difference? *Resources Policy*. **32**(3), 116–125 (2007).

[14] R. Lumley and M. Zervos, A model for investing in the natural resource industry with switching costs, *Mathematics of Operations Research*. **26**(4), 637–653 (2001).

[15] R. Pindyck, The optimal exploitation and production of nonrenewable resources, *Journal of Political Economy*. **86**(5), 841–861 (1978).

[16] R. Pindyck, The optimal production of an exhaustible resource when price is exogenous and stochastic, *The Scandinavian Journal of Economics*. **83**(2), 277–288 (1981).

[17] N. Secomandi, Optimal commodity trading with a capacitated storage asset, *Management Science*. **56**(3), 449–467 (2010).

[18] M. Slade, Valuing managerial flexibility: An application of real-option theory to mining investments, *Journal of Environmental Economics and Management*. **41**(2), 193–233 (2001).

[19] F. Black and M. Scholes, The pricing of options and corporate liabilities, *Journal of Political Economy*. **81**(3), 637–654 (1973).

[20] J. Hull, *Options, Futures and Other Derivative Securities*. Pearson Prentice-Hall, Upper Saddle River, NJ, USA (2006).

[21] M. Brennan and E. Schwartz, Evaluating natural resources investments, *Journal of Business.* **58**(2), 135–157 (1985).

[22] G. Cortazar and J. Casassus, Optimal timing of a mine expansion: Implementing a real options model, *The Quarterly Review of Economics and Finance.* **38**(3), 755–769 (1998).

[23] G. Cortazar, E. Schwartz, and J. Casassus, Optimal exploration investments under price and geological-technical uncertainty: A real options model, *R&D Management.* **31**(3), 181–189 (2001).

[24] R. Gibson and E. Schwartz, Stochastic convenience yield and the pricing of oil contingent claims, *The Journal of Finance.* **45**(3), 959–976 (1990).

[25] J. Smith and K. McCardle, Options in the real world: Lessons learned in evaluating oil and gas investments, *Operations Research.* **47**(1), 1–15 (1999).

[26] W. Hustrulid, M. Kuchta, and R. Martin, *Open Pit Mine Planning and Design*, Third edn. CRC Press/Balkema, Leiden, The Netherlands (2013).

[27] C. Alford, M. Brazil, and D. Lee. Optimization in underground mining. In (eds.), A. Weintraub, C. Romero, T. Bjørndal, and R. Epstein, *Handbook on Operations Research in Natural Resources*, pp. 561–578. Springer-Verlag, New York, NY, USA (2007).

[28] K. Lane, *The Economic Definition of Ore: Cut-Off Grades in Theory and Practice.* Mining Journal Books Limited, London, England, UK (1988).

[29] R. Caldentey and S. Mondschein, Policy model for pollution control in the copper industry, including a model for the sulfuric acid market, *Operations Research.* **51**(1), 1–16 (2003).

[30] R. Caro, R. Epstein, P. Santibanez, and A. Weintraub. An integrated approach to the long-term planning process in the copper mining industry. In (eds.), A. Weintraub, C. Romero, T. Bjørndal, and R. Epstein, *Handbook of Operations Research in Natural Resources*, pp. 595–609. Springer-Verlag, New York, NY, USA (2007).

[31] P. Samuelson, Rational theory of warrant pricing, *Industrial Management Review.* **6**(2), 13–39 (1965).

[32] R. Merton, The theory of rational option pricing, *Bell Journal of Economics and Management Science.* **4**(1), 141–183 (1973).

[33] E. Schwartz and J. Smith, Short term variations and long-term dynamics in commodity prices, *Management Science.* **46**(7), 893–911 (2000).

[34] E. Schwartz, The stochastic behavior of commodity prices: Implications for valuation and hedging, *The Journal of Finance.* **52**(3), 923–973 (1997).

[35] M. Gersovitz and C. Paxson. The economics of Africa and the prices of their exports. Technical Report 68, Princeton University, Princeton, NJ, USA (1990).

[36] H. Geman, Energy commodity prices: Is mean-reversion dead? *The Journal of Alternative Investments.* **8**(2), 31–45 (2005).

[37] H. Geman. Mean reversion versus random walk in oil and natural gas prices. In (eds.), M. Fu, R. Jarrow, J. Yen, and R. Elliot, *Advances in Mathematical Finance*, Birkhäuser, Berlin, Germany (2007).

[38] H. Geman, *Commodities and Commodity Derivatives. Modeling and Pricing for Agriculturals, Metals and Energy.* John Wiley & Sons Ltd, Chichester, England, UK (2005).

[39] N. Secomandi and D. Seppi, Real options and merchant operations of energy and other commodities, *Foundations and Trends in Technology, Information and Operations Management.* **6**(3–4), 161–331 (2014).

[40] S. Shreve, *Stochastic Calculus for Finance II: Continuous-Time Models.* Springer-Verlag, New York, NY, USA (2004).

[41] M. Brennan. The price of convenience and the valuation of commodity contingent claims. In (eds.), D. Lund and B. Øksendal, *Stochastic Models and Option Values: Applications to Resources, Environment and Investment Problems*, pp. 33–72, North-Holland, New York, NY, USA (1991).

[42] J. Casassus and P. Collin-Dufresne, Stochastic convenience yield implied from commodity futures and interest rates, *The Journal of Finance.* **60**(5), 2283–2331 (2005).

[43] L. Evans and G. Guthrie. Commodity Price Behavior With Storage Frictions. In (ed.), N. Secomandi, *Real Options In Energy And Commodity Markets*, 3–29. Now Publishers, Boston, MA, USA and World Scientific Publishing, Hackensack, NJ, USA (2017).

[44] R. Caldentey and D. Saure. Network sequencing under market uncertainty. Working Paper, New York University, New York, NY, USA (2015).

[45] P. Pincheira. The price-stock relationship in the copper market, a surprising approach. In *Fourth International Conference Copper 99, Phoenix, AZ*, Minerals, Metals, and Materials Society, Warrendale, PA, USA (1999).

[46] D. Cuoco and J. Cvitanić, Optimal consumption choices for a "large" investor, *Journal of Economic Dynamics and Control.* **22**(3), 401–436 (1998).

[47] R. Frey, Perfect option hedging for a large trader, *Finance and Stochastics.* **2**(2), 115–141 (1998).

[48] B. Felix, O. Woll, and C. Weber, Gas storage valuation under limited market liquidity: An application in Germany, *The European Journal of Finance.* **19**(7), 715–733 (2013).

[49] V. Martínez-de Albéniz and J. M. Vendrell Simón. A capacitated commodity trading model with market power. In (ed.), N. Secomandi, *Real Options In Energy And Commodity Markets*, 31–60. Now Publishers, Boston, MA, USA and World Scientific Publishing, Hackensack, NJ, USA (2017).

[50] P. Protter, *Stochastic Integration and Differential Equations*, Second edn. Springer, Berlin, Germany (2005).

[51] S. Asmussen, *Applied Probability and Queues.* Springer-Verlag, New York, NY, USA (2003).

Chapter 5

Real Option Management
of Hydrocarbon Cracking Operations

Selvaprabu Nadarajah,*,¶ Nicola Secomandi,†,‖
Gary Sowers,‡,** and John M. Wassick§,††

*College of Business Administration, University of Illinois at Chicago
601 South Morgan Street, Chicago, IL 60607, USA

†Tepper School of Business, Carnegie Mellon University
5000 Forbes Avenue, Pittsburgh, PA 15213, USA

‡Light Hydrocarbons Technology Center, The Dow Chemical Company,
21255 LA Hwy 1, Plaquemine, LA 70765, USA

§Supply Chain Center of Excellence, The Dow Chemical Company,
715 East Main Street, Midland, MI 48674, USA

¶selvan@uic.edu
‖ns7@andrew.cmu.edu
**GMSowers@dow.com
††JMWassick@dow.com

Commodity conversion assets play important economic roles. It is well known that the market value of these assets can be maximized by managing them as real options on the prices of their inputs and/or outputs. In particular, when futures on these inputs and outputs are traded, managing such real options, that is, valuing, hedging, and exercising them, is analogous to managing options on such futures, using risk neutral valuation and delta hedging methods. This statement holds because dynamically trading portfolios of these futures and a risk less bond can replicate the cash flows of these assets. This basic principle, which forms the basis of commodity merchant operations, is not always appreciated by managers of commodity conversion assets. Moreover, determining the optimal operational cash flows of such an asset

requires optimizing the asset operating policy. This issue complicates
the real option management of commodity conversion assets. This chapter illustrates the application of this approach to manage a hydrocarbon
cracker, a specific commodity conversion asset, using linear programming and Monte Carlo simulation. The discussion is based on a simplified representation of the operations of this asset. However, the material
presented here has potential applicability to the real option management
of more realistic models of hydrocarbon cracking assets, as well as other
energy and commodity conversion assets.

5.1. Introduction

Basic commodities include agricultural products, such as oranges and coffee, energy sources, such as crude oil and natural gas, and metals, such as
gold and aluminum. Conversion of such commodities generates derived commodities, e.g., chemicals and plastic manufactured from natural gas, and
electricity generated from coal. Commodities and their conversions play
important economic roles [1].

Commodity conversions are performed by assets that transform one or
more commodities into additional commodities. An example is the refining
of oil into products, such as diesel, gasoline, and naphtha. The prices of
these inputs and/or outputs typically evolve in an uncertain fashion, due to
uncertain market dynamics. It follows that commodity conversion assets can
be managed as real options on the prices of their inputs and/or outputs [1–
3], an approach dubbed as commodity merchant operations in [4]. This
approach enables the managers of these assets to maximize the market
value of the assets under their control.

Specifically, when futures are traded on the inputs and/or outputs of
a commodity conversion asset, managing such an asset as a real option is
equivalent to managing an option on these futures; that is, valuing, finan-
cially hedging, and exercising this option using *risk neutral valuation* and
delta hedging methods. (Financial hedging need not be implemented by an
option manager, but it can add value under some conditions, as discussed
later.) This equivalence holds because the conversion asset cash flows can be
replicated by dynamically trading portfolios of such futures and a risk less
bond. This basic principle, which lies at the heart of commodity merchant
operations [4], is not always appreciated by managers of commodity conversion assets. Further, optimization is needed to determine the cash flows

of a commodity conversion asset. This feature adds a layer of complexity to the real option management of such an asset.

Hydrocarbon cracking plays an important economic role; e.g., the United States production of ethylene, the main output of this activity, is currently valued at about \$21 billion a year [5]. This chapter focuses on the real option management of a simplified hydrocarbon cracker (HC). This HC is a specific commodity conversion asset that converts naphtha and propane into ethylene and other co-products. We consider a single conversion time, labeled as T. With some simplifications, this conversion can be modeled as a linear program. The optimal objective function value of this linear program is a deterministic function of the input and output prices at the conversion time, since these prices are known at this time. In other words, the time T market value of this conversion corresponds to the optimal value of this objective function, and is thus known at time T. However, this value is not known with certainty at earlier times, because the naphtha, propane, ethylene, and co-product prices evolve in an uncertain fashion over time. Consequently, the market value of the time T conversion cash flows fluctuates as the current time t approaches the conversion time T.

The basic principle underlying the real option approach to determine the time $t < T$ market value of the time T conversion cash flows is their replication via appropriately constructed portfolios of futures contracts on the HC inputs and outputs and a risk less bond. These portfolios are dynamically traded between times t and T. The time t market value of the conversion is the time t market value of the replicating portfolio. One of the main results underlying the real option approach is that these portfolios need not be explicitly computed to determine this value. In particular, the time t market value of the time T conversion is a special mathematical expectation of the time T conversion cash flows, discounted back to time t using the risk free rate (see, e.g., [6,7]). This expectation is taken under a so-called *risk neutral* probability distribution of the input and output prices. This distribution is a *risk adjusted* version of the distribution that represents the uncertainty in these prices. This approach is the risk neutral valuation method.

Due to credit rationing considerations (see, e.g., [8, §5.4] and references therein), eliminating the fluctuations of the market value of the conversion asset between times t and T can be advantageous. In these situations the replicating portfolios become practically useful. The so called deltas [9, Chapter 18] of the conversion asset market value represent the number of each type of futures contracts that should be held in the replicating portfolio at each given time t before the conversion time T. Shorting these futures at each such time t eliminates the fluctuations of the market value of the time T conversion cash flows. This strategy is the delta hedging method.

This chapter exemplifies the application of risk neutral valuation and delta hedging to manage a simplified HC, based on the integration of linear programming and Monte Carlo simulation techniques, as in [10], the authors of which instead focus on natural gas transportation. It provides numerical examples based on a simple model of the evolution of the prices of the HC inputs and outputs, which we calibrate to market data. The approach presented here requires minor modifications when using more advanced models of commodity price evolution.

Whereas the discussion in this chapter is specific to a given conversion asset, the material presented here has potential relevance for the real option management of more realistic HCs, as well as other energy and commodity conversion assets. We thus hope that this material will be of interest to managers of commodity conversion assets, and improve their understanding of the real option approach for managing such assets. Indeed, HCs are only one example of commodity conversion assets. Other examples include natural gas and oil production facilities [2], electricity transmission capacity [11], natural gas pipelines [10,12], natural gas storage facilities [13–20], liquefied natural gas storage terminals [21], various cross-commodity conversion assets [22–29], and energy swing (acquisition) assets [18,30]. Additional examples and references to the literature are available in [1,3,4,31–34].

The rest of this chapter is organized as follows. Section 5.2 provides an elementary introduction to risk neutral valuation and delta hedging. This section sets the stage for the presentation of our model in Sec. 5.3. We discuss our numerical results in Sec. 5.4. Section 5.5 concludes.

5.2. Elementary Introduction to Risk Neutral Valuation and Delta Hedging

In this section, we provide an elementary illustration of risk neutral valuation and delta hedging, which, as discussed in Sec. 5.1, form the basis of the real option management of commodity and energy conversion assets. In particular, this section provides a road map for the discussion of more advanced models in Sec. 5.3. The ensuing development is in part based on material presented in [4, §2.4] and [7, pp. 383–386].

The current time is 0. The conversion time T is simplified to 1 in this section. We assume that the HC converts only propane into ethylene, which we abbreviate as PR and EL, respectively. The risk less discount factor from time 1 back to time 0 is $\delta \in [0, 1]$. The time 0 price of a propane futures with time 1 delivery is F_{PR}. The time 1 spot price of propane, S_{PR}, which is also the time 1 price of a propane futures with immediate delivery, can be either $S_{\mathrm{PR}}^u := u \cdot F_{\mathrm{PR}}$ with probability p or $S_{\mathrm{PR}}^d := d \cdot F_{\mathrm{PR}}$ with probability $1 - p$, with $0 < d < 1 < u$. For simplicity, we fix the time 1 spot price of ethylene to S_{EL} (the example can be generalized to make this price uncertain, but the notation becomes more involved), and set the marginal conversion cost to 0. The HC conversion yield and input capacity are normalized to 1 unit of ethylene per unit of propane and 1 unit of propane per unit of time, respectively.

The market value of the HC cash flows at time 1 is the value of an optimal solution of the following *trivial* linear program:

$$v := \max_{x}(S_{\mathrm{EL}} - S_{\mathrm{PR}})x \quad \text{s.t. } 0 \leq x \leq 1, \tag{5.1}$$

where x is the amount of propane purchased and processed at time 1. Clearly, it holds that $v = \max\{S_{\mathrm{EL}} - S_{\mathrm{PR}}, 0\}$. Define $v^u := \max\{S_{\mathrm{EL}}^u - S_{\mathrm{PR}}, 0\}$ and $v^d = \max\{S_{\mathrm{EL}}^d - S_{\mathrm{PR}}, 0\}$.

To obtain the time 0 market value of the time 1 HC cash flows, at time 0 we set up a portfolio of N propane futures contracts with time 1 delivery and take a position equivalent to a dollar amount B in a risk less bond, such that the time 1 cash flows of this portfolio match the HC cash flows for each realization of the propane spot price. That is, this portfolio replicates the time 1 HC cash flows. Thus, the time 0 market value of this portfolio is also the one of HC.

To determine the values of N and B, we point out that the time 1 payoff from the futures position N is $(S_{\mathrm{PR}} - F_{\mathrm{PR}})N$, which is called marking to market the position N, and the position B in the bond increases to B/δ in between times 0 and 1. The sought values of N and B can thus be obtained by solving the two following linear equations:

$$(S_{\mathrm{PR}}^u - F_{\mathrm{PR}})N + \frac{B}{\delta} = v^u,$$

$$(S_{\mathrm{PR}}^d - F_{\mathrm{PR}})N + \frac{B}{\delta} = v^d.$$

Substituting the expressions that define S_{PR}^u and S_{PR}^d into these equations yields

$$F_{PR}(u-1)N + \frac{B}{\delta} = v^u,$$

$$F_{PR}(d-1)N + \frac{B}{\delta} = v^d.$$

Defining $q := (1-d)/(u-d)$, the solution to these equations is

$$N = \frac{v^u - v^d}{S_{PR}^u - S_{PR}^d}, \tag{5.2}$$

$$B = \delta \left[qv^u + (1-q)v^d \right]. \tag{5.3}$$

The market value of a futures position is zero when this position is transacted, because a futures contract derives value from changes in its price over time and at time 0 no such change has yet occurred (this argument does not mean that the price of the futures contract is zero at this time). The time 0 market value of this portfolio, V, is thus B as given by (5.3):

$$V = \delta \left[qv^u + (1-q)v^d \right].$$

Remarkably, the time 0 market value of HC does not depend on the probability p. However, this value can be interpreted as an expectation under a modified probability distribution. That is, since q is a number between 0 and 1, it can be interpreted as the modified probability that the propane spot price at time 1, S_{PR}, is equal to S_{PR}^u. Hence, V is the expected value of the cash flows from optimally operating HC at time 1 obtained using the probability mass function $(q, 1-q)$ for the random variable $S_{PR} := (S_{PR}^u, S_{PR}^d)$, discounted back to time 0 using the risk free discount factor δ.

We now discuss the relationship between the probabilities p and q. Define as $\mathbb{E}^p[S_{PR}]$ the expectation at time 0 of the propane spot price at time 1 using the probability mass function $(p, 1-p)$ for the random variable $S_{PR} \equiv (S_{PR}^u, S_{PR}^d)$: $\mathbb{E}^p[S_{PR}] := pS_{PR}^u + (1-p)S_{PR}^d$. We can define the difference $\mathbb{E}^p[S_{PR}] - F_{PR}$ normalized by the spread of the support of the random variable S_{PR} as the percentage risk premium on propane price risk (PRP$_{PR}$):

$$PRP_{PR} := \frac{\mathbb{E}^p[S_{PR}] - F_{PR}}{S_{PR}^u - S_{PR}^d}. \tag{5.4}$$

Define as $\mathbb{E}^q[S_{PR}]$ the expectation at time 0 of the propane spot price at time 1 using the probability mass function $(q, 1-q)$ for the random variable

$S_{PR} \equiv (S_{PR}^u, S_{PR}^d)$: $\mathbb{E}^q[S_{PR}] := qS_{PR}^u + (1-q)S_{PR}^d$. Simple calculations based on the definition of q show that this expectation is equal to the time 0 propane futures price with time 1 delivery, that is, $\mathbb{E}^q[S_{PR}] = F_{PR}$. It then follows that

$$
\begin{aligned}
PRP_{PR} \cdot \left(S_{PR}^u - S_{PR}^d\right) &= \mathbb{E}^p[S_{PR}] - F_{PR} \\
&= \mathbb{E}^p[S_{PR}] - \mathbb{E}^q[S_{PR}] \\
&= pS_{PR}^u + (1-p)S_{PR}^d - \left[qS_{PR}^u + (1-q)S_{PR}^d\right] \\
&= (p-q)\left(S_{PR}^u - S_{PR}^d\right).
\end{aligned}
$$

This sequence of equalities implies that

$$
PRP_{PR} = p - q,
$$

or, equivalently, that

$$
q = p - PRP_{PR}. \tag{5.5}
$$

We can thus interpret the probability q as the original probability p adjusted by the percentage risk premium PRP_{PR}. In this sense, the probability mass function $(q, 1-q) = (p - PRP_{PR}, (1-p) + PRP_{PR}))$ is a *risk adjusted* probability mass function for the random variable S_{PR}.

To summarize, applying risk neutral valuation to determine the time 0 market value of the HC time 1 uncertain cash flows entails the following steps:

(1) Determine the HC cash flows at time 1 by solving the linear program (5.1) for each possible realization of the propane spot price;
(2) Risk adjust the probability mass function $(p, 1-p)$ of the time 1 propane spot price S_{PR};
(3) Compute the expected value of these cash flows using this risk adjusted probability mass function, and discount this value back to time 0 using the risk free discount factor.

These steps generalize directly to more realistic models of hydrocarbon and commodity price evolution, as discussed later in this section and in Sec. 5.3.

As long as risk adjusting the relevant probability distribution does not require determining a replicating portfolio, applying risk neutral valuation does not involve actually constructing this portfolio, even though this portfolio is at the heart of this valuation technique. However, trading in the futures market by shorting the *futures part* of this portfolio eliminates changes in the combined market value of HC and this futures portfolio between times 0 and 1, as now explained. The quantity V is the time 0 combined market value of HC and a portfolio that includes a position $-N$, with N given by (5.2), in propane futures contracts with time 1 delivery (as this futures position is worthless at time 0). The combined time 1 cash flow from operating HC at time 1 and holding this position through time 1 is $v - N(S_{\mathrm{PR}} - F_{\mathrm{PR}})$. We now show that this value is equal to V/δ irrespective of the realization of S_{PR}. That is, *with probability 1* it holds that

$$v - N(S_{\mathrm{PR}} - F_{\mathrm{PR}}) = \frac{V}{\delta}. \tag{5.6}$$

When $S_p = S_{\mathrm{PR}}^u$ it holds that

$$
\begin{aligned}
v^u - N(S_{\mathrm{PR}}^u - F_{\mathrm{PR}}) &= v^u - \left(\frac{v^u - v^d}{S_{\mathrm{PR}}^u - S_{\mathrm{PR}}^d} \right)(S_{\mathrm{PR}}^u - F_{\mathrm{PR}}) \\
&= v^u - (v^u - v^d)\left(\frac{u-1}{u-d} \right) \\
&= \frac{(1-d)v^u + (u-1)v^d}{u-d} \\
&= qv^u + (1-q)v^d \\
&= \frac{V}{\delta}.
\end{aligned}
$$

When $S_p = S_{\mathrm{PR}}^d$ we have

$$
\begin{aligned}
v^d - N(S_{\mathrm{PR}}^d - F_{\mathrm{PR}}) &= v^d - \left(\frac{v^u - v^d}{S_{\mathrm{PR}}^u - S_{\mathrm{PR}}^d} \right)(S_{\mathrm{PR}}^d - F_{\mathrm{PR}}) \\
&= v^d - (v^u - v^d)\left(\frac{d-1}{u-d} \right) \\
&= \frac{(1-d)v^u + (u-1)v^d}{u-d} \\
&= qv^u + (1-q)v^d \\
&= \frac{V}{\delta}.
\end{aligned}
$$

These expressions state that the combined time 0 market value of HC and the futures position $-N$, with N given by (5.2), is equal to V irrespective of the realization of the propane spot price at time 1. That is, *shorting* the futures position $N \equiv (v^u - v^d)/(S_{\mathrm{PR}}^u - S_{\mathrm{PR}}^d)$ perfectly hedges the change in the market value of HC. This method is delta hedging, as the quantity $(v^u - v^d)/(S_{\mathrm{PR}}^u - S_{\mathrm{PR}}^d)$ is known as delta.

To obtain more insight into both delta hedging and the delta label, we emphasize that the quantity $\left(v^u - v^d\right) / \left(S_{\mathrm{PR}}^u - S_{\mathrm{PR}}^d\right)$ is the ratio of the *contemporaneous changes* in the time 1 market value of HC, v, and the spot price of propane, S_{PR}, respectively. Thus, this ratio can be interpreted as a finite difference that approximates the derivative of v with respect to S_{PR}, when S_{PR} is treated as a continuous variable.

Consider now a slightly richer model of the evolution of the propane futures price. That is, consider an intermediate time $1/2$. Between time 0 and $1/2$, F_{PR} can either increase by a factor of u or decrease by a factor of d with probabilities p and $1 - p$, respectively. Contingent on having increased by u or decreased by d at time $1/2$, between times $1/2$ and 1 this resulting price can further increase by u or decrease by d with probabilities p and $1 - p$, respectively. Thus, at time $1/2$ the propane futures price with time 1 delivery can be equal to either $F_{\mathrm{PR}}^u := uF_{\mathrm{PR}}$ or $F_{\mathrm{PR}}^d := dF_{\mathrm{PR}}$, and at time 1 this price, which is also the time 1 propane spot price, can take one of the following values: $S_{\mathrm{PR}}^{u^2} := u^2 F_{\mathrm{PR}}$, $S_{\mathrm{PR}}^{ud} := udF_{\mathrm{PR}}$, and $S_{\mathrm{PR}}^{d^2} := d^2 F_{\mathrm{PR}}$. The market value of the time 1 HC cash flows in each of these three cases is

$$v^{u^2} := \max\left\{ S_{\mathrm{PR}}^{u^2} - S_{\mathrm{EL}}, 0 \right\},$$

$$v^{ud} := \max\left\{ S_{\mathrm{PR}}^{ud} - S_{\mathrm{EL}}, 0 \right\},$$

$$v^{d^2} := \max\left\{ S_{\mathrm{PR}}^{d^2} - S_{\mathrm{EL}}, 0 \right\}.$$

It is possible to extend the previous analysis to the current setting, and show that the time 0 market value of the time 1 HC cash flows now is

$$V = \delta \left[q^2 v^{u^2} + 2q(1 - q)v^{ud} + (1 - q)^2 v^{d^2} \right].$$

This value is again obtained by applying risk neutral valuation, since V is the expectation of the random variable $v := (v^{u^2}, v^{ud}, v^{d^2})$ taken using the risk adjusted probability mass function $(q^2, 2q(1 - q), (1 - q)^2)$ and discounted back to time 0 at the risk free discount factor δ. Moreover, the time 0 delta is $(v^u - v^d)/(S_{\mathrm{PR}}^u - S_{\mathrm{PR}}^d)$, with v^u and v^d *redefined* as

$$v^u := \sqrt{\delta} \left[qv^{u^2} + (1 - q)v^{ud} \right],$$

$$v^d := \sqrt{\delta} \left[qv^{ud} + (1 - q)v^{d^2} \right].$$

These redefinitions are evidently based on risk neutral valuation. Delta hedging involves shorting the time 0 delta at time 0 and rebalancing the corresponding futures position at time $1/2$. In particular, the time $1/2$ delta is $(v^{u^2} - v^{ud})/(S_{\mathrm{PR}}^{u^2} - S_{\mathrm{PR}}^{ud})$ when the propane futures price with time 1 delivery is equal to F_{PR}^u; it is equal to $(v^{ud} - v^{d^2})/(S_{\mathrm{PR}}^{ud} - S_{\mathrm{PR}}^{d^2})$ when this price is equal to F_{PR}^d. Rebalancing the futures position at time $1/2$ involves changing the futures position established at time 0 to equal the negative of these deltas in these respective cases at time $1/2$.

Suppose that we keep adding additional intermediate times in between times 0 and 1, e.g., time $1/4$ between times 0 and $1/2$, time $3/4$ between times $1/2$ and 1, and so on. When the number of such times goes to infinity, the process for the propane futures price with time 1 delivery converges (in some sense) to a continuous time and space stochastic process [35]. We use the suffix (t) to indicate quantities associated with this process at time $t \in [0,1]$. Moreover, the time 0 market value of HC, $V(0)$, can be differentiated with respect to the time 0 propane futures price with time 1 delivery, $F_{\mathrm{PR}}(0)$, to obtain the time 0 delta Delta(0):

$$\mathrm{Delta}(0) := \frac{\partial V(0)}{\partial F_{\mathrm{PR}}(0)}.$$

At each subsequent time t in the interval $(0,1)$ the delta of the HC time t market value, $V(t)$, is given by $\mathrm{Delta}(t) := \partial V(t)/\partial F_{\mathrm{PR}}(t)$, where $F_{\mathrm{PR}}(t)$ is the time t price of the propane futures with time 1 delivery. This discussion explains the label delta given to the futures replicating positions. Further, delta hedging consists of continuously shorting $\mathrm{Delta}(t)$ from time 0 up to, but excluding, time 1.

To summarize, implementing delta hedging when using a continuous time and space model of the propane futures price evolution involves the following steps:

(1) A time 0, determine the HC market value $V(0)$ using risk neutral valuation, compute Delta(0), and take a position equal to $-\mathrm{Delta}(0)$ in propane futures with time 1 delivery.
(2) At each subsequent time t before the conversion time, that is, $t \in (0,1)$, determine the HC market value $V(t)$ using risk neutral valuation, compute Delta(t), and rebalance the futures position by making it equal to $-\mathrm{Delta}(t)$.
(3) At the conversion time 1, close the resulting futures position.

In practice, continuous rebalancing of the futures portfolio is not possible, and rebalancing is thus performed a finite number of times.

These steps generalize directly to the case when the HC market value depends on more prices than the propane spot price. In this case, the important issues that need to be resolved when applying risk neutral valuation and delta hedging at time t are

(1) Risk adjusting the distribution of the relevant futures prices;
(2) Determining the time 1 HC conversion cash flows;
(3) Computing the time t discounted expectation of these cash flows using this risk adjusted distribution; and
(4) Computing the time t delta positions.

We discuss these issues in a more general setting in Sec. 5.3.

5.3. Model

In this section, we present our model for the real option management of a simplified HC asset. This model integrates a conversion model, a price model, a risk neutral valuation model, and a delta hedging model, which we discuss in Secs. 5.3.1–5.3.4, respectively. Our model exemplifies the application of the modeling framework discussed at the end of Sec. 5.2.

Throughout this section, T denotes the conversion time. Although we use the suffix (t) to indicate the dependence of a given quantity on time t, we omit this suffix when this dependence is obvious from the context.

5.3.1. *Conversion Model*

Our simplified HC converts naphtha and propane into ethylene and co-products. The co-products are benzene, crude C4s, fuel oil, hydrogen, natural gas, propylene, and pygas. Table 5.1 summarizes these inputs, outputs, and their abbreviations. We include the input and output abbreviations in sets $\mathcal{I}$ and $\mathcal{J}$, respectively.

Conversion decisions are made with full knowledge of the realized spot prices of these commodities at time T, which we take as realized futures prices. Since futures contracts entail delivery/receipt of given daily quantities, we assume that HC operates in the same manner on every day of the month that starts at time T. In reality, one could make the conversion model more granular, e.g., by allowing four weekly conversion decisions

Table 5.1 Simplified HC inputs, outputs, and their abbreviations.

	Abbreviation
Input	
Naphtha	NA
Propane	PR
Output	
Benzene	BN
Crude C4s	C4
Ethylene	EL
Fuel Oil	FO
Hydrogen	HY
Natural Gas	NG
Propylene	PL
Pygas	PG

within a month using four weekly "spot" price realizations. We denote by S_i and S_j the spot prices of input $i \in \mathcal{I}$ and output $j \in \mathcal{J}$ at time T. We assume here that futures contracts and liquid spot markets exist for each co-product. This assumption is not entirely realistic. At the beginning of Sec. 5.3.2 we discuss how we deal with this assumption to make our model operational.

We let $y_{i,j} \in [0,1]$ be the yield of product $j \in \mathcal{J}$ obtained from cracking one unit of input $i \in \mathcal{I}$. We denote by c_i the energy cost in dollars per pound (\$/lb) of cracking one unit of input i. We define the per unit variable margin obtained from cracking one unit of input $i \in \mathcal{I}$ as

$$M_i = \left(\sum_{j \in \mathcal{J}} y_{i,j} S_j \right) - (S_i + c_i).$$

We let the decision variable x_i represent the flow rate of input i, the parameter Q_i the processing capacity on the flow rate of input i, and the parameter $Q^{\mathcal{I}}$ the processing capacity on the sum of the flow rates of the two inputs, that is, naphtha and propane. This decision variable and these parameters are measured in pounds per hour (lbs/hr). The market value of the HC cash flows at the conversion time T is

$$v := \max_x \sum_{i \in \mathcal{I}} M_i x_i, \tag{5.7}$$

$$\text{s.t. } x_i \leq Q_i, \ \forall i \in \mathcal{I}, \tag{5.8}$$

$$\sum_{i \in \mathcal{I}} x_i \leq Q^{\mathcal{I}}, \tag{5.9}$$

$$x_i \geq 0, \ \forall i \in \mathcal{I}. \tag{5.10}$$

That is, v is the optimal solution value of a linear program, which extends the linear program (5.1) discussed in Sec. 5.2. The objective function (5.7) maximizes the total cracking margin, measured in \$/hr (it can be scaled to a monthly figure accordingly). Constraints (5.8) restrict the flow rate of each input to be no more than its associated processing capacity. The constraint (5.9) limits the sum of the two inputs' flow rates to be no more than the total processing capacity. Constraints (5.10) are non-negativity restrictions on each input flow rate.

It is easy to see that an optimal solution $(x^*_{\mathrm{NA}}, x^*_{\mathrm{PR}})$ to the linear program (5.7)–(5.10) is as follows:

(1) If $\max\{M_{\mathrm{NA}}, M_{\mathrm{PR}}\} \leq 0$, then $x^*_{\mathrm{NA}} = x^*_{\mathrm{PR}} = 0$.
(2) If $\max\{M_{\mathrm{NA}}, M_{\mathrm{PR}}\} > 0$ and $M_{\mathrm{PR}} \geq M_{\mathrm{NA}}$, then $x^*_{\mathrm{PR}} = \min\{Q_{\mathrm{PR}}, Q^{\mathcal{I}}\}$; further, if $M_{\mathrm{NA}} > 0$, then $x^*_{\mathrm{NA}} = \min\{Q_{\mathrm{NA}}, Q^{\mathcal{I}} - x^*_{\mathrm{PR}}\}$, otherwise, $x^*_{\mathrm{NA}} = 0$.
(3) If $\max\{M_{\mathrm{NA}}, M_{\mathrm{PR}}\} > 0$ and $M_{\mathrm{NA}} > M_{\mathrm{PR}}$, swap the indices NA and PR in the optimal solution stated in the previous case.

5.3.2. *Price Model*

Reasonably liquid futures and spot markets exist for ethylene, naphtha, natural gas, propylene, and propane. We include the abbreviations of these commodities in the set $\mathcal{L} := \{\mathrm{EL}, \mathrm{NA}, \mathrm{NG}, \mathrm{PL}, \mathrm{PR}\}$. However, there are either no futures markets or liquid forward markets, as well as spot markets for the following co-products: hydrogen, crude C4s, benzene, pygas, and fuel oil. We thus use the price of naphtha as a proxy for the prices of benzene, crude C4s, fuel oil, and pygas, and the price of natural gas as a proxy for the price of hydrogen. Table 5.2 summarizes our proxying approach.

Table 5.2   Price proxies and associated outputs.

Price Proxy	Output
Naphtha	Benzene, Crude C4s, Fuel Oil, Pygas
Natural Gas	Hydrogen

For simplicity, we model the evolution of the futures prices for the commodities in set $\mathcal{L}$ using correlated one factor models, as in [10]. Let, $\sigma_l \exp\left[-\kappa_l(T-t)\right]$ be the volatility function of the price of the futures contract with maturity T for commodity $l \in \mathcal{L}$ (the parameters σ_l and κ_l are discussed after expression (5.13)). Denote by $dZ_l(t)$ the increment of a standard Brownian motion for commodity l. The *risk neutral* dynamics of the maturity T futures price for commodity l, $F(t)$, are described by the following stochastic differential equation:

$$\frac{dF_l(t)}{F_l(t)} = \sigma_l e^{-\kappa_l(T-t)} dZ_l(t). \tag{5.11}$$

Moreover, the standard Brownian motion increments for each pair of distinct commodities l and $l' \in \mathcal{L}$ have instantaneous correlation coefficient $\rho_{l,l'}$, that is,

$$dZ_l(t)dZ_{l'}(t) = \rho_{l,l'}dt. \tag{5.12}$$

Under the price model (5.11)–(5.12), conditional on the time t vector of futures prices $F(t) := (F_l(t), l \in \mathcal{L})$, the risk neutral distribution of the natural logarithm of the time T vector of futures prices $F(T) := (F_l(T), l \in \mathcal{L})$ is jointly normal. In particular, the mean of $\ln F_l(T)$ is

$$\ln F_l(t) - \frac{[1 - e^{-2\kappa_l(T-t)}]\sigma^2}{4\kappa_l},$$

the variance of $\ln F_l(T)$ is

$$\frac{[1 - e^{-2\kappa_l(T-t)}]\sigma^2}{2\kappa_l},$$

and the covariance of $\ln F_l(T)$ and $\ln F_{l'}(T)$ is

$$\rho_{l,l'}\sigma_l\sigma_{l'} \frac{[1 - e^{(\kappa_l+\kappa_{l'})(T-t)}]}{\kappa_l + \kappa_{l'}}.$$

As discussed in [30], the futures price model (5.11) can be obtained by assuming that the dynamics of the natural logarithm of the spot price $S_l(t)$, denoted by $X_l(t)$, are governed by a mean-reverting process. (When price seasonality is modeled using a commodity specific deterministic function of time, as in [30], $X_l(t)$ is the natural logarithm of the deseasonalized spot price of commodity l, that is, $S_l(t)$ divided by the seasonality function of commodity l evaluated at time t. We do not model seasonality in this chapter.) The mean-reverting process for $X_l(t)$ is

$$dX_l(t) = \kappa_l \left[\xi_l^* - X_l(t)\right] dt + \sigma_l dZ_l(t), \tag{5.13}$$

where the parameter ξ_l^* is the *risk adjusted* level toward which $X_l(t)$ reverts to. Thus, we can interpret the parameters σ_l and κ_l in (5.13) as the volatility and speed of mean reversion, respectively, of $X_l(t)$. Moreover, the term $dZ_l(t)$ in (5.13) is the same term that appears in (5.11); that is, the spot and futures prices of a given commodity are subject to the same random shocks.

The price model (5.13) corresponds to a risk adjusted version of a mean-reverting model that governs the "actual" dynamics of the natural logarithm of the spot price. Such mean-reverting process is identical to (5.13), except that the parameter ξ_l^* is replaced with the parameter ξ_l. The relationship between these two parameters is

$$\xi_l^* = \xi_l - \lambda_l,$$

where λ_l is the risk premium associated with the (natural logarithm of the) price of commodity l [36,37]. This risk adjustment is conceptually analogous to the adjustment for risk in (5.5) of the probability p into q in the spot price model of Sec. 5.2.

It practice, futures prices are observed in the market. However, it is sometimes useful for analysis to be able to generate futures prices for a particular maturity starting from spot price information. Under model (5.13), this task can be accomplished using the following formula (see, e.g., [30]):

$$\ln F_l(t) = X_l(t)e^{-\kappa_l(T-t)} + \xi_l^*[1 - e^{-\kappa_l(T-t)}]$$
$$+ \frac{[1 - e^{-2\kappa_l(T-t)}]\sigma_l^2}{4\kappa_l}. \tag{5.14}$$

When seasonality is relevant, then one should add to this value of $\ln F_l(t)$ the natural logarithm of the seasonality function evaluated at time T.

5.3.3. *Risk Neutral Valuation Model*

We discuss the application of risk neutral valuation to estimate the time 0 market value of the time T HC conversion cash flows. Doing so at a later time t is analogous.

We redefine δ as $\exp(-rT)$, with r the risk free discount rate. We denote by $\mathbb{E}$ expectation computed using the *risk adjusted* distribution of the natural logarithm of the vector of time T futures prices, $\ln F(T)$, conditional on the time 0 vector of futures prices, $F(0)$, under price model (5.11)–(5.12).

By risk neutral valuation, the value that we seek is

$$V = \delta\mathbb{E}[v], \tag{5.15}$$

where v is the optimal objective function value of the linear program (5.7)–(5.10), a random variable as of time 0. To be precise, v is the optimal objective function value of the linear program (5.7)–(5.10) formulated by using the proxying approach explained in Sec. 5.3.2. That is, let, $\mathcal{J}(\mathrm{NA})$ be the set of labels for the outputs whose prices are proxied by the price of naphtha: $\mathcal{J}(\mathrm{NA}) := \{\mathrm{BN}, \mathrm{C4}, \mathrm{FO}, \mathrm{PG}\}$. Then, in (5.7) we replace the price S_j for each $j \in \mathcal{J}(\mathrm{NA})$ with the price S_{NA}. In (5.7) we also replace the price S_{HY} with the price S_{NG}.

We estimate V by integrating linear programming and Monte Carlo simulation to estimate the expectation in (5.15). Given the time 0 vector of futures prices $F(0)$, we generate a given number of samples of the time T vector of futures prices $F(T)$. We do this by Monte Carlo sampling from the distribution of $\ln F(T)$ conditional on $F(0)$. The vector $F(T)$ is identical to the time T vector of spot prices $S(T) := (S_l(T), l \in \mathcal{L})$. For each such sample, we solve the linear program (5.7)–(5.10) to obtain a sample of the market value of the HC cash flows at time T, that is, v. We then average these sample market values, and discount the resulting average back to time 0 using the risk free discount factor δ.

5.3.4. *Delta Hedging Model*

Delta hedging involves shorting the deltas of the HC market value at a given set of trading times before the conversion time. We thus focus on the computation of these deltas at these trading times. To simplify the discussion we focus on time 0. However, our results extend directly when time 0 is replaced with any other time t in the interval $(0, T)$.

The quantity of interest is

$$\mathrm{Delta}_l \equiv \frac{\partial V}{\partial F_l}, \ \forall l \in \mathcal{L}.$$

An expression for this quantity can be obtained by applying the pathwise derivative method [38, Chapter 7] as follows

$$\begin{aligned} \mathrm{Delta}_l &= \frac{\partial V}{\partial F_l} \\ &= \frac{\partial \delta\mathbb{E}[v]}{\partial F_l} \end{aligned}$$

$$= \delta\mathbb{E}\left[\frac{\partial v}{\partial F_l}\right]$$

$$= \delta\mathbb{E}\left[\frac{\partial v}{\partial S_l}\frac{\partial S_l}{\partial F_l}\right], \tag{5.16}$$

where the second equality holds under some technical conditions [38, Chapter 7], which can be verified to hold in our application using arguments similar to the ones used in [10, proof of Proposition 4], and the last equality follows from the chain rule.

The first partial derivative in (5.16) can be determined from an optimal solution of the linear program (5.7)–(5.10). Let x_i^* be the component of an optimal solution of this linear program corresponding to input i. Given our price proxying approach, the optimal objective function value of this linear program, v, can be written as

$$v = \sum_{i\in\mathcal{I}} M_i x_i^*$$

$$= \left[\left(\sum_{j\in\mathcal{J}(\mathrm{NA})} y_{\mathrm{NA},j}S_{\mathrm{NA}}\right) + y_{\mathrm{NA,HY}}S_{\mathrm{NG}} + \left(\sum_{j\in\mathcal{J}\setminus\{\mathcal{J}(\mathrm{NA})\cup\{\mathrm{HY}\}\}} y_{\mathrm{NA},j}S_j\right)\right.$$

$$\left. - (S_{\mathrm{NA}} + c_{\mathrm{NA}})\right]x_{\mathrm{NA}}^* + \left[\left(\sum_{j\in\mathcal{J}(\mathrm{NA})} y_{\mathrm{PR},j}S_{\mathrm{NA}}\right) + y_{\mathrm{PR,HY}}S_{\mathrm{NG}}\right.$$

$$\left. + \left(\sum_{j\in\mathcal{J}\setminus\{\mathcal{J}(\mathrm{NA})\cup\{\mathrm{HY}\}\}} y_{\mathrm{PR},j}S_j\right) - (S_{\mathrm{PR}} + c_{\mathrm{PR}})\right]x_{\mathrm{PR}}^*.$$

It then follows that

$$\frac{\partial v}{\partial S_l} = \begin{cases} -x_l^*, & l = \mathrm{PR}, \\ \left[\left(\sum_{j\in\mathcal{J}(\mathrm{NA})} y_{l,j}\right) - 1\right]x_l^* + (\sum_{j\in\mathcal{J}(\mathrm{NA})} y_{\mathrm{PR},j})x_{\mathrm{PR}}^*, & l = \mathrm{NA}, \\ \sum_{i\in\mathcal{I}} y_{i,l}x_i^*, & l \in \{\mathrm{EL, PL}\}, \\ \sum_{i\in\mathcal{I}}(y_{i,\mathrm{HY}} + y_{i,\mathrm{NG}})x_i^*, & l = \mathrm{NG}. \end{cases} \tag{5.17}$$

The second partial derivative in (5.16) can be expressed in closed form. First, it is well known (see, e.g., [10, Section B in the Online Appendix]) that

$$S_l = F_l \exp\left\{ -\sigma^2 \left[\frac{1 - \exp(-2\kappa T)}{4\kappa} \right] + \sigma \sqrt{\frac{1 - \exp(-2\kappa T)}{2\kappa}} W \right\},$$

where W is a standard normal random variable — S_l and F_l here stand for $S_l(T)$ and $F_l(0)$. Abbreviating by $\exp\{\cdot\}$ the term that multiplies F_l in this expression, it follows that

$$\frac{\partial S_l}{\partial F_l} = \frac{\partial F_l \exp\{\cdot\}}{\partial F_l} = \exp\{\cdot\} = \frac{F_l \exp\{\cdot\}}{F_l} = \frac{S_l}{F_l}. \qquad (5.18)$$

Substituting (5.17) and (5.18) into (5.16) yields

$$\text{Delta}_l = \begin{cases} -\dfrac{\delta \mathbb{E}[S_l x_l^*]}{F_l}, & l = \text{PR}, \\[2ex] \dfrac{\delta\{[(\sum_{j \in \mathcal{J}(\text{NA})} y_{l,j}) - 1]\mathbb{E}[S_l x_l^*] + (\sum_{j \in \mathcal{J}(\text{NA})} y_{\text{PR},j})\mathbb{E}[S_l x_{\text{PR}}^*]\}}{F_l}, & l = \text{NA}, \\[2ex] \dfrac{\delta \mathbb{E}[S_l (\sum_{i \in \mathcal{I}} y_{i,l} x_i^*)]}{F_l}, & l \in \{\text{EL}, \text{PL}\}, \\[2ex] \dfrac{\delta\{\sum_{i \in \mathcal{I}} (y_{i,\text{HY}} + y_{i,\text{NG}})\mathbb{E}[S_l x_i^*]\}}{F_l}, & l = \text{NG}. \end{cases}$$

$$(5.19)$$

Expression (5.19) can be used to easily estimate the quantity Delta$_l$ by Monte Carlo simulation, *simultaneously* with the estimation of the time 0 HC market value, V.

5.4.   Numerical Results

In this section, we illustrate the application to data of the model discussed in Sec. 5.3. We discuss our price model calibration results in Sec. 5.4.1, and our valuation and hedging results in Sec. 5.4.2.

5.4.1.   *Price Model Calibration*

Recall that our price model involves the following commodities in set $\mathcal{L}$: ethylene, naphtha, natural gas, propane, and propylene. We calibrate this model by applying the method discussed in [10] to historical spot prices observed from January 2008 to December 2010 for each of these commodities. This method is based on simple linear regression and is detailed in [32, §3.2.2]. This calibration yields estimates of the speed of mean reversion, long term mean-reverting level, and volatility parameters, κ_l, ξ_l^*, and σ_l, for each commodity $l \in \mathcal{L}$, as well as the instantaneous correlation coefficient, $\rho_{l,l'}$, for any two distinct commodities $l, l' \in \mathcal{L}$ ($\rho_{l,l} := 1$ for each $l \in \mathcal{L}$).

Table 5.3 Results of the price model calibration: parameter estimates ($\hat{\cdot}$) and their standard errors (in parenthesis).

Commodity (l)	$\hat{\kappa}_l$	$\hat{\xi}_l$	$\hat{\sigma}_l$	$\hat{\rho}_{l,l'}$ Commodity (l')			
				NA	NG	PR	PL
EL	1.659	−0.986	0.681	0.366	0.135	0.351	0.370
	(1.053)	(0.5162)	(0.055)	(0.078)	(0.069)	(0.100)	(0.097)
NA	1.682	−1.231	0.626		0.117	0.0642	0.548
	(1.261)	(0.4789)	(0.039)		(0.081)	(0.064)	(0.092)
NG	2.657	−2.186	0.948			0.358	−0.003
	(1.618)	(0.8070)	(0.104)			(0.076)	(0.077)
PR	1.281	−3.027	0.496				0.371
	(1.155)	(0.7816)	(0.026)				(0.092)
PL	0.952	−0.714	0.605				
	(0.798)	(0.5560)	(0.120)				

Table 5.3 displays the resulting parameter estimates and their standard errors. Comparing the reported estimates and standard errors indicates that the volatilities and instantaneous correlations coefficients are estimated more precisely than the speeds of mean reversion and long term mean-reversion levels. Except for a marginally negative estimate of the instantaneous correlation coefficient for natural gas and propylene, the estimates of the other instantaneous correlations coefficients are positive.

Estimation of each risk adjusted long term mean-reverting parameter, ξ_l^*, which is needed to apply risk neutral valuation and delta hedging, would entail the use of futures prices. Since we lacked such prices at the time when this study was performed, we proceed under the *simplifying* assumption of zero risk premium for each considered commodity, that is, $\xi_l^* \equiv \xi_l$ for each $l \in \mathcal{L}$.

5.4.2. Valuation and Hedging

We set the valuation date (time 0) to January 25, 2008, and the conversion date (time T) to six months later, that is, July 25, 2008. The operational parameters that characterize the simplified HC are not reported here for confidentiality reasons. We estimate all the relevant futures prices based on spot prices using formula (5.14). We use 100,000 time T spot price samples for valuation purposes.

It is useful to decompose the time 0 HC market value, V, into two components, its intrinsic and extrinsic values, V^{I} and V^{E}, respectively.

The intrinsic value is the time 0 market value of the HC cash flows obtained under the assumption that the conversion decisions are made at time 0 only with knowledge of the time 0 futures prices for delivery on the conversion date, time T. Specifically, the intrinsic value is the optimal solution value of the following linear program:

$$
\begin{aligned}
V^{\mathrm{I}} := \max_x \Bigg\{ &\left[\sum_{j \in \mathcal{J}(\mathrm{NA})} y_{\mathrm{NA},j} F_{\mathrm{NA}}(0) \right] + y_{\mathrm{NA,HY}} F_{\mathrm{NG}}(0) \\
&+ \left[\sum_{j \in \mathcal{J} \setminus \{\mathcal{J}(\mathrm{NA}) \cup \{\mathrm{HY}\}\}} y_{\mathrm{NA},j} F_j(0) \right] - [F_{\mathrm{NA}}(0) + c_{\mathrm{NA}}] \Bigg\} x_{\mathrm{NA}} \\
&+ \Bigg\{ \left[\sum_{j \in \mathcal{J}(\mathrm{NA})} y_{\mathrm{PR},j} F_{\mathrm{NA}}(0) \right] + y_{\mathrm{PR,HY}} F_{\mathrm{NG}}(0) \\
&+ \left[\sum_{j \in \mathcal{J} \setminus \{\mathcal{J}(\mathrm{NA}) \cup \{\mathrm{HY}\}\}} y_{\mathrm{PR},j} F_j(0) \right] - [F_{\mathrm{PR}}(0) + c_{\mathrm{PR}}] \Bigg\} x_{\mathrm{PR}},
\end{aligned}
$$

$$\tag{5.20}$$

$$\text{s.t. } (5.8)-(5.10). \tag{5.21}$$

The extrinsic value is obtained by subtracting the intrinsic value from the HC market value V:

$$
V^{\mathrm{E}} := V - V^{\mathrm{I}}.
$$

It is thus the part of the HC market value attributable to uncertainty in the commodity prices.

The computed intrinsic value, V^{I}, and the estimated extrinsic value, $\hat{V}^{\mathrm{E}}$, are roughly 97.58% and 2.42%, respectively, of the estimated time 0 HC market value, $\hat{V}$ (the standard error of $\hat{V}$ is 0.11% of $\hat{V}$). Thus, the contribution of price uncertainty to the HC market value is small. This finding is due to the combination of two reasons. First, the estimated time 0 HC market value obtained by ignoring the possibility of converting naphtha is 94.86% of the estimated time 0 HC market value. That is, there is a 5.14% loss in market value by cracking propane only, rather than both naphtha and propane: even though ignoring naphtha as an input to the conversion entails a possibly substantial flow rate reduction, the resulting monetary loss is much smaller because the margin from converting naphtha is small.

Second, the *intrinsic* propane conversion margin, that is, the quantity

$$\left[\sum_{j\in\mathcal{J}(\mathrm{NA})} y_{\mathrm{PR},j}F_{\mathrm{NA}}(0)\right] + y_{\mathrm{PR,HY}}F_{\mathrm{NG}}(0)$$

$$+ \left[\sum_{j\in\mathcal{J}\setminus\{\mathcal{J}(\mathrm{NA})\cup\{\mathrm{HY}\}\}} y_{\mathrm{PR},j}F_{j}(0)\right] - [F_{\mathrm{PR}}(0) + c_{\mathrm{PR}}]$$

is positive and large. Hence, there are little chances of observing a negative realization of the propane conversion margin at time T, that is, a negative value of the quantity

$$\left(\sum_{j\in\mathcal{J}(\mathrm{NA})} y_{\mathrm{PR},j}S_{\mathrm{NA}}\right) + y_{\mathrm{PR,HY}}S_{\mathrm{NG}}$$

$$+ \left(\sum_{j\in\mathcal{J}\setminus\{\mathcal{J}(\mathrm{NA})\cup\{\mathrm{HY}\}\}} y_{\mathrm{PR},j}S_{j}\right) - (S_{\mathrm{PR}} + c_{\mathrm{PR}}).$$

The resulting extrinsic value is consequently small.

However, this conclusion does not mean that there is little variability in the time T market value of the HC conversion cash flows. This phenomenon is illustrated in Fig. 5.1, which displays the empirical probability mass function of these sample conversion market values discounted to time 0, δv, relative to the time 0 HC market value estimate, $\hat{V}$. Delta hedging can reduce (ideally eliminate) this variability. We implement delta hedging by shorting at time 0 the deltas computed at this time for the commodities in set $\mathcal{L}$, and subsequently recomputing these deltas and rebalancing the futures positions at each of a finite number of times in the interval $(0, T)$.

We denote by t_k a delta rebalancing time. We indicate by ω a sample path of futures price realizations during the time interval $[0, T]$. Focusing on commodity l, we let $\mathrm{Delta}_l(t)(\omega)$ and $F_l(t)(\omega)$ be the delta and futures price computed and realized, respectively, at time t along sample path ω (more precisely we estimate $\mathrm{Delta}_l(t)(\omega)$ rather than computing it exactly; we do not show this fact in our notation to avoid using the cumbersome $\widehat{\mathrm{Delta}_l(t)(\omega)}$ notation). The kth delta hedging cash flow, h_k, arises from marking-to-market the negative of the delta positions taken at time t_{k-1}, that is, multiplying the delta hedging position $-\mathrm{Delta}_l(t_{k-1})$ for each commodity l by its futures price change from time t_{k-1} to time t_k, $F_l(t_k) - F_l(t_{k-1})$, and cumulating the resulting cash flows — this computation is analogous to how a futures position cash flow is determined in

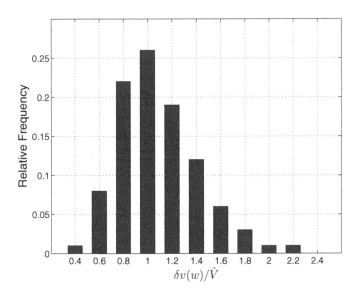

Fig. 5.1 Empirical probability mass function of the discounted sample time T HC market values relative to the time 0 HC market value estimate $(\delta v(\omega)/\hat{V})$.

Sec. 5.2. Specifically, the kth delta hedging cash flow along sample path ω is defined as

$$h_k(\omega) := -\sum_{l \in \mathcal{L}} \text{Delta}_l(t_{k-1})(\omega) \left[F_l(t_k) - F_l(t_{k-1})\right](\omega).$$

We include in set $\mathcal{K} := \{1, \ldots, K\}$ the labels of K dates in the time interval $(0, T]$ when these delta hedging cash flows are generated. That is, we rebalance the deltas at times t_1 through t_{K-1} and time t_K corresponds to the conversion date T. The time 0 market value of the total hedging cash flows along sample path ω is

$$H(\omega) := \sum_{k \in \mathcal{K}} \exp(-rt_k)h_k(\omega).$$

If delta hedging were performed continuously, and $H(\omega)$ were redefined correspondingly, it would hold that

$$H(\omega) + \delta v(\omega) \equiv V \tag{5.22}$$

on (almost) every sample path ω — this equality is analogous to the equality (5.6) in the spot price model of Sec. 5.2. Since we only rebalance the deltas a finite number of times and we estimate the deltas, this equality only holds approximately in our simulation.

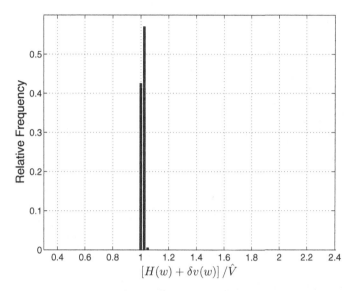

Fig. 5.2 Empirical probability mass function of the sum of the discounted cumulative hedging cash flows (H) and the discounted time T HC market values relative to the time 0 HC market value estimate ($[H(\omega) + \delta v(\omega)]/\hat{V}$) with weekly rebalancing.

Figures 5.2 and 5.3 display the empirical probability mass functions of the sample realizations of the left hand side of (5.22) as a fraction of the estimated time 0 HC market value when the deltas are rebalanced weekly and monthly, respectively. (These figures are based on 200 sample paths, ω. We use 100,000 additional time T spot price samples to estimate the deltas at each rebalancing time along a given sample path ω.) These figures show that delta hedging is effective even when estimates of the deltas are used and the deltas are rebalanced a finite number of times. In particular, delta hedging with weekly rebalancing is somewhat more effective than delta hedging with monthly rebalancing, as expected.

Despite its effectiveness, in this case delta hedging is not needed to almost completely reduce the variability of the time T HC cash flow values. This claim is true because transacting at time 0 by trading in the forward market according to an optimal solution of the intrinsic value linear program (5.20)–(5.21) yields a *sure* value equal to 97.58% of the estimated time 0 HC market value, that is, irrespective of the realizations of the relevant spot prices at time T. This approach entails purchasing forward, for delivery at the conversion time T, an amount of propane equal to the value of the decision variable x_{PR} in an optimal solution of this linear program,

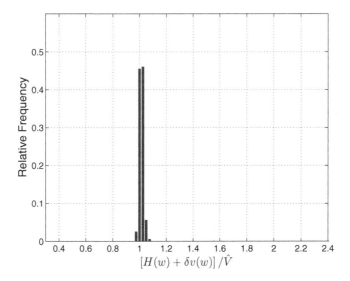

Fig. 5.3   Empirical probability mass function of the sum of the discounted cumulative hedging cash flows (H) and the discounted time T HC market values relative to the time 0 HC market value estimate $([H(\omega) + \delta v(\omega)]/\hat{V})$ with monthly rebalancing.

and simultaneously selling forward, for the same delivery time, the corresponding values of ethylene and co-products. We call this approach intrinsic hedging.

Of course, intrinsic hedging does not entail an appreciable market value loss only when nearly all the time 0 HC market value is intrinsic. When the HC intrinsic value is substantially less than the time 0 HC market value, which can happen for some conversion dates due to the variability in commodity prices, such a hedging strategy entails a substantial market value loss. In contrast, in theory delta hedging allows the HC managers to recover the entire time 0 HC market value, irrespective of the magnitude of the HC intrinsic value. Being able to estimate the time 0 HC market value is thus important to decide whether one should employ intrinsic hedging or delta hedging for specific future conversion dates.

To make these considerations more concrete, we modify our example by changing the time zero input spot prices to make the time 0 margins M_{NA} and M_{PR} zero and double the volatility estimates of the spot input and output prices. The resulting intrinsic value, V^{I}, and the estimated extrinsic value, $\hat{V}^{\mathrm{E}}$, are roughly 90.80% and 9.20%, respectively, of the estimated time 0 HC market value, $\hat{V}$ (the standard error of $\hat{V}$ is 0.29% of $\hat{V}$). In this

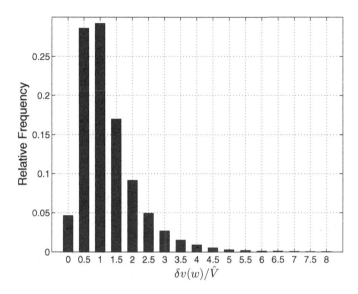

Fig. 5.4   Empirical probability mass function of the discounted sample time T HC market values relative to the time 0 HC market value estimate $(\delta v(\omega)/\hat{V})$ for the modified example.

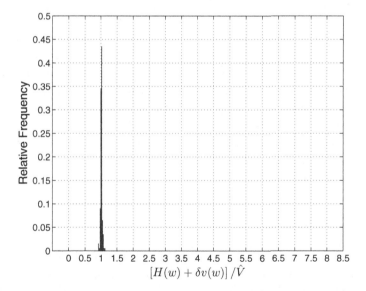

Fig. 5.5   Empirical probability mass function of the sum of the discounted cumulative hedging cash flows (H) and the discounted time T HC market values relative to the time 0 HC market value estimate $([H(\omega) + \delta v(\omega)]/\hat{V})$ with weekly rebalancing for the modified example.

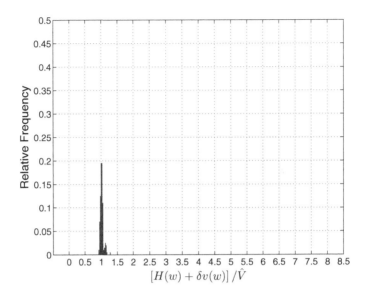

Fig. 5.6 Empirical probability mass function of the sum of the discounted cumulative hedging cash flows (H) and the discounted time T HC market values relative to the time 0 HC market value estimate ($[H(\omega) + \delta v(\omega)]/\hat{V}$) with monthly rebalancing for the modified example.

case the intrinsic hedge strategy incurs a substantial loss of the estimated time 0 HC market value. Moreover, Figs. 5.4–5.6, which are analogous to Figs. 5.1–5.3, show that, compared to the base case, the empirical probability mass function of the discounted sample time T HC market values relative to the time 0 HC market value estimate is more skewed to the right, and there is more variability in the ability of delta hedging to eliminate the change in the time 0 HC market value estimate. Despite this increased variability, Figs. 5.5 and 5.6 indicate that delta hedging remains effective in this case, especially with weekly, rather than monthly, rebalancing.

5.5. Conclusion

Commodity conversion assets play important economic roles. They can be managed as real options on the prices of futures contracts on their input and output commodities. This basic principle, which is a foundational element of commodity merchant operations [4], is not always appreciated by the managers of these assets. In this chapter we discuss the real option management of a simplified HC. Specifically, we illustrate the application of risk neutral valuation and delta hedging to estimate the HC market value and to reduce the variability in the market value of the HC cash flows, respectively. We hope that this chapter will be of interest to managers of HCs and other commodity and energy conversion assets, and increase the awareness of these managers of the real option approach to manage the assets under their control.

The one factor price model used in this chapter is a simple model of energy price evolution. More advanced models of commodity price evolution include additional factors (see, e.g., the models presented in [36, 39]). Our calibration of the parameters of the one factor model is based on simple linear regression applied to spot prices. There are other calibration methods available in the literature, such as approaches based on Kalman filtering and principal component analysis also using prices of traded commodity and energy derivatives, such as futures contracts and options on the prices of these contracts (see, e.g., [36, 39, 40]). In applications, it is advisable to explore the sensitivity of the valuation and hedging results to the chosen price model and the method and data used to calibrate its parameters. It is also important to investigate the possible effects of errors in the model specification and its parameter estimates on the resulting valuation and hedging. This issue is explored in [17] in the context of merchant commodity, in particular natural gas, storage.

Acknowledgments

This work was originally accepted for publication in the collection of chapters *Optimization and Analytics in the Oil and Gas Industry* edited by Kevin C. Furman, Jin-Hwa Song, and Amr El-Bakry, which, however, was not and never will be published. We thank Kevin C. Furman and two anonymous referees for their feedback on an earlier version of this chapter. The inclusion of this chapter in *Real Options in Energy and Commodity Markets* is by permission of Zac Rolnik, editor of the World Scientific — Now Publishers Series in Business. The support for this work by the Enterprise-wide Optimization Project at Carnegie Mellon University is gratefully acknowledged. The second author is a Faculty Affiliate of the Scott Institute of Energy Innovation at Carnegie Mellon University.

References

[1] H. Geman, *Commodities and Commodity Derivatives: Modeling and Pricing for Agriculturals, Metals and Energy*. John Wiley & Sons Ltd., Chichester, England, UK (2005).

[2] J. E. Smith and K. F. McCardle, Options in the real world: Lessons learned in evaluating oil and gas investments, *Operations Research*. **47**(1), 1–15 (1999).

[3] A. Eydeland and K. Wolyniec, *Energy and Power Risk Management: New Developments in Modeling, Pricing, and Hedging*. John Wiley & Sons Inc., Hoboken, NJ, USA (2003).

[4] N. Secomandi and D. J. Seppi, Real options and merchant operations of energy and other commodities, *Foundations and Trends in Technology, Information and Operations Management*. **6**(3–4), 161–331 (2014).

[5] J. R. Hagerty, Shale-gas boom spurs race, *The Wall Street Journal*. p. A3 (December 27, 2011).

[6] D. J. Seppi. Risk-neutral stochastic processes for commodity derivative pricing: An introduction and survey. In (ed.), E. Ronn, *Real Options and Energy Management Using Options Methodology to Enhance Capital Budgeting Decisions*, pp. 3–60. Risk Publications, London, England, UK (2002).

[7] D. G. Luenberger, *Investment Science*, Second edn. Oxford University Press, New York, NY, USA (2014).

[8] J. Tirole, *The Theory of Corporate Finance*. Princeton University Press, Princeton, NJ, USA (2006).

[9] J. C. Hull, *Options, Futures, and Other Derivatives Securities*, Eight. edn. Prentice Hall, Englewood Cliffs, NJ, USA (2012).

[10] N. Secomandi and M. Wang, A computational approach to the real option management of network contracts for natural gas pipeline transport capacity, *Manufacturing & Service Operations Management*. **14**(3), 441–454 (2012).

[11] S.-J. Deng, B. Johnson, and A. Sogomonian, Exotic electricity options and the valuation of electricity generation and transmission assets, *Decision Support Systems*. **30**(3), 383–392 (2001).

[12] N. Secomandi, On the pricing of natural gas pipeline capacity, *Manufacturing & Service Operations Management*. **12**(3), 393–408 (2010).

[13] M. Thompson, M. Davison, and H. Rasmussen, Natural gas storage valuation and optimization: A real options application, *Naval Research Logistics*. **56**(3), 226–238 (2009).

[14] N. Secomandi, Optimal commodity trading with a capacitated storage asset, *Management Science*. **56**(3), 449–467 (2010).

[15] G. Lai, F. Margot, and N. Secomandi, An approximate dynamic programming approach to benchmark practice-based heuristics for natural gas storage valuation, *Operations Research*. **58**(3), 564–582 (2010).

[16] S. Nadarajah, F. Margot, and N. Secomandi, Relaxations of approximate linear programs for the real option management of commodity storage, *Management Science*. **61**(12), 3054–3076 (2015).

[17] N. Secomandi, G. Lai, F. Margot, A. Scheller-Wolf, and D. J. Seppi, Merchant commodity storage and term structure model error, *Manufacturing & Service Operations Management*. **17**(3), 302–320 (2015).

[18] S. Nadarajah, F. Margot, and N. Secomandi. Comparison of least squares Monte Carlo methods with applications to energy real options. *European Journal of Operational Research*, **256**(1), 196–204 (2017).

[19] M. Thompson. Natural gas storage valuation, optimization, market and credit risk management. Working Paper, Queen's School of Business, Queen's University, Kingston, Ontario, CA (2012).

[20] O. Wu, D. Wang, and Z. Qin, Seasonal energy storage operations with limited flexibility: The price-adjusted rolling intrinsic policy, *Manufacturing & Service Operations Management*. **14**(3), 455–471 (2012).

[21] G. Lai, M. X. Wang, S. Kekre, A. Scheller-Wolf, and N. Secomandi, Valuation of storage at a liquefied natural gas terminal, *Operations Research*. **59**(3), 602–616 (2011).

[22] C. L. Tseng and G. Barz, Short-term generation asset valuation: A real options approach, *Operations Research*. **50**(2), 297–310 (2002).

[23] C. L. Tseng and K. Y. Lin, A framework using two-factor price lattices for generation asset valuation, *Operations Research*. **55**(2), 234–251 (2007).

[24] W. J. Hahn and J. S. Dyer, Discrete time modeling of mean-reverting stochastic processes for real option valuation, *European Journal of Operational Research*. **184**(2), 534–548 (2008).

[25] O. Boyabatli, P. R. Kleindorfer, and S. R. Koontz, Integrating long-term and short-term contracting in beef supply chains, *Management Science*. **57** (10), 1771–1787 (2011).

[26] S. K. Devalkar, R. Anupindi, and A. Sinha, Integrated optimization of procurement, processing and trade of commodities in a network environment, *Operations Research*. **59**(6), 1369–1381 (2011).

[27] O. Wu and H. Chen, Optimal control and equilibrium behavior of production-inventory systems, *Management Science*. **56**(8), 1362–1379 (2010).

[28] R. Adkins and D. Paxon, Reciprocal energy switching options, *The Journal of Energy Markets*. **4**(1), 91–120 (2011).

[29] J. Dockendorf and D. Paxon, Continuous rainbow options on commodity outputs: What is the real value of switching facilities? *The European Journal of Finance*. **19**(7–8), 645–673 (2013).

[30] P. Jaillet, E. I. Ronn, and S. Tompaidis, Valuation of commodity-based swing options, *Management Science*. **50**(7), 909–921 (2004).

[31] A. K. Dixit and R. S. Pindyck, *Investment under Uncertainty*. Princeton University Press, Princeton, NJ, USA (1994).

[32] L. Clewlow and C. Strickland, *Energy Derivatives: Pricing and Risk Management*. Lacima Publications, London, England, UK (2000).

[33] E. Ronn, (ed.), *Real Options and Energy Management Using Options Methodology to Enhance Capital Budgeting Decisions*. Risk Publications, London, England, UK (2002).

[34] V. Kaminski, (ed.), *Managing Energy Price Risk*, Third edn. Risk Publications, London, England, UK (2004).

[35] J. C. Cox, S. A. Ross, and M. Rubinstein, Option pricing: A simplified approach, *Journal of Financial Economics*. **7**(3), 229–263 (1979).

[36] E. S. Schwartz and J. E. Smith, Short-term variations and long-term dynamics in commodity prices, *Management Science.* **46**(7), 893–911 (2000).

[37] J. E. Smith, Alternative approaches for solving real-options problems (comment on Brandão *et al.*, 2005), *Decisions Analysis.* **2**(2), 89–102 (2005).

[38] P. Glasserman, *Monte Carlo Methods in Financial Engineering.* Springer, New York, NY, USA (2004).

[39] G. Cortazar and E. S. Schwartz, The valuation of commodity-contingent claims, *Journal of Derivatives.* **1**(4), 27–39 (1994).

[40] A. Roncoroni, R. I. Brik, and M. Cummins. Estimating commodity term structure volatilities. In (eds.), G. F. A. Roncoroni and M. Cummins, *Handbook of Multi-Commodity Markets and Products: Structuring, Trading and Risk Management*, pp. 635–657. John Wiley & Sons Ltd., Chichester, England, UK (2015).

Chapter 6

Contract Portfolio Optimization for a Gasoline Supply Chain

Daniel Adelman* and Shanshan Wang[†]

The University of Chicago, Booth School of Business,
5807 S Woodlawn Avenue, Chicago, IL 60637, USA.
*dan.adelman@ChicagoBooth.edu
[†]swang5@ChicagoBooth.edu

Major oil companies sell gasoline through three channels of trade: Branded (associated with long-term contracts), unbranded (associated with short-term contracts), and the spot market. The branded channel provides them with a long-term secured and sustainable demand source, but requires an inflexible long-term commitment with demand and price risks. The unbranded channel provides a medium level of allocation flexibility. The spot market provides them with the greatest allocation flexibility to the changing market conditions, but the spot market's illiquidity mitigates this benefit. In order to sell the product in a profitable and sustainable way, they need a dynamic contract portfolio strategy that would enable them to adjust the supply contract portfolio over time in anticipation of the future market conditions in each individual channel while satisfying the contractual obligations. We propose a multi-period model to dynamically rebalance the contract portfolio according to changing market dynamics with the objective of maximizing total expected discounted profit. We represent the evolution of product prices using a common real option model. We characterize the structure of an optimal state-dependent base-share contract portfolio policy for both finite and infinite planning horizons. Our computational results provide managerial insights into the structure of optimal policies and the benefit of using dynamic rather than static policies, and illustrate the sensitivity of the optimal contract portfolio and corresponding profit value in terms of the different parameters of our model.

6.1. Introduction

A manufacturer rarely produces a single product and sells to a single type of customer. Rather, a typical firm is likely to produce a portfolio of products for a variety of different customers and market segments, and sell them through different types of contracts. Suppliers in capital-intensive industries typically have a variety of different contracts with customers in order to sell the plant's output in a profitable way through time. For example, many manufacturers sell their own branded and unbranded products, that is, private label goods, from the same factory with different time scales for the contracts in the different channels. Having the right supply contract portfolio has been recognized, both in industry and academia, to play an important role in suppliers' abilities to improve profit, reduce cost, and manage risks [1].

The goal of this chapter is to find an optimal dynamic contract portfolio strategy that would enable gasoline suppliers to dynamically adjust their supply contract portfolio in anticipation of the future market conditions in each individual channel while satisfying their contractual obligations. The objective is to maximize the total discounted expected profits from all three channels of trade.

We explicitly model the contract formation process and capture its dynamics, with decisions contingent on product prices that evolve stochastically over time. We employ a common model used in the real option literature to represent the evolution of these prices. In particular, we consider the time persistence of the contract commitment, evolving price/demand processes, and customer defection. These basic elements appear in contract portfolios across many industries, but in this chapter they combine in a way that is specific to gasoline. We illustrate the tradeoffs between various factors that determine the portfolio of the supply contracts. These factors include customer type (contracting in various channels or markets), duration (long-term, short-term and spot), commitment type (share based and volume based), investment cost (with or without investment cost), and pricing (exogenous price and endogenous price).

We provide insights into what drives the contract portfolio and how to manage it. Specifically, we characterize a simple and easily implementable dynamic contractportfolio policy characterized by a branded base-share level and an unbranded contract commitment combination that would enable suppliers to dynamically rebalance their supply contract portfolio. We estimate some of our model parameters using market data. We assess the value of incorporating dynamic market conditions in contract portfolio decision-making versus using a static policy, as well as the value of spot market trading, illustrating that market illiquidity reduces the supplier's incentive to trade in the spot market as the trading cost increases. We also find that less supply should be committed to the long-term contract as the underlying price process becomes more volatile.

Our research is motivated by our work with British Petroleum (BP), one of the largest integrated gasoline suppliers in the world, but it has broad application to gasoline suppliers across the industry, which collectively generate around \$300 billion in annual revenue in the United States alone. Further, the challenge of optimizing a portfolio of these contracts in order to maximize profit is not unique to gasoline supply chains.

The most salient difference between our analysis and earlier work, reviewed in Sec. 6.3, is that our model considers a dynamic contract portfolio optimization problem from the supplier's perspective. In particular, we analyze how suppliers dynamically allocate the capacity to different channels whose demands and prices are subject to individual trends by building a portfolio of long-term contracts, short-term contracts, and spot trading.

In Sec. 6.2 we describe the gasoline supply chain in more detail. In Sec. 6.3 we review the extant literature. In Sec. 6.4 we formulate and analyze dynamic programming models. In Sec. 6.5 we discuss data input and present numerical results. We conclude in Sec. 6.6. All proofs are in Appendix A.

6.2.   Gasoline Supply Chain

The petroleum industry is usually divided into two main sectors on a functional basis: The upstream market that includes exploration and production and the downstream market that includes refining, transportation, and marketing. The downstream supply chain is a competitive and complex network. As illustrated in Fig. 6.1, gasoline is produced by refiners and then transported to distribution and storage facilities called terminals, which are located near large cities in metropolitan areas. The terminals serve as the wholesale market for the supply of gasoline to retail stations.

Major oil companies sell gasoline through three channels of trade to the wholesale market. Two types of gasoline, are sold, branded, and unbranded. Whereas branded gasoline (with company-specific additives)

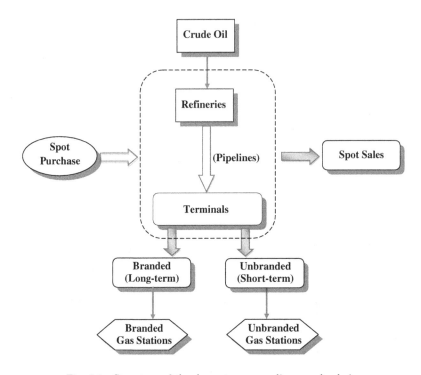

Fig. 6.1   Structure of the downstream gasoline supply chain.

bears the name of a major supplier, such as BP, Exxon or Shell, unbranded gasoline is a generic commodity and does not bear any brand name.

Branded gasoline is sold primarily through branded jobbers, independent firms that own and/or supply the branded gas stations, but in some cases through independent dealers that resell branded gasoline to the end customers. Contracts associated with the branded channel are long-term. Branded jobbers are obligated to sell only branded gasoline under contract, and gasoline suppliers must satisfy the realized demand at branded gas stations. Branded jobber contracts generally feature 10-year commitments and renewal is the jobbers' option. The Petroleum Marketing Practice Act (PMPA) prohibits suppliers in the United States from terminating or failing to renew contracts. Therefore, technically, these contracts last forever until the customer defects. This type of contract is in essence a supply commitment for gasoline suppliers, which are locked in once a long-term contract is signed.

Gasoline is also sold in the unbranded channel at outlets such as Costco, Walmart and Safeway, or to unbranded jobbers. Contracts associated with the unbranded channel are short-term, usually for one-year. Suppliers are obligated to deliver a fixed volume of gasoline contracted in the unbranded channel. Unbranded jobbers can buy gasoline based on the wholesale market rather than being forced to accept gasoline from a particular gasoline supplier. That is, they have the flexibility of shopping around for the cheapest available gasoline. This freedom makes the unbranded channel demand more volatile because unbranded jobbers might not continue to do business with suppliers if they can find better deals. Furthermore, they can purchase gasoline from the spot market without any contract if the short-term contract cannot cover the demand at their unbranded gas stations.

The third channel of trade for gasoline is the spot market. Spot sales are mostly unbranded sales. Unbranded jobbers, other refiners, and distributors buy gasoline in the spot market. There is no contract and no supply obligations for gasoline suppliers to sell gasoline in the spot market. The spot market is also used by gasoline suppliers to leverage their inventory. Gasoline suppliers sell the leftover product into the spot market after satisfying contract commitments, due to storage constraints and the working capital tied up when holding inventory. They purchase from the spot market to meet unsatisfied contract commitments. The spot market is illiquid because it is relatively small, having only a few market participants, and access to this market is imperfect, due to transportation constraints, the difficulty of locating a counter party, and search friction. An important characteristic of such a market is price impact. Each unit traded in the spot market drives the market price against the trader, which means that the spot price goes up when buying and down when selling. Such impact increases with the size of the trade. If gasoline suppliers want to sell leftover products, they may have to do so through the spot market at unfavorable prices.

The supply contracts described above are dynamic contracts (state-dependent), as opposed to the traditional static (state-independent) contracts, which have fixed prices. As gasoline prices are highly volatile, primarily due to the fluctuations of crude oil prices, they are pegged to some price index to help the suppliers shift some of the price risk to the customers. Gasoline prices in the United States are linked to the Oil Price Information Service (OPIS) Price Index. For example, unbranded gasoline can be priced at OPIS Low 2 plus 2 cents per gallon. Both because of the government's concern about gasoline price manipulation and the competition in gasoline markets, gasoline suppliers are price takers in the gasoline contract markets. When trading in the spot market, gasoline suppliers experience temporary price impact.

Refineries are extremely capital extensive. For instance, it costs approximately $4–6 billion to build a large refinery. Additionally, the costs to upgrade and modernize a refinery with follow-up maintenance costs are significant. For example, in 2013 BP's Whiting refinery completed a $4.2 billion upgrade in order to be able to process more and a wider variety of heavy crude oils. Process shutdowns and restarts are very costly for a refinery. Therefore, efficient refineries tend to be run at full capacity.

Gasoline suppliers typically lack a scientific mechanism for deciding the appropriate ratio to be sold through different channels of trade. Among these three channels, the branded channel gives gasoline suppliers a long-term secure demand source, but requires an inflexible long-term commitment with demand and price risks. The unbranded channel provides them a medium level of allocation flexibility. The spot market offers them the greatest allocation flexibility, but its illiquidity reduces this benefit. Historically, the objective of continually increasing sales has driven gasoline suppliers toward maximizing branded sales. The key question that we study is whether gasoline suppliers should rely solely on secure long-term contracts to sell the refinery production, or also market this production through the other two channels of trade.

Various sources of uncertainty make answering this question challenging. In particular, managers must commit to the contracts before they know the following:

(1) *Profit margins for each channel of trade.* As crude oil costs and gasoline prices are highly volatile, profit margins for each channel of trade are stochastic. The dynamically changing prices complicate the optimal contract portfolio decisions and require a dynamic policy.

(2) *Branded demand.* The long-term contract commitment is determined in anticipation of having to meet future branded demand, or in anticipation of having more profitable opportunities in the unbranded and spot channels. If a gasoline supplier is under-committed to the branded channel, the spot market might hold it captive, as the supplier might need to sell the leftover products into the spot market at an unattractive price. Likewise, if a gasoline supplier is over-committed to the branded channel, this might limit its ability to flexibly allocate products across different channels and they might end up purchasing from the spot

market at an unfavorable price in order to satisfy the branded contract if the branded demand spikes.

(3) *Branded customer defection.* Customer defection includes cases in which contracts with branded jobbers are not renewed for various reasons, for example, jobbers' violation or inability to comply with any term or condition of the contract, or jobbers finding a better deal with other suppliers.

(4) *Production disruption.* Disruptions in refinery operations resulting from unscheduled maintenance and breakdowns lead to production short-falls. As a result, the production might not be sufficient to satisfy the contract obligations, and the supplier might be held captive in the spot market. While our model and theoretical analysis allow for supply uncertainty, we assume supply is deterministic in our numerical study.

6.3. Literature Review

One main branch of the supply chain management literature related to our chapter concentrates on analyzing the potential benefit of using long-term contracts versus short-term contracts. Most of the literature analyzes the procurement problem from the buyer's perspective considering the trade-offs among different types of contracts (e.g., [2–4]). Unlike our chapter, the problems described by these papers are not contract portfolio problems, but are part of the contract selection process, evaluating the costs or benefits of any contracting alternative and discussing conditions under which a given type of contract may be preferred to another.

Another stream of literature related to our chapter deals with contract portfolio management in the presence of spot markets. For a more complete review, see the survey papers [5,6]. This stream of work is mainly done from the buyer or the buyer–seller perspective. The buyer–focused papers deal with the procurement side of the supply chain, where the buyer maximizes its expected utility by using different supply sources. The authors of [7,8] address this type of scenario in single-period models. In [9] the authors investigate the dynamic aspects of the procurement problem for a buyer in a multi-period setting. Despite their multi-period environment, the contract portfolio is determined at the beginning of the first period, and there can be no contract adjustment and dynamic rebalancing of the portfolio in later periods. In contrast, we explicitly model the supplier's dynamic contract formation processes as market conditions change. The buyer–seller-focused papers mainly answer the question of how access to the spot market affects buyer–seller coordination (e.g., [10–12]). We do not consider coordination issues.

Management science has been widely and successfully applied in the petroleum industry in areas of crude oil acquisition and refinery planning, as well as scheduling, blending, and distribution planning (e.g., [13, 14]). Our results provide gasoline suppliers with managerial insights into the benefit of using dynamic rather than static policies.

There is a growing operations management literature that combines real option models of the evolution of commodity prices and models of inventory and production management (e.g., [15–19]). Much of this work also includes forward price curves, which we do not consider. Our approach to modeling long-term share contracts with random customer defection appears novel.

6.4. Model

In this section we formulate the contract portfolio problem. We develop our framework from the supplier's perspective at an aggregate level. In Secs. 6.4.1 and 6.4.2 we characterize the optimal dynamic contract portfolio policies and value functions in the finite- and infinite-horizon cases, respectively.

6.4.1. *The Finite Horizon Case*

Our finite-horizon model considers a supplier's contracting decisions over time. The planning horizon is finite and has T time periods indexed from T to 1 in decreasing order. In order to specify a discrete time contract portfolio optimization model, we will introduce the following notation:

- x_t: The branded market share at the beginning of time period t before signing any contracts;
- f_t: Branded market share at the beginning of time period t after signing the branded contracts;
- y_t: Quantity contracted in the unbranded channel at the beginning of time period t;
- z_t: Quantity traded in the spot market in time period t;
- D_t^b: Aggregate branded industry demand in time period t, which depends on the branded price p_t^b and the random component ϵ_t^b; $D_t^b = d_t^b(p_t^b, \epsilon_t^b)$;

- D_t^u: Unbranded demand the supplier faces at the end of time period $t+1$ (that is, previous period), which depends on the unbranded price p_{t+1}^u and the random component ϵ_{t+1}^u; $D_t^u = d_t^u(p_{t+1}^u, \epsilon_{t+1}^u)$;
- r_t: Random defection fraction at the end of time period t; $r_t \in [0,1]$;
- Q_{t+1}: Potentially random refinery supply in time period $t+1$;
- Φ_t: Information vector, which contains the production cost, the production quantity, the prices in the branded and unbranded channels and the spot market, and the random terms of the branded and unbranded demand models for time period $t+1$; $\Phi_t = (c_{t+1}, Q_{t+1}, p_{t+1}^b, p_{t+1}^u, p_{t+1}^s, \epsilon_{t+1}^b, \epsilon_{t+1}^u)$;
- β: Discount factor; $\beta \in (0,1)$.

The timing difference between the realization of D_t^b and D_t^u is due to the fact that at the beginning of time period t the supplier knows the unbranded demand D_t^u, which is a function of the unbranded price and the random components in time period $t+1$, whereas the supplier knows the branded demand D_t^b later in time period t after the branded price and the random components in time period t have been realized (recall that the time index runs backwards in our model).

The sequence of the decisions and information is shown in Fig. 6.2. At the beginning of time period $t, t = T, \ldots, 1$, the state space is defined by the current branded market share x_t and information vector Φ_t. We normalize the size of the entire branded channel to unity. The branded market share x_t indicates the prior period's branded supply commitment. Because of the nature of the long-term commitment and the fact that the supplier does not know the exact volume when contracting in the branded channel, the supplier chooses the new branded market share it wants to commit. The supplier decides on a new branded market share f_t, $x_t \leq f_t \leq \overline{f}$, where $\overline{f}$ denotes the maximum potential branded market share (this limit models competition). Whereas the supplier must satisfy all the consumer

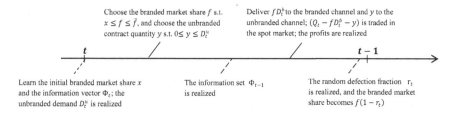

Fig. 6.2   Model timeline.

demand from the branded gas stations it contracts with, it can choose which gas stations to contract with, that is, $f_t < \overline{f}$. Thus, f_t is a proxy for the fraction of all gas stations operating in the market that are branded to our particular supplier. The quantity contracted in the unbranded channel y_t is constrained by the realized unbranded demand D_t^u. Different than D_t^b, D_t^u is the demand that the supplier faces rather than the industry demand. For example, Walmart may want to sign a short-term contract with BP for the delivery of 100 million gallons of gasoline. BP then decides the contract quantity y_t, $0 \leq y_t \leq D_t^u$, in the unbranded channel, and is obligated to deliver this fixed quantity. The associated investment cost (cost of the branding) $k_t(f_t - x_t)$ is proportional to the extra branded market share contracted. As the supplier is obligated to supply the contracted branded channel, if the future aggregate demand across the branded channel is D_t^b, it needs to deliver an amount $f_t D_t^b$ to the branded channel.

The information vector Φ_{t-1} then becomes known. After learning this information, the supplier delivers $f_t D_t^b$ to the branded channel, y_t to the unbranded channel, and trades $z_t = Q_t - f_t D_t^b - y_t$ in the spot market. Because suppliers carry on average seven days of inventory[a], which is negligible for a model applied on an annual basis as we assume here, we suppose there is no inventory carryover. The supplier thus sells the left-over product $z_t > 0$ to the spot market after satisfying contract commitments, and purchases $-z_t$ from the spot market to meet unsatisfied contract commitments.

At the end of time period t, customers may defect, in which case the branded market share shrinks by a fraction r_t; that is, a new branded market share $x_{t-1} = f_t \cdot (1 - r_t)$ is carried forward into the next time period $t-1$. As we attribute the price impact to imperfect market access, and it thus is a temporary price fluctuation induced by order flow, we adopt the assumption often made in the literature that this impact is temporary, moving the current price but having no effect on future spot prices (e.g., [20, 21]). Whereas the evolution of the spot price p_t^s then follows an exogenous price process that does not depend on the supplier's actions, they do affect the current spot market price: This price goes up when the supplier buys and

---

[a]The report by the United States Energy Information Administration, available at. http://www.eia.doe.gov/dnav/pet/pet_sum_mkt_dcu_nus_a.htm, accessed on October 25, 2015 shows that for Motor Gasoline 2009, about 363 million gallons per day were sold and motor gasoline stocks were 55 million barrels, which leads to 6.36 days of inventory.

goes down when it sells. The spot price impact function $P_t(z_t, p_t^s, \lambda_t)$ models the spot price when the supplier trades quantity z_t at a pre-trade price p_t^s via the price impact parameter $\lambda_t > 0$, which captures the level of market liquidity and is such that larger trades generate larger price impact, if everything else is constant. In the absence of price impact, that is, $\lambda_t = 0$, we have $P_t(z_t, p_t^s, 0) = p_t^s$. When $z_t = 0$, we have $P_t(0, p_t^s, \lambda_t) = p_t^s$ as no trading incurs no price impact. The spot revenue function, denoted by $R_t(z_t, p_t^s, \lambda_t)$, is defined by $R_t(z_t, p_t^s, \lambda_t) := z_t P_t(z_t, p_t^s, \lambda_t)$. We make the following assumptions on the spot price impact function and the spot revenue function.

Assumption 6.1. (a) $P_t(z_t, p_t^s, \lambda_t)$ is nonincreasing in z_t, satisfies $P_t(z_t, p_t^s, \lambda_t) \leq$ (resp. $\geq$) p_t^s for $z_t \geq$ (resp. $\leq$) 0, and is bounded below: $P_t(z_t, p_t^s, \lambda_t) \geq 0$ over all z_t for any fixed p_t^s and λ_t. (b) $P_t(z_t, p_t^s, \lambda_t)$ is decreasing in λ_t for $z_t > 0$, and increasing in λ_t for $z_t < 0$ for any fixed p_t^s. (c) $R_t(z_t, p_t^s, \lambda_t)$ is strictly concave in z_t for any fixed p_t^s and λ_t.

Assumption 6.1(a) says that each unit traded in the spot market drives the market price against the trader and the traded price cannot be negative. Assumption 6.1(b) states that the larger the λ_t, the greater the price impact. For any fixed z_t and p_t^s, the larger the value of λ_t, the more the market price moves against the trader. Assumption 6.1(c) states that the spot revenue function $R_t(z_t, p_t^s, \lambda_t)$ is strictly concave in z_t for any fixed p_t^s and λ_t. Commonly used spot price impact functions are linear, that is, $P_t(z_t, p_t^s, \lambda_t) = p_t^s - \lambda_t z_t$ (e.g., [20]); the authors of [22] obtain a linear price impact function in a linear symmetric trading equilibrium or negative exponential, that is, $P_t(z_t, p_t^s, \lambda_t) = p_t^s e^{-\lambda_t z_t}$ (e.g., [23,24]). The spot revenue function $R_t(z_t, p_t^s, \lambda_t)$ is concave for linear functions or negative exponential functions within a reasonable range of price impact parameters. This property is also satisfied by all concave spot price impact functions.

The objective of the supplier is to maximize the total discounted expected profit margin obtained from operating in the branded and unbranded channels and the spot market over the entire planning horizon. In this setting, the unbranded contract commitment is made after the unbranded demand D_t^u is realized. However, the commitment f_t to meet future branded demand is made upfront. Both decisions occur before knowing all the rest of the uncertainties. As a consequence, the commitment f_t will be determined in anticipation of having to meet future branded demand, or in anticipation of future opportunities in the unbranded and spot channels. The supplier can hurt itself by overcommitting to the branded channel, because it limits its ability to flexibly allocate product when margins fluctuate randomly across different channels, and profitable unbranded demand may emerge. Also, the supplier can hurt itself by under-committing to the branded channel, because it might cause the supplier to allocate the product to other less profitable channels. The choice of unbranded contract commitment can also influence the branded market share as well as the future contract portfolio composition.

We analyze these decisions using dynamic programming. Define

$$L_t(f, y, \Phi_t) := \mathbb{E}_{\Phi_{t-1}}[-c_t Q_t + (p_t^b - g_t) f d_t^b(p_t^b, \epsilon_t^b) + p_t^u y$$
$$+ z_t(f, y) P_t(z_t(f, y), p_t^s, \lambda_t) | \Phi_t], \qquad (6.1)$$

where

$$z_t(f, y) = Q_t - f d_t^b(p_t^b, \epsilon_t^b) - y \qquad (6.2)$$

denotes the expected profit margin from the branded, unbranded, and spot markets for period t, $t = 1, 2, \ldots, T$; here the conditional expectation is taken over the information vector at period t given the last period's produc-tion, prices, and demand information. In (6.1), the first term is the produc-tion cost; the second and third terms are the revenue from both branded and unbranded channels, where g_t is the extra cost associated with the branded product compared with the unbranded product; the fourth term is the spot revenue if $z_t(f, y) > 0$, or the payment for spot product purchases if $z_t(f, y) < 0$.

For technical reasons, in determining the optimal policy we make Assumptions 6.2–6.4 for $t = 1, 2, \ldots, T$ and any given Φ_t.

Assumption 6.2. The random variables c_t, Q_t, and p_t^u have finite condi-tional expectations.

Assumption 6.3. It holds that $\mathbb{E}_{\Phi_{t-1}}[d_t^b(p_t^b, \epsilon_t^b) | \Phi_t] < \infty$ and $\mathbb{E}_{\Phi_{t-1}}[p_t^b d_t^b(p_t^b, \epsilon_t^b) | \Phi_t] < \infty$.

Assumption 6.4. We have $\lim_{y \to \infty} \mathbb{E}_{\Phi_{t-1}}[p_t^u y + z_t(f, y) P_t(z_t(f, y), p_t^s, \lambda_t) | \Phi_t] = -\infty$ for all $f \in [0, \overline{f}]$ and $\mathbb{E}_{\Phi_{t-1}}[z_t(f, y) P_t(z_t(f, y), p_t^s, \lambda_t) | \Phi_t] < \infty$ for all $f \in [0, \overline{f}]$ and $y \in [0, \infty)$.

Assumption 6.2 is very mild. Assumption 6.3 states that the condi-tional expected demands and revenues from the branded channel are finite. The first part of Assumption 6.4 says that the expected cost tends to infinity when contracting an infinite amount of product in the unbranded channel.

In an illiquid spot market, the trading price is pushed up to infinity if a supplier wants to purchase an infinite amount of the product. The second part of Assumption 6.4 ensures that the conditional expected revenue from the spot market is finite. All of these assumptions are weak restrictions that are likely to be satisfied in a realistic market. These assumptions ensure that the functions L_t are well defined. In particular, for $t = 1, 2, \ldots, T$ and any given Φ_t, we have $\lim_{y \to \infty} L_t(f, y, \Phi_t) = -\infty$ for all $f \in [0, \overline{f}]$ and $L_t(f, y, \Phi_t) < \infty$ for all $f \in [0, \overline{f}]$ and $y \in [0, \infty)$.

Denote by $v_t(x_t, \Phi_t)$ the profit-to-go function at the beginning of time period t with initial branded market share x_t and information vector Φ_t. Let $v_0(x, \Phi_0) := 0$ for all x_0 and Φ_0. For each $t = 1, 2, \ldots, T$, we have

$$v_t(x_t, \Phi_t) = k_t x + \max_{\{x_t \le f \le \overline{f},\, 0 \le y \le d_t^u(p_{t+1}^u, \epsilon_{t+1}^u)\}} G_t(f, y, \Phi_t), \qquad (6.3)$$

where

$$G_t(f, y, \Phi_t) := -k_t f + L_t(f, y, \Phi_t)$$
$$+ \beta \mathbb{E}_{\Phi_{t-1}}[\mathbb{E}_{r_t}[v_{t-1}(f \cdot (1 - r_t), \Phi_{t-1}) | \Phi_{t-1}] | \Phi_t]. \qquad (6.4)$$

In words, starting period t in state (x_t, Φ_t), making contracting decisions f and y, and following an optimal policy thereafter yields an expected profit equal to the sum of the negative of the cost of raising the branded market share level to f, which is $-k_t(f - x_t)$, the expected profit margin from all three channels incurred at time period t, and the expected present value of starting period $t - 1$ in state $f \cdot (1 - r_t)$ and Φ_{t-1} and acting optimally over the remainder of the time horizon. In (6.4), the defection fraction r_t is conditional on the information vector realized in time period t, Φ_{t-1}.

Let $J_t(x_t, \Phi_t)$ denote the second term on the right-hand side of (6.3), that is,

$$J_t(x_t, \Phi_t) := \max_{\{x_t \le f \le \overline{f},\, 0 \le y \le d_t^u(p_{t+1}^u, \epsilon_{t+1}^u)\}} G_t(f, y, \Phi_t). \qquad (6.5)$$

We can rewrite (6.3) as

$$v_t(x_t, \Phi_t) = k_t x_t + J_t(x_t, \Phi_t). \qquad (6.6)$$

We define the set Ω_t as $\{(f, y) | f \in [0, \overline{f}], y \in [0, d_t^u(p_{t+1}^u, \epsilon_{t+1}^u)]\}$.

We now characterize the optimal contract portfolio strategy, which takes the form of *a state-dependent "base-share" contract portfolio policy*. It is analogous to a *"base-stock" policy* [25] where the base stock level in each period is $f_t^*(\Phi_t)$. This policy is characterized by a branded base-share level and an unbranded contract commitment pair, $(f_t^*(\Phi_t), y_t^*(\Phi_t))$, given as a function of the initial information state Φ_t. If the initial branded market share is below the base-share level, it is increased to that base-share level and an unbranded contract commitment is made. If the branded market share is above the base-share level, then nothing extra is contracted in the branded channel and the optimal quantity contracted in the unbranded channel $y_t^*(x_t, \Phi_t)$ is less than the unbranded contract commitment $y_t^*(\Phi_t)$. In addition, the higher the excess in the initial branded market share, the less should be contracted in the unbranded channel, that is, $y_t^*(x_t, \Phi_t)$ is nonincreasing in x for any given Φ_t. Theorems 6.1 and 6.2 summarize these properties.

Theorem 6.1. *Fix* $t = 1, \ldots, T$. *(a) For any fixed* Φ_t, *the function* $G_t(f, y, \Phi_t)$ *is jointly concave in* f *and* y, *and* $G_t(f, y, \Phi_t)$ *has a finite maximizer over set* Ω_t, *denoted by* $(f_t^*(\Phi_t), y_t^*(\Phi_t))$. *(b) For any fixed* Φ_t, $J_t(x_t, \Phi_t)$ *is concave and nonincreasing in* x_t; $v_t(x_t, \Phi_t)$ *is concave in* x_t *and* $v_t(x_t, \Phi_t) < \infty$ *for all* $x \in [0, \overline{f}]$. *(c) If* $x_t \leq f_t^*(\Phi_t)$ *it is optimal to contract up to* $f_t^*(\Phi_t)$ *in the branded channel; that is, bring the branded market share up to the base-share level* $f_t^*(\Phi_t)$ *and contract* $y_t^*(\Phi_t)$ *in the unbranded channel; if* $x_t > f_t^*(\Phi_t)$, *it is optimal to contract nothing extra in the branded channel.*

In this chapter, we assume that the investment cost is in the form of $k_t(x_t - f)$. Our results hold when the investment cost function is generalized to cost functions that are additively separable and jointly convex in the state x_t and decision variable f. The monotonicity of the optimal unbranded contract quantity, $y_t^*(\Phi_t, x_t)$, in the branded share x_t depends on the submodularity of the functions $G_t(f, y, \Phi_t)$ in (f, y) (see [26]).

Theorem 6.2. *Fix* $t = 1, \ldots, T$. *(a) For any fixed* Φ_t, *the function* $G_t(f, y, \Phi_t)$ *is submodular in the contract portfolio decisions* (f, y). *(b) For any fixed* Φ_t, *the optimal unbranded contract quantity* $y_t^*(\Phi_t, x_t)$ *is nonincreasing in* x_t *and* $y_t^*(\Phi_t, x_t) \leq y_t^*(\Phi_t)$.

We can interpret Theorem 6.2 by stating that the optimal branded market share and the unbranded contract quantity are strategic substitutes: Increasing the branded market share results in a decrease in the return from increasing the unbranded contract quantity and, hence, at a higher level of branded market share, a lower unbranded contract quantity is optimally chosen. For further discussion of this notion of substitutability, see [27].

6.4.2. *The Infinite Horizon Case*

Optimal policies fail to be stationary in finite-horizon models because of the end-of-the-horizon effect, even when the data are stationary. We now consider an infinite horizon stationary model, in which the cost parameters and revenue functions, as well as the cost, price, and demand processes are stationary. We show that a stationary state-dependent base-share contract portfolio policy is optimal for the infinite horizon model.

The approach we use to analyze the infinite horizon model is to treat it as the limit of the finite horizon model as the horizon tends to infinity. Infinite horizon models are often treated as three types of models based on the properties of the one-stage reward: Non-negative, nonpositive, and bounded. The one-stage expected profit in our model is

$$h(x, f, y, \Phi) = -k(f - x) + L(f, y, \Phi), \ x \leq f \leq \overline{f}, \ 0 \leq y \leq d_t^u(p^u, \epsilon^u).$$

Since $L(f, y, \Phi) < \infty$ for all $f \in [0, \overline{f}]$ and $y \in [0, \infty)$, there exists a real valued function $M(\Phi)$ such that $L(\cdot, \cdot, \Phi) \leq M(\Phi)$. Let $M < \infty$ be the maximum over all Φ (assuming it exists). Since $-k(f - x) \leq 0$, by subtracting M uniformly from the one-stage expected profit, we transform the original model with the one-stage reward bounded above to a new model with a nonpositive one-stage reward. Thus, the new value functions for the finite horizon model satisfy $\widehat{v}_t(x, \Phi) \leq 0$, and we have

$$\widehat{v}_t(x, \Phi) = v_t(x, \Phi) - \frac{M(1 - \beta^t)}{1 - \beta},$$

$$\widehat{G}_t(f, y, \Phi) = G_t(f, y, \Phi) - \frac{M(1 - \beta^t)}{1 - \beta}.$$

The infinite horizon optimality equation for the modified model is given by

$$\widehat{v}(x, \Phi) = kx + \max_{\{x \leq f \leq \overline{f}, \ 0 \leq y \leq d^u(p^u, \epsilon^u)\}} \widehat{G}(f, y, \Phi), \qquad (6.7)$$

where

$$\widehat{G}(f, y, \Phi) := -kf + L(f, y, \Phi) - M + \beta \mathbb{E}_{\Phi'}$$
$$\times [\mathbb{E}_r[\widehat{v}(f \cdot (1 - r), \Phi') | \Phi'] | \Phi], \qquad (6.8)$$

and

$$L(f, y, \Phi) := \mathbb{E}_{\Phi'}[-c'Q + (p^{b'} - g)fd^b(p^{b'}, \epsilon^{b'}) + p^{u'}y$$
$$+ z(f, y)P(z(f, y), p^{s'}, \lambda) | \Phi],$$
$$z(f, y) := Q - fd^b(p^{b'}, \epsilon^{b'}) - y.$$

Let $v^*(x, \Phi)$ and $\widehat{v}^*(x, \Phi)$ denote the maximum infinite-horizon expected total discounted profit in the original and the modified models when starting with an initial branded market share x and information vector Φ, respectively. Then it follows that $\widehat{v}^*(x, \Phi) = v^*(x, \Phi) - M/(1 - \beta)$ and $\widehat{G}^*(f, y, \Phi) = G^*(f, y, \Phi) - M/(1 - \beta)$.

Theorem 6.3 states that the maximum finite horizon expected total discounted profit function, $v_t(x, \Phi)$, converges to the maximum infinite horizon expected total discounted profit function, $v^*(x, \Phi)$, associated with the optimal stationary policy $(f^*(\Phi), y^*(\Phi))$, and, as a consequence, this policy is optimal for the infinite horizon model.

Theorem 6.3. *(a) It holds that* $v_\infty = v^*$, $\widehat{v}_\infty = \widehat{v}^*$, $G_\infty = G^*$, *and* $\widehat{G}_\infty = \widehat{G}^*$. *The functions* $\widehat{v}^*$ *and* $\widehat{G}^*$ *(v^* and G^*) satisfy the infinite horizon optimality equation in the modified (original) model. (b) The function* $G^*(f, y, \Phi)$ *is jointly concave and submodular in f and y, and $G^*(f, y, \Phi)$ has a finite maximizer over set Ω, denoted by $(f^*(\Phi), y^*(\Phi))$. The function $v^*(x, \Phi)$ is concave in x. (c) A state-dependent base-share contract portfolio policy with base-share level and unbranded contract commitment combination $(f^*(\Phi), y^*(\Phi))$ is optimal for the infinite horizon model.*

6.5. Numerical Study

The state-dependent base-share contract portfolio policy that is optimal for the finite horizon models in Sec. 6.4.1 can be computed by the recursions (6.3) and (6.4). By Theorem 6.3, when the length of the horizon is sufficiently long, the recursive schemes converge to the infinite horizon value function under the expected total discounted profit criteria, and the associated optimal contract portfolio policies also converge to an optimal policy for the infinite horizon model. In this section, we focus on computing the stationary state-dependent base-share contract portfolio policy for the infinite horizon model using modified policy iteration methods (see [28]).

As the infinite horizon model discussed in Sec. 6.4.2 has high dimensional and continuous state spaces, it becomes computationally intractable. We reduce the effective dimensions by pegging other price processes to one particular price process, and we introduce discretizations of the domains of the relevant state variables and their stochastic transition functions. By doing so, we reduce the effective dimensions of the state space to two, that is, the underlying price and the branded market share. Another difficulty we face is that even though we discretize the branded market share, because of the customer defection fraction, the new branded market share at the beginning of the next period might not be on the prescribed grid. Therefore, we use Chebyshev polynomials to approximate the value function, which allows us to evaluate the value function for any point not on this grid.

In this numerical study we use some data provided by BP, our industrial partner. BP is one of the largest oil and gas producers in the United States and also a top refiner with a total processing capacity of 1.5 million barrels of crude oil per day. It is also the second largest gasoline marketer in the United States, selling more than 15 billion gallons of gasoline each year through 11,000 service stations around the country. The results provide BP with valuable managerial insights on their contract portfolio optimization.

In Sec. 6.5.1 we discuss how we calibrate input parameters to our model, and then in Sec. 6.5.2 we present numerical results.

6.5.1. *Data Input and Modeling*

Price evolution and discretization. As discussed in [29, p. 893], commodity prices exhibit mean reversion (see also, [30, 31]):

> "Intuitively, when the price of a commodity is higher than some long-run mean or equilibrium price level, the supply of the commodity will increase because higher cost producers of the commodity will enter the market — new production comes online, older production expected to go off line stays on line — thereby putting downward pressure on prices. Conversely, when prices are relatively low, supply will decrease since some of the high-cost producers will exit, putting upward pressure on prices. When these entries and exits are not instantaneous, prices may be temporarily high or low but will tend to revert toward the equilibrium level."

To capture this phenomenon, we use a stochastic mean-reverting process for gasoline prices where future prices are expected to drift back to a specified long-run average price. The particular form we use assumes the logarithm of the time t gasoline price $X_t = \ln(p_t)$, evolves in continuous time as an Ornstein–Uhlenbeck (OU) process (see [32]); that is, future gasoline prices are described by the following stochastic differential equations (here, with some abuse of notation t denotes continuous time):

$$dX_t = \kappa(\mu - X_t)dt + \sigma dW_t,$$

where μ denotes the equilibrium or long-term mean to which log-prices revert, $\sigma > 0$ is the volatility of the process, $\kappa > 0$ is the rate of mean reversion, and W_t is a standard Brownian motion. Hence, given X_0, with time running forward X_t is normally distributed with mean

$$\mu_N = \mu + (X_0 - \mu)e^{-\kappa t},$$

and variance

$$\sigma_N^2 = \frac{\sigma^2}{2\kappa}(1 - e^{-2\kappa t}).$$

The corresponding distribution of the gasoline price is lognormal with mean

$$e^{\mu_N + \frac{1}{2}\sigma_N^2},$$

and variance

$$e^{2\mu_N + \sigma_N^2}\left(e^{\sigma_N^2} - 1\right).$$

Using monthly gasoline prices expressed in dollars per gallon, from January 1983 through July 2009 adjusted to July 2009 dollars,[b] we estimate a long-run mean (μ) of 0.166, a mean-reversion coefficient (κ) of 39.2% per year, and a volatility (σ) of 32.6% per year. Letting $t \to \infty$ in the above formulae, these parameter estimates imply that the long-run distribution of unbranded gasoline price has a mean of $1.26 per gallon and a standard deviation of $0.48.

In order to construct a discrete-time stationary transition probability matrix for the unbranded price process for use in our dynamic programming model, we discretize the unbranded price levels concentrating on a reasonably wide range from $0.5 to $4.5 for each time period. Given this unbranded price, we truncate the conditional distribution of each next period's unbranded price and normalize it, taking the duration of a period to be 1 in the continuous-time model above. We thereby construct a transition probability matrix for the unbranded price process. The authors of [32] use a similar method, employing three-point approximations for the conditional distributions. Using this stationary transition matrix, the induced unbranded price process has a long-run stationary distribution whose mean and standard deviation match those of the exact long-run distribution.

---

[b]These are Midwest (PADD2) regular gasoline wholesale/resale price by all sellers, as reported by the Energy Information Administration (EIA). We use them as unbranded prices in the Midwest as they represent the wholesale prices of the homogeneous commodity shipped by the pipeline.

We assume the following simple linear relationships between unbranded price and other prices and cost:

$$p^b = \alpha^b + \gamma^b p^u + \varepsilon^b, \tag{6.9}$$

$$p^s = \alpha^s + \gamma^s p^u + \varepsilon^s, \tag{6.10}$$

$$c = \alpha^c + \gamma^c p^u + \varepsilon^c, \tag{6.11}$$

where ε^b, ε^s, and ε^c are independent and identically distributed normal random variables with zero means. Using monthly gasoline prices and costs from June 2004 through June 2008,[c] we estimate (6.9) and (6.11) by ordinary least squares. For (6.9), the estimate of α^b is 0.0486 and that of γ^b is 0.9894. Both estimates are statistically significant with p-value less than 0.00001. The regression gives an R^2 of 0.9987 and a standard error of 0.0187. For (6.11), the estimate of α^c is not statistically different from zero, and the estimate of γ^c is 0.9650 with p-value less than 0.00001. The regression gives an R^2 of 0.9810 and a standard error of 0.0716. As spot prices are not available, we assume $\alpha^s = -0.02, \gamma^s = 1.01$, and set the standard deviation of ε^s to 0.02, which provide a reasonable level of the expected profit margin and the variance for the spot price compared to the branded and unbranded prices.

Recall that in our dynamic programming models, the time index runs backwards. Thus, let p_{t-1}^m denote the price of channel $m \in \{b, u, s\}$ in period $t - 1$, which follows period t. Figure 6.3 displays the expected next period's profit margin for each channel of trade conditional on the current underlying price, that is, $\mathbb{E}[(p_{t-1}^m - c)|p_t^u], m \in \{b, u, s\}$. The extra cost g (for additives) associated with the branded product is considered when computing the branded profit margin. When the current underlying price is at a low level, the branded channel has the highest expected profit margin in the next period and the spot market has the lowest expected profit margin. When the current underlying price is at a high level, the order of the profit margins is reversed. All three channels exhibit a higher expected profit margin at a higher current price level. The gasoline prices are usually larger during periods of supply scarcity, such as when a pipeline or refinery breakdown causes a supply disruption, which leads to higher

---

[c]These are BP branded price, unbranded price, and refinery gate prices (which we use as the product cost) in Chicago, collected by the Oil Pricing Information Service (http:/opisnet.com) and made available to us by BP.

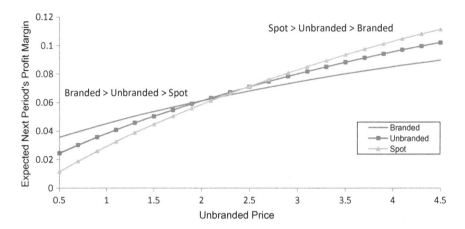

Fig. 6.3   The expected next period's profit margin for each channel of trade conditional on the current underlying price, $\mathbb{E}[(p_{t-1}^m - c)|p_t^u]$, $m \in \{b, u, s\}$.

profit margins for gasoline. When the gasoline supplies are very tight, unbranded jobbers may end up paying higher wholesale prices than branded jobbers that have long-term supplier commitments, and the spot market becomes even more profitable for the suppliers. We also computed the conditional variance of the profit margin in the next period for each channel of trade and found that, for each current underlying price, the spot market has the highest variance and the branded channel has the lowest variance.

Even though the channels of trade have different variances, we assume that the decision-maker is risk-neutral and discount cash flows using the risk-free rate. This modeling choice is consistent with typical performance measures given to managers with profit and loss responsibility within a corporation. In future work, one could take an investor perspective and either discount cash-flows from the different channels using different risk-adjusted rates or use risk-neutral (risk-adjusted) probabilities for price evolution and discount using a risk-free rate to study the impact of risk on contract portfolio decisions.

Other data. Table 6.1 summarizes the base scenario parameters used in the infinite horizon model. We normalize the refinery supply Q to 100 million gallons, and assume it is deterministic. We further use the following parameter values: The maximum potential branded market share $\overline{f} = 30\%$; the investment cost for contracting 1% of the branded market share $k = \$20$ million; the extra cost associated with branded gasoline $g = \$0.03$; and

Table 6.1   Summary of Model Parameters.

Unbranded Price Process Parameters		Base Case Value
Long-term level	μ	0.166
Mean-reversion coefficient	κ	0.392
Volatility	σ	0.326
Other Prices and Cost Parameters		
Branded price $p^b = \alpha^b + \gamma^b p^u + \varepsilon^b$	α^b	0.0486
	γ^b	0.9894
	Std Deviation of ε^b	0.0187[a]
Spot price $p^s = \alpha^s + \gamma^s p^u + \varepsilon^s$	α^s	−0.02
	γ^s	1.01
	Std Deviation of ε^s	0.02
Cost $c = \alpha^c + \gamma^c p^u + \varepsilon^c$	α^c	0
	γ^s	0.9650
	Std Deviation of ε^c	0.0716[a]
Demands Parameters		
Branded demand $D^b = a^b - b^b p^b$	a^b	500
	b^b	50
Unbranded demand $D^u = a^u - b^u p^u$	a^u	35
	b^u	5
Other Parameters		
Refinery capacity	Q	100 million gallons
Maximum potential branded market share	$\bar{f}$	30%
Investment cost for contracting the entire branded channel	k	\$20 million
Extra cost associated with branded product	g	\$0.03
Customer defection fraction r follows uniform distribution on the interval $[\underline{r}, \bar{r}]$	$\underline{r}$	0
	$\bar{r}$	10%
Price impact parameter (linear price impact function)	λ	0.002
Discount factor	β	93.24%

[a]Unbiased estimator of the error term standard deviation in the linear regression.

the discount factor $\beta = 93.24\%$.[d] We assume that the customer defection fraction is uniformly distributed with left and right support ends $\underline{r} = 0\%$ and $\bar{r} = 10\%$, respectively. We use a linear price impact function with

---

[d]This discount factor is based on an annual internal rate of return equal to 7%.

parameter $\lambda = 0.002$. We stipulate the following linear demand functions for the branded and unbranded channel: $D^b = a^b - b^b p^b$ and $D^u = a^u - b^u p^u$, respectively. We expect demand for branded gasoline to be less elastic than demand for unbranded gasoline. Because the product sold at unbranded gas stations is not identified with an individual refiner, jobbers are free to purchase unbranded gasoline from any seller of unbranded product in response to price changes [33]. In the base scenario case, we use $a^b = 500$, $b^b = 50$, $a^u = 35$, and $b^u = 5$. Thus, the demand for branded gasoline is less elastic than the demand for unbranded gasoline at the same price. The elasticities fall within the range of known empirical estimates of the price elasticity of the gasoline demand.[e]

6.5.2. *Results*

We discuss our computational results with the goal of bringing to light insights into the structure of optimal policies and illustrating the sensitivity of the expected profit and corresponding optimal portfolio to changes in the values of the various parameters. We specifically focus on

(1) the benefit of a dynamic contract portfolio policy compared with a static branded market share policy;
(2) the impact of the spot market liquidity level, the customer defection fraction, and the coefficients of the underlying price process.

Base Scenario. Figure 6.4 displays our results for the base case scenario. The top left panel reports the total expected profit for each pair of states, namely, initial underlying price and branded market share. For each given underlying price state, the total expected profit is concave in the branded market share, as proved in Theorem 6.1(b), which means the marginal expected profit is decreasing in the initial branded market share. The total expected profit is relatively high for higher underlying price states, as the conditional expected profit margins for all three channels are higher at a high underlying price level, as illustrated in Fig. 6.3. The top right panel illustrates the branded market base-share level as a function of the underlying price: The base-share level initially decreases and then increases in the

---

[e]The author of [34] reviews the literature and finds that the reported short-run price elasticity estimates for the demand for gasoline range from 0 to -1.36, with an average of -0.26 and a median of -0.23, and the reported long-run price elasticity estimates range from 0 to -2.72, with an average of -0.58 and a median of -0.43.

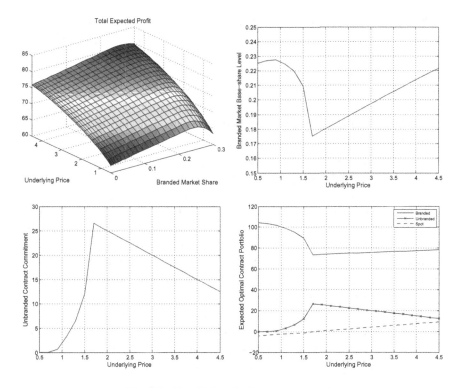

Fig. 6.4   Results for the base case scenario.

underlying price. Two effects primarily cause this behavior. First, as the underlying price increases the branded channel is expected to become relatively less profitable, which provides BP an incentive to reduce the branded market share and allocate the product to more profitable channels. Second, as the underlying price increases, both the branded and the unbranded demand shrinks; as a consequence, BP tends to seek more branded market share, and this effect dominates the expected profitability effect when the underlying price is high. The bottom left panel shows the unbranded contract commitment as a function of the underlying price. Because of the same effects discussed for the base-share level, we observe an increase of the unbranded contract commitment in the underlying price and then a decrease as the shrinking unbranded demand constrains the unbranded contract commitment. This finding suggests the potential for profit opportunities in the unbranded channel for the suppliers. Given the optimal contract portfolio strategy, we compute the expected allocation by channel of trade. The bottom right panel displays the expected optimal contract portfolio as a function of the underlying price. At a low underlying price, because the spot market has a relatively low expected profit margin, spot purchasing (indicated by a negative quantity) is more attractive than it is at a higher underlying price. Spot selling becomes more profitable as the underlying price increases. When the underlying price is low, more product should be allocated to the most profitable channel, that is, the branded channel. Furthermore, spot purchasing should also be used to meet contractual obligations. As the underlying price increases, the unbranded channel becomes more profitable, but the decreasing unbranded demand constrains the allocation to this channel. The profitability of the spot market also increases, but the illiquidity of the spot market dampens this benefit. As a consequence, even though the branded channel becomes less profitable, the corresponding expected allocation to this channel increases slightly. As the branded demand also decreases, to keep even the same level of the allocation in the branded channel, BP needs to expand its branded market share, as we can observe in the top right panel.

Comparison of Static and Dynamic Policies. The base case scenario discussed above established the intuition for the optimal dynamic contract portfolio policy structure and corresponding optimal expected profit. We now turn to the comparison of static and dynamic policies. The objective of this analysis is to ascertain the value of dynamically incorporating commodity price information in contract portfolio decision-making. The static policy is a simple policy that uses a fixed (state independent) branded base-share level and unbranded contract commitment. Regardless of the initial underlying price, if the initial market share is less than the target level, the static policy brings it up to the target level; otherwise, it does not contract for any new branded market share until the branded market share drops below the target level due to customer defection. According to the static policy, the unbranded allocation is the minimum of a fixed unbranded contract commitment and the realized unbranded demand. Figure 6.5 compares the optimal dynamic contract portfolio policy with static policies with different fixed branded base-share levels ($f = 0.15, 0.17, 0.19, 0.21, 0.23$, and 0.25) and fixed unbranded contract commitments ($y = 5, 10, 15$, and 20). The numbers on the top of the bars are the average percentage increase in total expected profits achieved by the optimal dynamic contract policy compared with the static policies across the state space. The optimal dynamic policy attains substantially higher total expected profit than either a conservative branded market strategy or an aggressive branded market

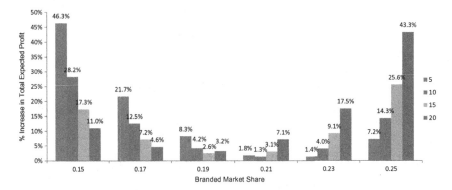

Fig. 6.5   The average percentage increase in total expected profits achieved by the optimal dynamic contract portfolio policy compared with different static policies. (Colors correspond with fixed levels of unbranded contract commitments.)

strategy. For example, the expected profit advantage varies between 11% and 46.5%, compared to the conservative branded market strategy with 15% of the branded market share, and ranges from 7.2% to 43.3% relative to the aggressive branded market strategy with 25% of the branded market share. For both these conservative and aggressive branded market strategies, the impact of different levels of the unbranded contract commitment on the expected profits is much greater than it is for the median branded market strategies. This finding implies that diversification in a static policy/portfolio can somewhat mitigate the relative benefits of a dynamic policy. Both branded market strategies require a high volume of spot trading in order to either get rid of leftover product or cover unmet contractual obligations, and which is costly due to the spot market illiquidity; therefore an appropriate unbranded contract commitment can be used in combination with the branded market strategy to reduce the reliance on the spot market.

Effect of Spot Market Liquidity. We now examine how spot market illiquidity influences the optimal contract portfolio and the corresponding expected profit. We consider different spot market liquidity levels. The top right panel of Fig. 6.6 exhibits the impact of the spot market liquidity on the expected total profit. The percentage change is the average across the state space and is measured relative to the base case scenario ($\lambda = 0.002$). The expected total profit increases with the spot market liquidity level. The left panels show the expected allocations in the branded, unbranded, and spot market channels (top, middle, bottom) under different spot market liquidity

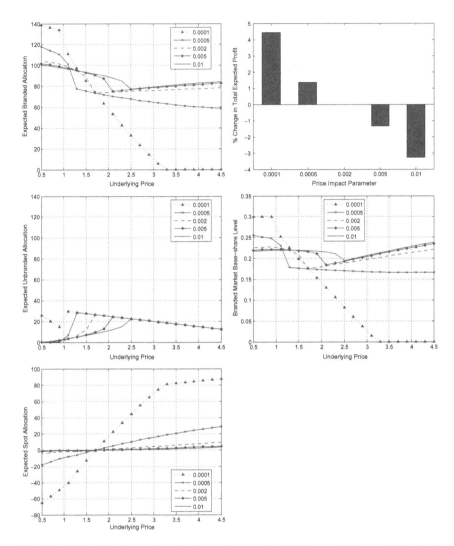

Fig. 6.6   Effect of spot market price impact parameter λ (values of λ shown in the chart legends).

levels ($\lambda = 0.0001$, 0.0005, 0.002, 0.005, and 0.01). These results indicate that the lower the spot market liquidity, the lower the quantities traded in the spot market, as expected. When the spot market liquidity increases (lower market impact), the amount traded in the spot market increases. Spot trading cannot eliminate the contracting channels even if the spot market is highly liquid. In order to take advantage of the highly liquid spot market, however, the suppliers are more aggressive in the branded channel at the price states where the contracting channels have relatively higher expected profit margin. As we can see in the middle right panel, for high spot market liquidity the branded market base-share level is much more dispersed across the underlying price states than for lower spot market liquidity. This finding suggests that the dynamic policy may be more beneficial compared with the static policies when the spot market is more liquid. As trading in the more liquid spot market is less costly, however, the overcommitment and undercommitment costs are relatively low, which may diminish the value provided by the dynamic policy.

Effect of Customer Defection Fraction. The top and middle panels of Fig. 6.7 illustrate the impact of the mean of the customer defection fraction under the base scenario as well as four alternative scenarios with respective means equal to 0%,[f] 0.075, 0.1, and 0.125, keeping the variance constant. The top left panel shows that the total expected profit decreases in the customer defection fraction mean. The top right panel shows that at a low underlying price, the higher the customer defection fraction mean, the lower the branded market base-share level. With high customer defections, contracting is costly in the branded channel, so more product is allocated to the unbranded channel. At a high underlying price, we observe no significant impact because the unbranded channel is constrained and the costs of selling more product to the spot market outweigh the costs of selling to the branded channel. In the case of no customer defection, we notice a stable branded market base-share level as a function of the underlying price, with a maximum base-share level across the considered underlying price levels of 20.7%. The middle left panel displays the corresponding total expected profit for the case of no customer defection (displayed as "Mean = 0" above the fig.). In this case the total expected profit is significantly lower at a high initial branded market share due to the overcommitment costs. The middle right panel depicts the total expected profit for the case when the customer defection fraction mean is 0.125. In contrast to the no-customer-defection case, the total expected profit is less dispersed across visited states, and is lower for a low initial branded market share and higher for a high initial branded market share. The bottom panels of Fig. 6.7 consider the impact of the customer defection fraction variance. The total expected profit decreases with the customer defection fraction variance, whereas the

---

[f]In this case no customer defection occurs and we assume the variance is zero.

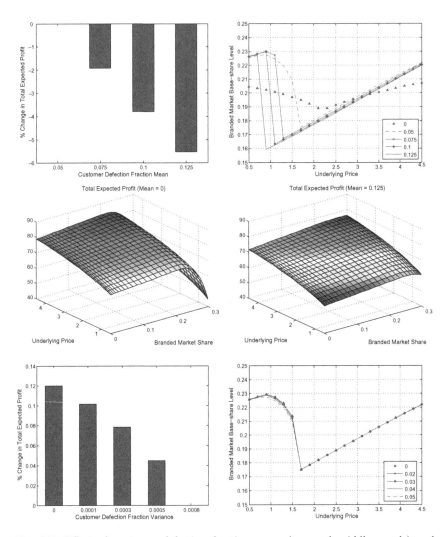

Fig. 6.7   Effect of customer defection fraction mean (top and middle panels) and variance (bottom panels); the chart legends show the respective values of these parameters.

impact of the variance on the branded market base-share level is fairly small.

Effect of the Underlying Price Process Parameters. In Figs. 6.8 and 6.9 we investigate the impact of the underlying (unbranded) price process parameters. The top panels of Fig. 6.8 consider the impact of different

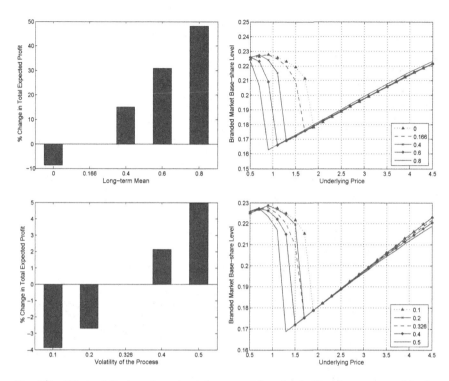

Fig. 6.8 Effect of the long-term level (top panels) and volatility (bottom panels); the chart legends indicate the respective values of these parameters.

values for the long-run level parameter μ equal to 0, 0.166, 0.4, 0.6, and 0.8, where 0.166 corresponds to the base scenario. The considered values for this parameter correspond to long-run gasoline prices equal to 1.07, 1.26, 1.60, 1.95, and 2.38 dollars per gallon. As the long-run gasoline price rises from \$1.07 to \$2.38, we observe a substantial increase in the total expected profit, as depicted in the top left panel of Fig. 6.8, since all channels are more profitable at a high underlying price. An increase in the long-run price implies that the unbranded and spot channels become relatively more profitable, which leads to higher allocations to the unbranded and spot channels and a lower commitment to the branded channel, as shown in the top right panel of Fig. 6.8. The bottom panels of Fig. 6.8 consider the impact of different values of the volatility σ (0.1, 0.2, 0.326, 0.4, 0.5, where 0.326 corresponds to the base scenario). The optimal branded market base-share level drops across the considered underlying prices as the volatility increases. The drop is obvious at a low underlying price, because the overcommitment cost is

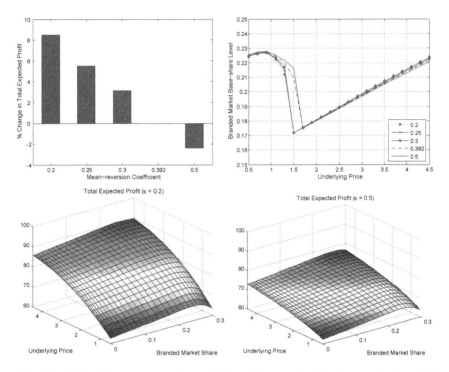

Fig. 6.9   Effect of the mean-reversion coefficient; the legend of the chart in the top right panel indicates the values of this parameter.

higher than the undercommitment cost. Purchasing from the spot market to satisfy the unmet branded commitment is more costly than selling more product to the unbranded channel. As the volatility becomes smaller, the price is concentrated on the long-run level of \$1.26. The total expected profit becomes lower as compared with a more volatile underlying price process, which leads to a more wide spread distribution of the long-run price. This behavior implies that as the underlying price process becomes more volatile, less should be optimally committed to the long-term contract. Figure 6.9 considers the impact of different values of the mean-reversion coefficients κ (0.2, 0.25, 0.3, 0.392, and 0.5, where 0.392 corresponds to the base scenario). We can interpret $-\ln(0.5)/\kappa$ years as representing the "half-life" of the mean-reverting process; that is, in $-\ln(0.5)/\kappa$ years, we would expect the log price to have reverted half-way back to the long-run level (see [32]). The considered mean-reversion coefficients correspond to half-lives equal to 3.47, 2.77, 2.31, 1.77, and 1.39 years. The bigger the mean-reversion coefficient, the faster the process reverts to the long-run gasoline price of $1.26. At a high underlying price, the expected total profit drops dramatically in the mean-reversion coefficient as the price reverts quickly from highly profitable price states to the long-run level. At a low underlying price, the expected total profit increases slightly in the mean-reversion coefficient. The decrease at a high underlying price dominates the increase at a low underlying price, which leads to a decrease on average as noted in the top left panel.

6.6. Conclusion

We develop a new framework for dynamically modeling the contract portfolio decisions of gasoline suppliers. Using this model, we characterize a simple and easily implementable contract portfolio policy that would enable such suppliers to dynamically rebalance their contract portfolio in anticipation of future market conditions in each individual channel while satisfying the contractual obligations. We establish that the optimal dynamic policy is characterized by a branded base-share level and an unbranded contract commitment combination, given as functions of the information state. We estimate some of the parameters of our model on market data and compute and illustrate the corresponding optimal contract portfolio policy and expected profit. A static portfolio can sometimes be competitive with a dynamically rebalanced portfolio if it achieves good diversification. As the spot market price impact increases, that is, liquidity decreases, the expected total profit decreases. Furthermore, as the underlying price process becomes more volatile, less should be committed to the long-term contract. Even though the dynamic contract portfolio framework we have built is specific to the gasoline supply chain, it can be applied to other industries.

Acknowledgments

Both authors gratefully acknowledge the financial support of the University of Chicago Booth School of Business. Also, we would like to thank BP, and in particular the Strategy and Planning Group for the Midwest Fuels Value Chain, for providing access to data and information that made this work possible. The authors also thank an anonymous reviewer and the editor for detailed comments that substantially improved this chapter.

Appendix A. Proofs

A.1. *Proof of Theorem 6.1*

By induction. By assumption, the terminal value function $v_0(x_0, \Phi_0)$ equals 0. Suppose parts (a)-(c) hold for $t - 1$. By part (b) for $t - 1$ we know that $v_{t-1}(f \cdot (1 - r_t), \Phi_{t-1})$ is concave in f for any given Φ_{t-1} and r_t. By Assumption 6.1(c), $R_t(z_t, p_t^s, \lambda_t)$ is strictly concave in z_t for any fixed p_t^s and λ_t. Since a concave function of an affine function is concave, the revenue function $R_t(z_t(f, y), p_t^s, \lambda_t)$ is strictly and jointly concave in f and y for any fixed p_t^s and λ_t, and $L_t(f, y, \Phi_t)$ is also jointly concave in f and y because expectation preserves concavity. The function $G_t(f, y, \Phi_t)$ is therefore the sum of three concave functions and hence itself jointly concave in f and y. From $v_{t-1}(f \cdot (1 - r_t), \Phi_{t-1}) < \infty$, $\lim_{y \to \infty} L_t(f, y, \Phi_t) = -\infty$, and $L_t(f, y, \Phi_t) < \infty$, it follows that $v_t(x_t, \Phi_t) < \infty$ and $\lim_{y \to \infty} G_t(f, y, \Phi_t) = -\infty$ for all $f \in [0, \overline{f}]$, which implies that $G_t(f, y, \Phi_t)$ has a finite maximizer $(f_t^*(\Phi_t), y_t^*(\Phi_t))$ over set Ω_t. So part (a) holds for t, which yields part (c) immediately for t. When $x_t \leq f_t^*(\Phi_t)$, $(f_t^*(\Phi_t), y_t^*(\Phi_t))$ is the optimal decision pair. If $x_t > f_t^*(\Phi_t)$, it is optimal to choose $f = x_t$. Thus, we have following cases:

Case 1. If $f_t^*(\Phi_t) = \overline{f}$, $v_t(x_t, \Phi_t) = k_t x_t + G_t(f_t^*(\Phi_t), y_t^*(\Phi_t), \Phi_t)$;
Case 2. If $f_t^*(\Phi_t) < \overline{f}$, $v_t(x_t, \Phi_t) = k_t x_t + J_t(x_t, \Phi_t)$, where

$$J_t(x_t, \Phi_t) = \begin{cases} G_t(f_t^*(\Phi_t), y_t^*(\Phi_t), \Phi_t), & \text{if } x_t \leq f_t^*(\Phi_t), \\ G_t(x_t, y_t^*(x_t, \Phi_t), \Phi_t), & \text{if } x_t > f_t^*(\Phi_t). \end{cases}$$

In Case 1, part (b) holds for t since $G_t(f_t^*(\Phi_t), y_t^*(\Phi_t), \Phi_t)$ is a constant. In Case 2, $v_t(x_t, \Phi_t)$ is continuous at $x_t = f_t^*(\Phi_t)$. Since $(f_t^*(\Phi_t), y_t^*(\Phi_t))$ is an interior maximizer of the concave function $G_t(\cdot, \cdot, \Phi_t)$, the vector 0 is a subgradient of $G_t(\cdot, \cdot, \Phi_t)$ at $(f_t^*(\Phi_t), y_t^*(\Phi_t))$. Therefore, $J_t(x_t, \Phi_t)$ is concave and nonincreasing in x_t since the constraints in (6.5) become tighter as x_t increases, which implies that $v_t(x_t, \Phi_t)$ is concave in x_t. This argument establishes part (b) for t. The claimed properties hold by the principle of mathematical induction.

A.2. *Proof of Theorem 6.2*

The feasible region for (f, y) in (6.3) separates component-wise, and thus forms a lattice. Since the sum of submodular functions on a lattice is submodular, it suffices to establish submodularity of each of the terms in (6.4). The first and third terms are submodular because they depend on only one of the two variables f and y. Similarly, to show sub-modularity of $L_t(f, y, \Phi_t)$ in (f, y), it suffices to show submodularity of $R_t(z_t(f, y), p_t^s, \lambda_t) = z_t(f, y) P_t(z_t(f, y), p_t^s, \lambda_t)$ in (f, y) since taking expectation preserves this property. Because $R_t(\cdot, p_t^s, \lambda_t)$ is concave, from [26, Lemma 2.6.2] we have that

$$R_t(z_t(f, y), p_t^s, \lambda_t) = R_t\left(Q_t - f d_t^b(p_t^b, \epsilon_t^b) - y, p_t^s, \lambda_t\right)$$

is submodular in (f, y), which establishes part (a).

Since $G_t(f, y, \Phi_t)$ is submodular, it follows from [35, Theorem 8.4] that the optimal unbranded contract quantity $y_t^*(x_t, \Phi_t)$ is nonincreasing in $f_t^*(x_t, \Phi_t)$. From Theorem 6.1(c), we know that

$$f_t^*(x_t, \Phi_t) = \begin{cases} f_t^*(\Phi_t) & \text{if } x_t \le f_t^*(\Phi_t), \\ x & \text{if } x_t > f_t^*(\Phi_t). \end{cases}$$

Hence, $y_t^*(x_t, \Phi_t)$ is nonincreasing in x_t, and $y_t^*(x_t, \Phi_t) \le y_t^*(\Phi_t)$, which completes the proof.

A.3. *Proof of Theorem 6.3*

In order to prove part (a), by [36, Proposition 9.17], it suffices to verify that for all $t = 1, 2, \ldots, \infty$, for each x, Φ, and $\delta \in R$, the set

$$U_t(x, \Phi, \delta) = \{(f, y) | x \le f \le \overline{f}, \ 0 \le y \le d^u(p^u, \epsilon^u) \quad \text{and}$$

$$kx + \widehat{G}_t(f, y, \Phi) \ge \delta\}$$

is compact. Since $\widehat{v}_t(x, \Phi) \le 0$, for $t = 1, 2, \ldots, \infty$, we have

$$kx + \widehat{G}_t(f, y, \Phi) = -k(f - x) + L(f, y, \Phi) - M$$

$$+ \beta \mathbb{E}_{\Phi'} \left[\mathbb{E}_r \left[\widehat{v}(f \cdot (1 - r), \Phi') | \Phi' \right] | \Phi \right]$$

$$\le L(f, y, \Phi) - M. \tag{A.1}$$

Since $L(f, y, \Phi)$ is concave, and for all $f \in [x, \overline{f}]$ we have $\lim_{y \to \infty} L(f, y, \Phi) = -\infty$, a constant $\overline{y}(\Phi, \delta)$ exists such that for $y > \overline{y}(\Phi, \delta)$, $L(f, y, \Phi) - M < \delta$. By (A.1), $kx + \widehat{G}_t(f, y, \Phi) \ge \delta$ implies $L(f, y, \Phi) - M \ge \delta$. Then we have $U_t(x, \Phi, \delta) \subseteq \{(f, y) | x \le f \le \overline{f}, \ 0 \le y \le \overline{y}(\Phi, \delta)\}$. Thus, the set $U_t(x, \Phi, \delta)$ is bounded. The function $G_t(f, y, \Phi)$ is concave in (f, y) by Theorem 6.1(a); hence, it is continuous in the interior of its domain, and so is $\widehat{G}_t(f, y, \Phi)$. This property implies that the set $U_t(x, \Phi, \delta)$ is closed and hence compact. It follows that $\widehat{v}^*$ and $\widehat{G}^*$ satisfy the infinite horizon optimality equation in the modified model. Since $\widehat{v}^*(x, \Phi) = v^*(x, \Phi) - M/(1 - \beta)$ and $\widehat{G}^*(f, y, \Phi) = G^*(f, y, \Phi) - M/(1 - \beta)$, it is easy to check that v^* and G^* also satisfy the infinite horizon optimality equation in the original model.

By Theorem 6.1(a)–(b), $G_t(f, y, \Phi_t)$ is jointly concave and submodular in f and y, and $v_t(x, \Phi_t)$ is concave in x. Then the claimed concavity of $G^*(f, y, \Phi)$ and $v^*(x)$ and the submodularity of $G^*(f, y, \Phi)$ follow from part (a), so that $G^* = G_\infty$ and $v^* = v_\infty$. Since the one-stage expected profit in the modified model is nonpositive, we have $\widehat{G}^* = \widehat{G}_\infty \leq \widehat{G}_1$. From the proof of Theorem 6.1, $\lim_{y \to \infty} G_1(f, y, \Phi_1) = -\infty$ for all $f \in [0, \overline{f}]$, so that $\lim_{y \to \infty} \widehat{G}_t(f, y, \Phi_t) = -\infty$. By the concavity of $G^*(f, y, \Phi)$ in (f, y) it follows that $G^*(f, y, \Phi)$ has a finite maximizer over set Ω, denoted by $(f^*(\Phi), y^*(\Phi))$, which establishes part (b).

Part (c) follows immediately from the proof of Theorems 6.1(c) and 6.2(b).

References

[1] M. Fisher, What is the right supply chain for your products? *Harvard Business Review.* **75**(2), 105–116 (1997).

[2] M. Cohen and N. Agrawal, An analytical comparison of long and short term contracts, *IIE Transactions.* **31**(8), 783–796 (1999).

[3] C. Li and L. Debo, Strategic dynamic sourcing from competing suppliers with transferable capacity investment, *Naval Research Logistics.* **56**(6), 540–562 (2009).

[4] R. Swinney and S. Netessine, Long-term contracts under the threat of supplier default, *Manufacturing & Service Operations Management.* **11**(1), 109–127 (2009).

[5] P. R. Kleindorfer and D. Wu, Integrating long and short-term contracting via business-to-business exchanges for capital-intensive industries, *Management Science.* **49**(11), 1579–1615 (2003).

[6] C. Haksoz and S. Seshadri, Supply chain operations in the presence of a spot market: A review with discussion, *Journal of the Operational Research Society.* **58**(11), 1412–1429 (2007).

[7] R. Akella, V. F. Araman, and J. Kleinknecht. B2B markets: Procurement and supplier risk management in e-business. In (eds.), J. Geunes, P. Pardalos, and H. Romeijn, *Supply Chain Management: Models, Applications, and Research Directions*, 33–66. Kluwer Academic Publishers, Dordrecht, The Netherlands (2002).

[8] R. Seifert, U. Thonemann, and W. Hausman, Optimal procurement strategies for online spot markets, *European Journal of Operational Research.* **152**(3), 781–799 (2004).

[9] V. Martínez de Albéniz and D. Simchi-Levi, A portfolio approach to procurement contracts, *Production and Operations Management.* **14**(1), 90–114 (2005).

[10] D. Wu, P. Kleindorfer, and J. Zhang, Optimal bidding and contracting strategies for capital-intensive goods, *European Journal of Operational Research.* **137**(3), 657–676 (2002).

[11] S. Spinler, A. Huchzermeier, and P. Kleindorfer, Risk hedging via options contracts for physical delivery, *OR Spectrum.* **25**(3), 379–395 (2003).

[12] D. Wu and P. Kleindorfer, Competitive options, supply contracting, and electronic markets, *Management Science.* **51**(3), 452–466 (2005).

[13] D. Klingman, N. Phillips, D. Steiger, R. Wirth, R. Padman, and R. Krishnan, An optimization based integrated short-term refined petroleum product planning system, *Management Science.* **33**(7), 813–830 (1987).

[14] D. Klingman, N. Phillips, D. Steiger, and W. Young, The successful deployment of management science throughout Citgo petroleum corporation, *Interfaces.* **17**(1), 4–25 (1987).

[15] Q. Wu and H. Chen, Optimal control and equilibrium behavior of production-inventory systems, *Management Science.* **58**(6), 1362–1379 (2010).

[16] A. Goel and G. Gutierrez. Integrating commodity markets in the optimal procurement policies of a stochastic inventory system. Working Paper, University of Austin, Austin, TX, USA (2007).

[17] N. Secomandi, On the pricing of natural gas pipeline capacity, *Manufacturing & Service Operations Management.* **12**(3), 393–408 (2010).

[18] N. Secomandi, Optimal commodity trading with a capacitated storage asset, *Management Science.* **51**(3), 452–466 (2010).

[19] G. Lai, F. Margot, and N. Secomandi, An approximate dynamic programming approach to benchmark practice-based heuristics for natural gas storage valuation, *Operations Research.* **58**(3), 564–582 (2010).

[20] D. Bertsimas and A. Lo., Optimal control of execution costs, *Journal of Financial Markets.* **1**(4), 1–15 (1998).

[21] R. W. Holthausen, R. W. Leftwich, and D. Mayers, Large block transactions, the speed of response, and temporary and permanent stock-price effects, *Journal of Financial Economics.* **26**(1), 71–95 (1990).

[22] H. Mendelson and T. Tunca, Strategic spot trading in supply chains, *Management Science.* **53**(5), 742–759 (2007).

[23] H. He and H. Mamaysky, Dynamic trading policies with price impact, *J. Economic Dynamics & Control.* **29**(5), 891–930 (2005).

[24] V. L. Vath., M. Mnif, and H. Pham, A model of optimal portfolio selection under liquidity risk and price impact, *Finance and Stochastics.* **11**(1), 51–90 (2007).

[25] E. Porteus, *Foundations of Stochastic Inventory Theory.* Stanford Business Books, Stanford, CA, USA (2002).

[26] D. Topkis, *Supermodularity and Complementarity*. Princeton University Press, Princeton, NJ, USA (1998).

[27] P. Milgrom and J. Roberts, The economics of modern manufacturing: Technology, strategy, and organization, *American Economic Review*. **80**(3), 511–528 (1990).

[28] M. Puterman, *Markov Decision Processes: Discrete Stochastic Dynamic Programming*. John Wiley & Sons Inc., Hoboken, NJ, USA (2005).

[29] E. Schwartz and J. E. Smith, Short-term variations and long-term dynamics in commodity prices, *Management Science*. **46**(7), 893–911 (2000).

[30] G. Cortazar and E. S. Schwartz, The evaluation of commodity contingent claims, *Journal of Derivatives*. **1**(4), 27–39 (1994).

[31] A. K. Dixit and R. S. Pindyck, *Investment Under Uncertainty*. Princeton University Press, Princeton, NJ, USA (1994).

[32] J. Smith and K. F. McCardle, Options in the real world: Lessons learned in evaluating oil and gas investments, *Operations Research*. **47**(1), 1–15 (1999).

[33] S. Borenstein and A. Shepard, Sticky prices, inventories, and market power in wholesale gasoline markets, *Rand Journal of Economics*. **33**(1), 116–139 (2002).

[34] M. Espey, Gasoline demand revisited: An international meta-analysis of elasticities, *Energy Economics*. **20**(3), 273–295 (1998).

[35] H. D. and M. Sobel, *Stochastic Models in Operations Research, Volume II*. McGraw Hill, New York, NY, USA (1984).

[36] D. Bertsekas and S. Shreve, *Stochastic Optimal Control: The Discrete-Time Case*. Academic Press, New York, NY, USA (1978).

Index

Printed in the United States
By Bookmasters